FAMILY RELATIONSHIPS IN LATER LIFE

SOME PAST VOLUMES IN THE
SAGE FOCUS EDITIONS

Family Relationships in Later Life

edited by
TIMOTHY H. BRUBAKER

SAGE PUBLICATIONS
Beverly Hills / London / New Delhi

For information address:

SAGE Publications, Inc.
275 South Beverly Drive
Beverly Hills, California 90212

SAGE Publications India Pvt. Ltd.
C-236 Defence Colony
New Delhi 110 024, India

SAGE Publications Ltd
28 Banner Street
London EC1Y 8QE, England

Printed in the United States of America

Library of Congress Cataloging in Publication Data

Main entry under title:

Family relationships in later life.

   (Sage focus editions)
   Bibliography: p.
   1. Aged—Family relationships—Addresses, essays,
lectures. 2. Aged—Social conditions—Addresses,
essays, lectures. 3. Family—Social conditions—
Addresses, essays, lectures. I. Brubaker, Timothy H.
HQ1061.F36   1983   306.8'7   83-13978
ISBN 0-8039-2104-7
ISBN 0-8039-2105-5 (pbk.)

FIRST PRINTING

CONTENTS

PREFACE

Family relationships in later life are an important concern to social gerontologists and family scholars. Research demonstrates that family members of various ages are actively involved in the support of their older members. Family members assist their elderly who live in the community as well as those who live in an institutionalized setting. In short, the family in later life is vital.

Within recent years, research has been directed toward specific family relationships of older people. Husband-wife, elderly parent-adult child, sibling and grandparent-grandchild relationships have been examined. In addition, a number of other issues concerning the relationship are emerging. Retirement, sexuality, sex roles, widowhood, divorce, abuse, and minority issues have been identified. The primary objective of this volume is to provide a review of research on these issues and family relationships in later life. In many cases, new research or theory is presented.

Another objective is to suggest practice and policy implications of the research. Family practice and policy can be grounded in the family relationships identified by the research. Services and policy can enhance older persons' family relationships. Knowledge of the husband-wife, adult child, sibling and grandparent relationships is necessary to build a service or policy that strengthens these relationships. For many older persons, the strength of their families is evidenced by the families' history. Consequently, practice and policy may want to recognize the family history of older clients. Strong families compliment services to older persons. One hopes that services compliment strong families.

This volume is organized into three sections. Part I considers specific family relationships (e.g., husband-wife, parent-child, sibling, grandparent) of older people. The second part focuses on a number of issues (types of couple relationship, sexuality, sex roles, widowhood, abuse, minority families) related to the later-life family. Part III focuses on policy and practice aspects.

Contributors represent research, theory, and/or practice emphases in gerontology and family studies. Sociology, psychology, and social work are the disciplines represented. This blend of emphases and disciplines will, it is hoped, bridge the gaps between research, theory, and practice.

A number of individuals contributed to the development of this volume. First and foremost, special appreciation is due to the contributors. Their willingness to make revisions and meet deadlines was admirable. Veronica Szczesny did a yeoman's job of developing the reference list. Debbie Rumpler, Joan McLaughlin, and Thelma Carmack typed a number of chapters. To them, I am grateful. Also, I wish to recognize the support of the Department of Home Economics and Consumer Sciences and the Scripps Foundation Gerontology Center, Miami University. These units have facilitated the completion of this volume.

Acknowledgments

Much of the encouragement for several of the chapters in this collection, and indeed, for the entire volume was provided by Edwin Zedlewski of the National Institute of Justice. Dr. Zedlewski had, for the past several years, coordinated a series of performance measurement projects at NIJ, focusing attention on the need for better measures of performance and for a fuller understanding of the role of performance measurement in public policy analysis. We thank Ed for his support and encouragement. We also thank Julie Daniel for her meticulous and cheerful assistance in manuscript preparation.

1

Introduction

TIMOTHY H. BRUBAKER

Family relationships in later life have recently received attention from family scholars and gerontologists. Research has demonstrated that the family is an important social group for older persons. Practitioners have suggested that families may be a key group that should be considered when working with older people. However, the complexity and dynamics of older persons's family relationships are not fully understood.

This chapter provides a definition of families in later life and discusses some of the unique features of these families. Viewing the families in later life as a system is also considered. Then, the demographics of older families are examined. Since the positive aspects of these families are usually noted, a section on positive *and* negative aspects of families in later life is included. This chapter concludes with a plan for this book.

Definition of Families in Later Life

Within gerontology and family studies, families in later life refer to families who have members who are beyond the child-rearing years and have launched their children. For couples who have been childless, living beyond the age of 50 years generally characterized later-life families. As Troll, Miller, and Atchley (1979) note, chronological age is not a reliable indicator. Families do not experience life events at the same chronological age. However, there are many people who follow similar life courses (Atchley, 1980; Neugarten, Moore, & Lowe, 1965). Within a range of several years, individuals marry, produce children, raise and launch children, make occupational choices, and retire. By age 50, many couples have seen their last child leave home and begin to phase out of their employment with the anticipation of retirement (Atchley, 1976a).

Families in later life have a number of unique characteristics that are important for researchers and practitioners. First, families in later life

9

are multigenerational. Many later-life families include three, four, or five generations. Increased longevity increases the opportunity to be a member of a multigenerational family. The existence and number of generations within a family unit are important, because the family is influenced by, and influences, the various generations (Troll & Bengtson, 1978). Neugarten (1979) suggests that the middle generation may be caught between the older and younger generations because both may need assistance. In some families, the adult-child generation is experiencing difficulty with aging at a time when the older generation may also need assistance. For other families, multigenerations create a group of people on whom older persons can rely. In any case, the multigenerational aspect is important for professionals to consider (Hirschfield & Dennis, 1979).

Another unique characteristic of later-life families is their lengthy family history. Older families may be experiencing new life events, but they have a large reservoir of experience. For instance, they have developed communication and coping patterns over their years as family members. The existence of a family history may be positive or negative. There may be unfinished business or tensions from earlier life experiences that influence behavior in later life (Peterson, 1979). An example of the importance of the family history of intrafamily relationships is when older parents reside in the same household as their adult children (Cohler & Grunebaum, 1981; Blazer, 1978; Glasser & Glasser, 1962. Brubaker and Brubaker (1981, p. 248) note that "the way that family members have previously dealt with stress, as individuals and as members of a family system, is likely to be similar to the way in which stress is handled in the intergenerational household." Therefore, the existence of a lengthy family history is important.

Older families are characterized by a number of life events that seldom occur in other families. Launching of children, becoming a grandparent, retiring from an occupation, experiencing normal aging processes, and coping with widowhood are life events that occur to families in later life (Duvall, 1977). These life events are important to the older persons as well as to other family members. For example, retirement may have an effect on the marital relationship of the older couple and may influence the relationship between the older couple and their children and grandchildren. Some retired couples have time to visit their children and grandchildren. The older family members may be able to help their adult children now that they are retired. Another example is that the death of an older family member is a crucial event to the surviving spouse and is important to the children, grandchildren, siblings, and other relatives. Families with older family members experience life events associated with the normal aging process.

The study of families in later life is focused on family systems in which a couple has launched their children (postchildbearing years) and anticipate or have experienced retirement. The later-life family continues until the death of both the husband and wife. As Duvall (1977, p. 385) suggests, "the aging couple continue to be 'family' to their grown children, grandchildren, and great-grandchildren." To study the family in later life it is important to examine the family relationships from the perspective of the older couple as well as from the vantage points of the other family members. Being a grandparent is important and having a grandparent is crucial to the grandchild. Thus, consideration of the family in later life needs to focus on the total family system.

Family in Later Life as a System

A number of studies indicate that older family members are a part of a family network. First, it is clear that older persons and their children maintain relationships throughout life (Hess & Waring, 1978; Cantor, 1975; Shanas, 1979b). In one study, Cantor (1975) reported strong family relationships in inner-city families. A second indicator of the family network is that family members, older persons and their children, expect to help an older family member in need of assistance. A number of studies (O'Brien & Wagner, 1980; Shanas, 1979b; Riley & Foner, 1968; Seelbach & Sauer, 1977) evidence the expectations of older parents and their adult children.

Another indication of the later-life family as a system is that family members are involved in helping their older relatives (Shanas, 1979a, 1979b; O'Brien & Wagner, 1980; Lebowitz, 1978; Brody, Poulshock, & Masciocchi, 1978). Family members assist older relatives before and after institutionalization (York & Caslyn, 1977). Studies of visiting patterns in nursing homes suggest that family members do most of the visiting (Hook, Sobal, & Oak, 1982; Greene & Monahan, 1982). In short, families with older members are interrelated.

Families in later life consist of a family system in which the eldest family members are experiencing postchildbearing years. There is a reciprocal relationship between the older and younger family members.

This family system provides an important support system for older persons as they experience their later years.

Demographics of Families in Later Life

Recent attention has been directed toward the increase in the number and proportion of older Americans within the twentieth century. There were 3.1 million persons aged 65 years and older in 1900. Eighty years later, the number had increased to 25 million. In 1900, individuals 65 years and older accounted for 4 percent of the total population. By 1980, 11 percent of our total population were 65 years and older (Brotman, 1981). Currently there are 46 million persons 55 years and older. This trend is expected to continue. Brotman (1982) reports that life expectancy at birth is expected to increase. In 1981, newborn males are expected to have a life expectancy of 70.7 years and newborn females are expected to live 78.3 years. By the year 2005, the male life expectancy is expected to increase to 73.3 years and for females to increase to 81.3 years. It is clear that the number and proportion of older persons are sizable and will increase in future years.

A large number of the older persons are members of family networks. Older persons are married and have siblings and/or children and grandchildren. Therefore, there are a large number of American families in which one member is experiencing later life.

Table 1.1 presents the distribution of men and women aged 55 and older by age group and marital status for 1980. Most men (85 percent) and women (70 percent) aged 55-64 years are married. There are more than 4.5 widows for each widower at this age. For ages 65-74 years, most of the men (83 percent) are married, while only one-half of the women are married. Approximately 40 percent of the women are widowed. Nearly 7 out of 10 men aged 75 years and over are married, and less than one-quarter are widowed. For women aged 75 years and over, less than one-quarter are married and nearly 7 out of 10 are widowed. These figures indicated that (1) most older men are married, (2) most of the women are married as long as they are 65 years and younger, and (3) most women over age 65 are widowed.

Two other characteristics are reported in these data. For all age groups, a small percentage (2-7 percent) are divorced. For both men and women, the older the group, the lower the percentage of divorce. Figure 1.1 indicates that the rate of divorce for older men and women has

TABLE 1.1   Distribution of Men and Women Aged 55 Years and Older by Age Group and Marital Status (March 1981)[a]

	Male		Female	
	Number	*%*	*Number*	*%*
55-64				
Married, spouse present	8,275	81.7	7,762	67.1
Married, spouse absent	310	3.1	371	3.2
Widowed	410	4.0	2,128	18.4
Divorced	615	6.1	827	7.1
Never married	520	5.1	486	4.2
65-74				
Married, spouse present	5,429	80.6	4,247	48.3
Married, spouse absent	159	2.4	154	1.7
Widowed	551	8.2	3,524	40.1
Divorced	261	3.9	389	4.4
Never married	333	4.9	475	5.4
75 and Over				
Married, spouse present	2,354	69.7	1,263	21.8
Married, spouse absent	75	2.2	84	1.4
Widowed	745	22.1	3,949	68.2
Divorced	83	2.4	133	2.3
Never married	119	3.5	359	6.2

a. Numbers in thousands.
SOURCE: U.S. Bureau of the Census (1981), "Marital Status and Living Arrangements: March 1981," Current Population Reports, Series p. 20, No. 372.

increased over the past twenty years. In 1960, there were 44 divorced older women per 1,000 married persons. By 1981, there were 95 per 1,000 married persons. For older men, there were 24 per 1,000 in 1960 and 44 per 1,000 in 1981. In 1980, the ratio for older men was 48. Therefore, there is a one-year decrease for the older men. In any case, divorce in later life is experienced by a small minority of older persons, and the size of the minority has more than doubled in the past twenty years.

Table 1.1 indicates that a small portion (4-6 percent) of older persons never experienced marriage. Data presented in Table 1.2 demonstrate that the percentage of single older persons has decreased over the past decade. For both men and women, a small portion were single in 1980

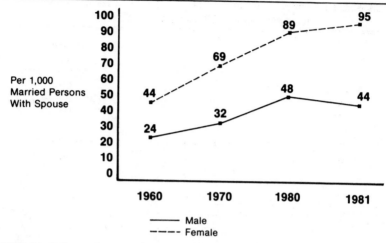

Per 1,000
Married Persons
With Spouse

———— Male
– – – – Female

SOURCE: "Marital Status and Living Arrangements: March, 1981." Current Population Reports, Series P. 20, No. 372, Bureau of Census, 1982, p. 3.

Figure 1.1   Divorced Persons Aged 65 years and Over per 1,000 Married Persons with Spouse Present

compared to 1970, and this trend continued into 1981. Unlike divorced older persons, the never-married elderly are a decreasing minority.

The living arrangements of older men and women are presented in Table 1.3. Most (79 percent) of the men aged 65-74 years live with spouses, while less than one-half of the women aged 65-74 years live with spouses. Nearly 40 percent of these women live alone or with a nonrelative. Few of the men (7 percent) and women (15 percent) live with other relatives. In the younger group of older persons, most are living in family relationships. This is not found in older persons aged 75 years and more. Less than 50 percent of the women live with a spouse or other relative. Nearly 52 percent of these women live alone or with a nonrelative. More than 75 percent of the older old men live in a family situation. The most common family arrangement is with a spouse. Less than one-quarter live alone or with a nonrelative.

These data suggest that most older men live in family settings, while most older old women live alone or with nonrelatives. It is important to note that older persons who live alone or with nonrelatives receive support from family and other kin. Cantor (1980) studied inner-city

TABLE 1.2   Percentage of Never-Married Men and Women
by Age: 1970, 1980, and 1981

	Men	Women
	55-64 Years	55-64 Years
1970	7.8	6.8
1980	5.3	4.5
1981	5.1	4.2
	65 Years and Over	65 Years and Over
1970	7.5	7.7
1980	4.9	5.9
1981	4.5	5.7

SOURCE: "Marital Status and Living Arrangements: March 1981," Current Population Reports, Series p. 20, No. 372. Bureau of the Census, 1982, p. 2.

elderly and reported that most had children. These children provided emotional support and companionship to their older parents. Thus, the family is an important group to older persons.

Although children provide support to their older parents, few elderly live with their children. Brotman (1981) reports that 6 percent of older men and 11 percent of older women live with their children. Further, there is a trend toward a decreasing number of older persons living with their children. For example, there were more than twice as many older women living independently in 1980 than in 1950. When older parents live with their children, they usually live with a daughter (Lopata, 1973; Shanas, Townsend, Wedderburn, Friis, Milhoj, & Stehouwer, 1968). The living arrangements of older men and women indicate that family relationships are significant even though few share in the same household.

The number of children within a family system has been declining in recent years. Fifty years ago, nearly 50 percent of older women had four or more children. Now, about 25 percent have four or more children (Brotman, 1981). Approximately 20 percent of older women have had at least one child. Data suggest that nearly 80 percent of persons 65 years and older have surviving children (Brotman, 1981). It appears that most older people have children, but the number of children in a family has decreased, and this trend is expected to continue. This suggests that the size of a family network may be decreasing.

TABLE 1.3   Living Arrangements of the 65+ Noninstitutional
Population by Sex and Age Group (1980 estimate)[a]

	Male		Female	
	Number	%	Number	%
65-74	6,549	100.0	8,549	100.0
Living with spouse	5,199	79.4	4,114	48.1
Living with other relative	426	6.5	1,243	14.5
Living alone or with nonrelative	924	14.1	3,192	37.3
75+	3,234	100.0	5,411	100.0
Living with spouse	2,190	67.7	1,197	22.1
Living with other relative	301	9.3	1,417	26.2
Living alone or with nonrelative	743	23.0	2,797	51.7

a. Numbers in thousands.
SOURCE: Herbert B. Brotman, "Supplement to the Chartbook on Aging in America,"
published by the 1981 White House Conference on Aging, p. 3.

Remarriage is an event that is experienced by few elderly. Two studies
(Cleveland & Gianturco, 1976; Treas & VanHilst, 1976) focused on the
possibility of remarriage in later life. Both report that the likelihood of
remarriage after widowhood or divorce is small. Men are more likely to
remarry than women. For example, Cleveland and Gianturco (1976)
report that less than one-quarter of widowers aged 65 years or older ever
remarry. For widows aged 55 years or more, less than 5 percent remarry.
Men are more likely to marry younger women than vice versa (Treas &
VanHilst, 1976). Most of the older men and women who marry are
marrying widows (Treas & VanHilst, 1976). Thus, remarriage in later
life may be attractive, but few elderly remarry in later life.

Demographic characteristics of older persons indicate that they are
or have been members of family networks. Most are married or have
been married. Most have children. Few have never married. Most older
women experience widowhood and few remarry. In any case, a family
network exists for most older persons.

Family:
Positive and Negative Aspects

The existence of a family network for older people provides a
reservoir of individuals. The family is available to help the older persons

Timothy H. Brubaker   17

in emergencies and to provide support for day-to-day activities. The family may provide financial assistance or advice. For emotional support, the family may be the primary resource for the older person. Lebowitz (1978) suggests that the family provides extraordinary amounts of support to older members. As a society, older persons' families contribute large sums of support to the elderly. As Nydegger (1983, p. 28) notes, "charity really does begin at home."

While the family provides support, it should be noted that there are negative aspects to close family involvement with the elderly. When an older parent and adult children reside in the same household, tensions may arise. The need to provide community support for intergenerational families is suggested by Brubaker and Brubaker (1981). The primary reason for such support relates to the negative aspects of family relationships. Family members may recall unpleasant family experiences or may be overwhelmed with the needs of the intergenerational household.

Another example of negative aspects of the family relationships in later life is reported by Quinn (1983). In a study of older parents and adult children, it was found that excessive filial expectations of older parents are negatively related to the communication patterns. The adult children may feel a burden from older parents' expectations; consequently, a strain is created on the family relationships.

Recently Nydegger (1983) cogently summarized the positive and negative aspects of family relationships in later life:

> supportive families can be found in all societies. So can their opposites. We must accept these negative aspects as natural outcomes and attempt to pinpoint those structural features that encourage conflict before we can fully understand the aged and their family ties. (p. 31)

Plan for This Book

This book is intended to provide an overview of family relationships in later life, to present research on specific family relationships (e.g., husband/wife, older parent/adult child), to focus on specific isues concerning families in later life (e.g., sexuality, marital interaction), and to discuss practice and policy concerns. The primary objectives of this book are to review research completed on a topic concerning family relationships in later life and present new research or applications of the topic.

The book is premised on the following:

(1) A viable family network exists for many older persons.
(2) Family relationships in later life are important to *both* older people and other family members.
(3) Positive *and* negative aspects characterize family relationships in later life.
(4) Policy and practice directed at older people need to recognize the importance of the family network in later life.

It is hoped that the chapters in this book will stimulate researchers and practitioners to consider family relationships in later life. Current research findings provide a broad description of later-life family relationships. Additional research is needed to understand the complexity of family relationships in later life.

PART I

Family Relationships

This part focuses on specific family relationships experienced by older persons. Each of the four contributions examines one important family relationship. In the first contribution, Linda Ade-Ridder and Timothy H. Brubaker consider the couple relationship in later life. For many older people, the husband-wife relationship is vital and long-standing. What does research indicate about the marital quality of these couples? Marital quality research is reviewed, and it is concluded that older couples experience different patterns of marital quality. For some, the later years are marked by an increase in marital quality; for others, a decrease. A theoretical discussion of the relationship between retirement, spouses' support of retirees' self-definitions, and marital quality is presented. It is suggested that the spouse's confirmation of the retiree's self-definition is a crucial factor in understanding marital quality in the later years.

Victor G. Cicirelli provides an in-depth review of the adult child and elderly parent relationship. He concludes that most adult children maintain a relationship with their adult parents because there are affection and bonds between them. Their relationship is characterized by close compatible and satisfying feelings between parents and children. At the same time, adult children need support in their relationships with their parents. Areas of need and ways to meet these needs are discussed.

Sibling relationships of older persons are reviewed in the next chapter. Jean Pearson Scott indicates that research on siblings is limited. However, studies report that 75 to 93 percent of people 65 years of age or older have at least one living brother or sister. Data gathered from 199 older persons are analyzed. Patterns of social interaction and assistance of siblings are compared to relationships with children and grandchildren. Although not as involved with older persons as adult children, siblings are supportive. Implications for working with older people are made.

The fourth relationship is grandparent. Lillian E. Troll suggests that grandparents play a central role in the family. Differences between parenting and grandparenting are explicated. It is concluded that the primary role of grandparents may be maintaining the family system. Grandparents may be the "watchdogs" of the family.

2

The Quality of Long-Term Marriages

LINDA ADE-RIDDER
TIMOTHY H. BRUBAKER

Understanding the marital relationships of older couples is important to family scholars and to gerontologists. Increased longevity and shrinking family size mean that more couples will survive into their retirement years. It is estimated that one out of every five first married couples will celebrate a fiftieth wedding anniversary (Glick & Norton, 1977). With the provision of basic survival assured for most, the focus of attention has shifted to include increased quality of life (Ade-Ridder, 1983). Research interest reflects the concern about marital quality across the life cycle and into the retirement years.

The primary objectives of this chapter are to review research on marital quality across the life cycle and in retirement and to present theoretical linkages of marital quality in retirement. Implications for researchers and practitioners are discussed.

Marital Quality Literature

Marital quality includes all of the variables contributing to it, such as happiness, success, satisfaction, and adjustment. Two subareas are reviewed: marriage across the family life cycle and marriage in retirement.

Marriage Across the Family Life Cycle

An issue that has received a great deal of attention is how marital quality varies over time. There is confusion in the literature surrounding marital quality in later life (Ade-Ridder, 1983). One problem is that very few studies have been longitudinal. Prior to the 1970s, few researchers used the family life cycle as an explanatory variable for marital quality, according to Hicks and Platt (1970).

TABLE 2.1   Patterns of Marital Quality Over the Family Life Cycle

Author	Year	N	Family Life Cycle Stage	Pattern of Marital Quality
Anderson, Russell, Schumm	1983	196	1-5	curvilinear
Axelson	1960	464	postparental	curvilinear
Blood & Wolfe	1960	909	all (1-8)	decrease
Bossard & Boll	1955	440	age 20-70	curvilinear
Burr	1970	116	postparental	curvilinear
Clark & Wallin[a] (also Dentler & Pineo, 1960; Pineo, 1961, 1969)	1965	1000 -428	1-middle	no change
Deutscher	1962 1964	49	postparental	increase
Gass	1959	85	age 25-50	increase
Glass & Wright	1965	831	1-12 years	decrease
Glenn	1975	1973	postparental	increase
Gurin, Veroff, & Feld	1960	1867	all	curvilinear
Luckey	1966	80	2-21 years	decrease
Miller	1976	140	all	bimodal
Orthner	1975	442	1-launching	curvilinear
Paris & Luckey[a]	1966	72	2-teenagers	decrease
Rollins & Cannon	1974	800	all	curvilinear
Rollins & Feldman	1970	799	all	curvilinear
Safilios-Rothschild	1967	320	pre-school	decrease
Smart & Smart	1975	476	all	curvilinear
Spanier, Lewis, & Cole	1975	1584	all	nothing and curvilinear
Stinnett, Carter, & Montgomery	1972	408	age 60-89	curvilinear
Stinnett, Collins, & Montgomery	1970	227	age 60+	curvilinear
Terman	1938	792	1-7	curvilinear
Tuckman & Lorge	1954	53	age 60-88	decrease

a. Longitudinal study.

Results from the studies of marital quality over the life cycle fall into three categories, according to Medley (1977): (1) A continual decline in marital happiness follows an initial period of satisfaction. (2) The initial period of marital happiness precedes a decline during the child-rearing years and is followed by an increase during the post-child-rearing years, or a curvilinear relationship. (3) Neither pattern is supported. Table 2.1

summarizes these studies according to the life-cycle stages studied and pattern of marital quality supported. Medley (1977) concluded that there was no one pattern of adjustment for retired couples. Any problems previously evident would be likely to intensify as fewer couple adjustments would be made over time.

Pattern of Decline in Marital Quality. Hicks and Platt (1970) reported that prior to the 1960s all studies showed a decline in marital happiness from the beginning of marriage onward. Most research (see Table 2.1) indicated that by age 50, most marriages had disintegrated a great deal (Tuckman & Lorge, 1954; Blood & Wolfe, 1960; Luckey, 1966; Safilios-Rothschild, 1969; Yarrow et al., 1971; Glass & Wright, 1977). Peterson and Payne (1975) suggested that marriages exhibit greater fragility and promise than ever before, as people's expectations for happiness increase; the continuing decline in marital happiness is primarily due to new roles. Husbands, however, reported that love reached its lowest point following retirement (Peterson & Payne, 1975).

Two prominent studies contributed support to the declining happiness position. Interviews with 909 Detroit-area women by Blood and Wolfe (1960) demonstrated a decline in marital quality over the life cycle. However, only 8 women in the sample were age 60 years or older; after 20 years of marriage, only 6 percent said they were fully satisfied with marriage. Blood and Wolfe (1960) reported a steady decline in marital love and companionship into the retirement years, and theorized that fewer shared activities combined with the husband's loss of power following retirement were responsible. Burgess and Wallin's (1953) longitudinal study, begun in 1954 on 1,000 engaged couples, also supported declining marital quality. These couples were interviewed five, fifteen, and twenty years after their marriages. Dentler and Pineo (1960; Pineo, 1961, 1969) attributed the decline in marital satisfaction and adjustment by middle age to disenchantment, "a process which appears to be generally an inescapable consequence of the passage of time in a marriage" (1961, p. 6). Pineo (1961) concluded that since we marry by "choice," the "fit" is best at marriage and declines thereafter.

Curvilinear Pattern of Marital Quality. The second category of marital adjustment or satisfaction supported by recent literature (see Table 2.1) is the curvilinear pattern, or U-shaped curve, from an initial period of happiness in very early marriage to a low during the early child-rearing years, followed by an increase in marital happiness during the later years (Terman, 1938; Bossard & Boll, 1955; Axelson, 1960; Gurin et al., 1960; Burr, 1970; Rollins & Feldman, 1970; Stinnett, Collins, &

Montgomery, 1970; Stinnett, Carter, & Montgomery, 1972; Rollins & Cannon, 1974; Orthner, 1975; Smart & Smart, 1975; Miller, 1976; Anderson, Russell, & Schumm, 1983). In a large, nationwide random sample, Gurin, Veroff, and Field (1960) found that older couples generally exhibited the same degree of marital happiness as did couples of younger ages; however, they were less likely to report problems. A decline in marital happiness was found until age 64, when an increase in marital happiness began with a sharp decline in marital problems after age 64. Increased education correlated with increased expectations for marriage and family, which led to greater opportunities for both gratification and distress. Couples were more apt to to share activities after their children had left and often developed a greater interdependence. They felt that the years after turning 65 were the happiest.

Harold Feldman (1964) has been involved with a series of studies starting in 1958, when he studied 852 middle- and upper-class couples at all stages of the family life cycle, finding a decrease in marital satisfaction from the start of marriage through the child-launching stages, followed by an increase in satisfaction, though not to the honeymoon level. Elderly couples without children were found to be happier than couples with children (Feldman, 1964; Troll, 1971). In 1970, Rollins and Feldman replicated Feldman's earlier findings, as did a 1974 study of 800 Mormons by Rollins and Cannon and a 1975 New Zealand study conducted by Smart and Smart.

Gould (1972) asserted that marital satisfaction increases somwhere around the fifth decade of life, as the perceived importance of self decreases and the importance of spouse increases. Miller (1976) noted that an upswing in marital satisfaction occurred earlier than had been previously documented, with the lowest satisfaction occurring between 6 and 10 years of marriage. Satisfaction then increased to a peak between 20 and 25 years before dropping off again to below early marriage levels at 36 or more years, resulting in a bimodel curve. In a study of marital quality over the family life cycle in three subsamples from Georgia, Iowa, and Ohio, a curvilinear pattern for one sample, Ohio, and insignificant results for the Georgia and Iowa samples were found by Spanier, Lewis, and Cole (1975). They concluded that longitudinal research is needed.

Other Patterns of Marital Quality. Finally, the third category of studies on marital satisfaction by family life cycle supported neither the continual decline nor the curvilinear relationship model (see Table 2.1). Some researchers found an apparent increase in marital quality, although all agreed that the child-rearing years are problematic (Gass, 1959; Axelson, 1960; Deutscher, 1964; Glenn, 1975). Deutscher (1962) stated that present cohorts of elderly people had few opportunities for anticipatory socialization with the relatively new phenomenon of both spouses surviving beyond the departure of the last child. Yarrow et al. (1971) reported that there was some degree of marital deterioration in up to one-third of the elderly couples sampled, leaving two-thirds as happy or happier than in earlier years. Clark and Wallin 1965) found that couples who had high levels of marital satisfaction previously tended to stay high, while couples exhibiting low levels of marital satisfaction previously also tended to stay low. A continuous pattern of marital quality across the life cycle is supported. While all couples experience a drop during their child-rearing years, marriages with high quality in early marriage are likely to bounce back, while marginal or lower-quality relationships are less likely to do so. Then again, is the tendency to report a later-life marriage as happier due to the greater length of time, energy, and resources invested in it by each partner so as not to feel that one has wasted his or her life (Spanier et al., 1975)? The theory of cognitive consistency may lead older individuals to rate their marriages as happier than those of younger people.

Marriage in Retirement

Butler and Lewis (1973, p. 112) wrote that "care during illness, household management, and emotional gratification are three expectations found in older marriages. The older couple married for many years will find they have a different marriage in old age than they had in middle or early life."

Morris Medley (1977), drawing from previous literature, proposed a theoretical framework to study marriage in the postretirement years. He proposed three types of postretirement marriages that would provide partners with a sense of self-fulfillment and a feeling of well-being. They do not necessarily last indefinitely, as marital adjustment is a creative process. Couples in the husband-wife relationship type of marriage emphasize the intimate and shared nature of their relationships. In the second type, parent-child relationships, the marriage is epitomized by one partner behaving in a nurturant, protective, and dominant role over the submissive and dependent spouse. In the third type, the associates, the spouses are friends, but each tends to find his or her most rewarding moments outside of the relationship. All three types of marital adjustment are influenced by earlier life experiences and patterns, although present activities sometimes enhance a relationship (Medley, 1977).

Adjustment to Retirement. The impact of retirement differs between men and women. Burgess (1960) suggested that the loss of status with retirement for men may negatively affect marital relationships. Cavan (1962, 1969) reported that retirement was the most acute adjustment most men had to make, due to the long-term buildup of their self-concept, centering on their role in the marketplace. For these men, retirement was a shattering experience (1962), offering no substitute for the "work role" (1969). This seemed to be particularly true for professionals (Kimmel, 1974). Keckhoff (1972) found that men expected and experienced more change with retirement than did women. Older women were found to be as work-oriented as men and were likely to take a longer time in adjusting to retirement than men (Atchley, 1976b). However, Jaslow (1976) found that morale was higher for retired women who had worked than for women who had never worked.

Marital Quality in Retirement. Considering the paucity of research studies on older married couples, Stinnett, Collins, and Montgomery (1970) concluded that a lack of appropriate instruments has hampered the few existing efforts, since previous instruments were written for an administered to younger samples. Yet the developmental needs and tasks of older persons may be significantly different from their needs and tasks in earlier years.

In a longitudinal study of upper-middle-class parents between 60 and 82 years, Maas and Kuypers (1974) found that 40 percent of the men were very involved with their spouses and claimed to have happy marriages, although 36 percent indicated low or declining marital satisfaction. These people seemed to organize their lives with little regard to the lifestyles of their spouses and were remarkably independent of one another (Parron & Troll, 1978).

On the other hand, marital quality among retired men and women has been found to increase after a dip around the actual retirement time (Lipman, 1962; Feldman, 1964; Rollins & Feldman, 1970). However, Feldman (1964) also reported that marital interaction among elderly couples was low, the women had the power, discussions were limited; both husband and wife were preoccupied with health, and a feeling of peace and lack of stress was evident.

Summary of Marital Quality Literature

The multiplicity of studies of marital quality over the family life cycle and into retirement presents widely varied and inconsistent findings. As Snyder (1979, p. 815) stated, researchers have utilized many different measures of marital quality with no real concurrence as to what that encompasses. In addition, many studies examined only one of two variables at a time, making comparisons between studies very difficult. Most earlier studies that reported a decline in marital quality did not study older men and women, or, if they did, the samples were too small for reliable inferences (Ade-Ridder, 1983). In addition, nearly all of the studies were cross-sectional in nature. Abelson's Cognitive Constancy Theory, as reported by Schram (1979), suggests that the longer a couple is married, the greater is the tendency to report the marriage as happy. The Cognitive Consistency Theory used by Spanier, Lewis, and Cole (1975; Streib & Beck, 1980) explains the curvilinear pattern of marital quality over the life cycle. This theory suggests that the more one invests in a relationship, the higher it will be valued, since not to do so would imply that one has wasted one's life. This tendency presents a special problem in studying older men and women and is complicated by the likelihood of obtaining socially desirable responses from them (Hawkins, 1966).

Theoretical Linkages of
Marital Quality in Retirement

Focusing on the retirement stage of the family life cycle may provide an understanding of marital quality in later life. Changes in a person's life situation as a result of retirement are seen as relevant to the couple relationship. For some retirees, the marital relationship contributes to their self-perceptions. For example, when changes occur in one's employment, a spouse may support or not support one's self-concept. The degree to which one's self-concept is supported during the retirement years may be related to the level of a couple's marital satisfaction. Factors external to the couple may support the self-concept in later life. For instance, an older person's view of old age may be crucial. Brubaker and Powers (1976) suggested that there is a relationship between an older person's self-concept and attitudes toward old age. An older person with a negative self-concept is likely to accept negative aspects of the stereotype of old. Conversely, an individual with a positive self-concept is likely to identify with positive aspects of old age.

The marital unit is the place where the retiree receives reinforcement of his or her self-concept. For example, the family member who retires, voluntarily or involuntarily, may turn to the spouse and possibly adult children for a redefinition of self. If work was the arena in which this older person received primary reinforcement of self, the family becomes the arena for support after retirement. In some cases, the marital partner may be the only person available to provide reinforcement.

Prior to retirement, the reinforcement of the spouse may not have been as important to marital quality. If a spouse did not agree with the retiree's self-assessment, confirmation may have been available at work. Upon retirement, self-confirmation may not be as readily available outside the family. Thus, spouses may need to turn to each other and, if confirmation is given, may increase marital quality in retirement.

The increase in marital quality may be a result of external family stress. One type of external family stress is retirement. For example, if a retiree's spouse provides support during retirement, then the marital relationship is enhanced. However, if support from the spouse is not evident, marital role strain may develop. Marital role strain refers to stress *within* the marital unit. Burr (1973) proposed that there is an inverse linear relationship between marital role strain and marital quality. Therefore, marital satisfaction is expected to decrease in retirement if the retiree's spouse does not provide a confirmation.

This may be applicable only to a retiree with a positive self-definition. If the retiree has a negative self-definition, confirmation may be readily available outside the marital unit. That is, a spouse may reinforce the existence of a negative self-definition and the opportunity for similar reinforcement outside the family appears to be greater than for a positive self-definition. Negative attitudes toward the old have been found to exist outside the family (Peters, 1971; McTavish, 1971), and these may reinforce an extant negative self-definition. Thus, if a retiree has a negative self-definition and reinforcement of it is not available within the marital dyad, such reinforcement may be obtained in social relationships external to the family. These negative attitudes toward the self may be in conflict with any reinforcement of a positive definition of the self that may be given within the family. Retirees may be particularly susceptible to negative external reinforcement, since most of their preretirement definitions of self are derived from external (work) rather than family sources.

Marital Quality in Retirement. Marital quality within the retirement stage of the family life cycle is related, as conceptualized here, to the type of reinforcement given to the retiree's self-concept. If the retiree's perception of self is confirmed by his other marital partner, marital quality during this stage is expected to increase. Marital quality is not expected to increase if confirmation of the retiree's self-definition is not found

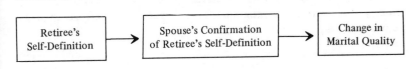

Figure 2.1   Theoretical Linkages of Marital Quality in Retirement

within the marital dyad. A graphic representation of the linkages of these variables is presented in Figure 2.1.

It is hypothesized that the quality of the marital relationship is dependent on the degree of congruency between the retiree's self-definition and the spouse's confirmation of the retiree's self-definition. Retirees are not expected to be satisfied with their marital relationships if their spouses do not support their own definitions of self.

It is also hypothesized that if retirees have positive self-concepts that are confirmed by their marital partners, marital quality will increase. This occurs because (1) both spouses agree on the definition of the retiree's self-definition and (2) a positive self-definition is incongruent with some definitions of retirement held by those outside the family. Also, it may be hypothesized that if retirees perceive their families as relatively deprived because they involuntarily retired, they may consider themselves and their families in conflict with society. Especially for retirees with positive self-definitions, perception of conflict with society contributes to increased solidarity of the marital dyad. Thus, the confirmation of a positive self-definition by the marital partner and the perception of conflict with society increase the family solidarity, thereby contributing to the increase in marital quality in retirement. This supports a curvilinear pattern of marital satisfaction.

A linear decline in marital quality, however, may be expected if the retiree's self-concept is negative. In this case, marital quality is expected to continue its gradual decline because acceptance of the negative stereotype of old is accepted. The negative stereotype defines retirement as less satisfying than previous life situations. Therefore, the retiree who accepts the negative elements of the stereotype of old might expect marital quality to decrease.

Implications

Implications for researchers and for practitioners in gerontology are discussed. This model suggests the need for self-definition measures paired with marital quality measures in research. Caregivers to the elderly may find these linkages useful in directing their efforts to problem areas and solutions that may enhance the quality of later-life marriages.

Implications of Theory for Research

Family research that focuses on marital quality within the retirement stage needs to include a measure of the self-definitions of each marital partner. This conceptualization emphasizes the saliency of the retiree's self-definition and the attitudes of the marital partner in relation to the level of marital quality experienced during this stage. Further, a longitudinal design is most appropriate because any change in both marital quality scores and self-definition measures can be evidenced. These changes are not evident in a cross-sectional analysis. This conceptualization may enable researchers to interpret their data more accurately because both linear and curvilinear patterns may be characteristic of the quality of the marital relationship over the family life cycle.

Implications of Theory for Applied Gerontology

This theoretical formulation has important implications for applied gerontology. It underscores the saliency of marital confirmation of the spouse's positive self-definition. If the spouse reinforces and confirms the extant positive self-definition, marital quality is expected to increase. Incidentally, this confirmation may be a result of verbal and/or nonverbal communication that has been positively related to marital quality (Navran, 1967; Kahn, 1970). Second, if a therapist is confronted with a situation in which a negative self-definition is characteristic of the retired member of the marital dyad, this formulation demonstrates the need to encourage this individual to accept responsibility to deal with this extant negative self-definition. If, then, the retiree learns to reject his or her negative self-concept, it is expected that the satisfaction with the marital relationship will increase. Finally, this formulation enables the applied gerontologist to determine the reason one couple experiences a continual decline and another evidences a gradual increase in marital quality during the retirement. This, it is hoped, will reduce the time involved in diagnosis and treatment of the problems existing within a retirement marriage.

3

Adult Children and Their Elderly Parents

VICTOR G. CICIRELLI

The second of the family relationships of elderly people to be taken up in this volume is that between adult children and their elderly parents. Ideally, such relationships should not be considered in isolation, since they constitute only one subsystem of a larger system in which the relationships within any one subsystem affect and are affected by the ongoing relationships within the other family subsystems. The larger family system may be looked upon as consisting of overlapping nuclear family subsystems (each consisting of two spouses and their children); thus, the middle-aged child of elderly parents in one subsystem may be the parent of young children in another. The larger family system may thus be a system of considerable complexity, which may change over time with shifting coalitions among family members as well as change in composition through birth and death. While it is recognized that interactions with other subsystems of the larger family system may influence the relationship between an adult child and the elderly parent, this chapter will focus on the parent-child relationship itself. The influence of other family subsystems on this relationship will be discussed only when particularly relevant.

This chapter will consider two major aspects of the parent-child relationship: the interpersonal relationship between them and the helping relationship. These aspects of the relationship will be considered from the perspective of life-span attachment theory. The chapter will begin by briefly reviewing attachment theory itself, and proceed by examining the adult child's proximity to and contact with the elderly parent, the quality of the relationship with the parent and whether it depends on the amount of interaction between the two, and the helping

Author's Note: Research herein presented was supported by grants from the AARP Andrus Foundation.

relationship. The test of a path model of helping behavior based on attachment theory will be presented. Next, some of the problem areas in helping elderly parents will be considered: communication on needs, absence of adult children, and stresses of helping. Finally, the effects of an adult child's marital disruption on the parent-child relationship will be discussed.

Attachment and the Relationship with Elderly Parents

Life-Span Attachment Theory

The extension of attachment theory over the life span can provide a conceptual framework that helps to explain the persistence of the parent-child relationship into old age. Attachment refers to an emotional or affectional bond between two people; it is essentially being identified with, in love with, and having the desire to be with another person. Although attachment is inferred from the infant's propensity to seek proximity and contact with the mother (Ainsworth, 1972), it is an internal state that is distinct from attachment behaviors. Protective behaviors that develop later in time are concerned with preserving or restoring the threatened existence of the attached figure (Bowlby, 1979, 1980).

Bowlby (1979, 1980) has extended this theory of attachment over the life span, holding that the child's attachment to the parent does not end in late childhood or adolescence but persists throughout life. Although separation from the parent is an inevitable part of the normal developmental sequence as the child moves out into the world to assume adult responsibilities, the propensity for closeness and contact is assumed to continue. As a way to deal with the conflict between this necessary separation and attachment, the child establishes symbolic closeness and contact with the parent through the mechanism of identification. Through love for the parent, the child incorporates part of the parent's personality into his own (Fromm, 1956; Hall & Lindzey, 1970). This makes it possible for the child to symbolize closeness to the parent in terms of ever-present personality features. Such a view of attachment leads to such criteria as feelings of closeness and perceived similarity to the parent as evidence of the child's attachment.

It should be noted that we are concerned here with the child's attachment to the parent, not new and multiple attachments that the individual develops or the mechanisms (e.g., conditioning, self-promoted feed-back) by which they develop (Hartup & Lempers, 1973; Kalish & Knudtson, 1976; Knudtson, 1976; Troll & Smith, 1976).

Attachment behaviors in adulthood may involve communication over a distance to make psychological closeness and contact as well as periodic visiting to reestablish physical contact (e.g., living close to the parent, visiting, telephoning, letter writing, and messages or informa-tion relayed by others). Obviously, such attachment behaviors as resi-dential proximity may be an expression of other factors than the child's attachment to the parent, such as employment opportunities or desires of a spouse. However, it is held that, other things being equal, the adult child who is more attached to the parent will have greater residential proximity than a less attached child in the same situation. One might thus expect a positive correlation between the child's feelings of attach-ment and residential proximity to the parent, although the correlation is likely to be only a moderate one.

Protective behaviors in adulthood occur in response to a threat or implied threat to the elderly parent's continued existence, such as illness, disability, increasing frailty, or economic deprivation. The adult child responds with some form of helping or caregiving behavior, which serves to diminish the threat, maintain the survival of the elderly parent, and preserve the emotional bond.

Proximity and Contact

An important preliminary question is whether most elderly people have living adult children. Approximately 80 percent of all elderly people have living children; most are middle-aged, although one should not forget the variability in age that exists among children of the elderly. Some adult children are themselves over age 65, while other children of elderly may be still minors or even preschool children (Cicirelli, 1979). The literature on geographic proximity of adult children to their parents and on amount of contact with them is large and has been amply reviewed elsewhere (Hill, Foote, Aldous, Carlson, & MacDonald, 1970; Riley & Foner, 1968; Shanas, Townsend, Wedderburn, Friis, Milhoj, & Stehouwer, 1968; Troll, 1971; Troll, Miller, & Atchley, 1979). Suffice it to say that from 78 to 90 percent of all older people with living children see their children once a week or more often and are in contact with them by telephone at about the same frequency. Rather than the telephone being used as a substitute form of contact by adult children who live too far away to visit, it appears that those who see their parents more frequently also telephone them more often. Thus, it is evident that most adult children maintain some level of attachment behaviors in regard to elderly parents and that the relationship is an ongoing and viable one. Only a very few elderly people have lost contact with their adult children.

Quality of the Parent-Child Relationship

Reports of case studies with problem families suggest that the relationships of older people and their adult children may be quite poor. However, studies of the general population tend to be in agreement that most adult children feel very close to their elderly parents, and vice versa. For example, we (Cicirelli, 1981a) found that 87 percent of adult children felt "close" or "very close" to their elderly fathers, and 91 percent felt "close" or "very close" to their elderly mothers; very few (2 and 0 percent, respectively) felt "not close at all," while the remainder felt a slight degree of closeness. Taking for granted the influence of social desirability on the responses, a general positive feeling toward parents is quite clear. Daughters felt closer than sons, while those at higher socioeconomic levels felt less close to parents than did those at lower socioeconomic levels.

Such feelings between parents and adult children seem to be mutual. However, as Bengtson (1979b) has pointed out, there seems to be a generational stake in the relationship, with parents feeling closer to their children than the children do in return.

For most adult children and their elderly parents, the relationship is a smooth and compatible one (Cicirelli, 1981a). Adult children gain a great deal of satisfaction from their relationships with their parents and report getting along well with them. However, we found that adult children were somewhat less likely to share intimate details of their lives and important decisions with their parents. Close as the relationship appears to be, many parents and children do not interact concerning these important areas of their lives.

When we looked at the extent of interpersonal conflict between adult children and their parents, only 5 percent reported frequent conflict with elderly mothers and 6 percent reported frequent conflict with elderly fathers, while 36 percent and 39 percent, respectively, reported no conflict at all. Conflict that occurred tended to center on one party's criticism of or intrusion into the other's habits or activities. Thus, most parents and children had little or no conflict in their relationships;

however, they did expect an increase in conflict if they were to live together. It may be that most parents and adult children are able to avoid conflict by limiting the scope of the relationship to less intimate and important areas of their personal lives. At the same time, they manage to enjoy certain satisfying aspects of the relationship, such as the sense of shared warmth and affectional closeness.

Interaction and Feelings of Attachment

The question of whether affection for the elderly parent is associated with closer proximity to parents and more frequent interaction is one about which there has been some controversy. Adams (1968), in a study of young to middle-aged adults, found that the degree of relationship between feelings of closeness and frequency of interaction depended on the distance between the residences of parent and child. When distances were very great, thus making it very difficult for interaction to take place, or when distances were very small, making accidental or obligatory contact more likely, Adams found no significant relationship between affectional closeness and frequency of interaction. However, at moderate distances that made contact more purely a reflection of volition, there was a significant positive relationship between frequency of interaction and feelings of closeness. Based on Adams's findings, it appears that when confounding influences have been removed, closeness of feeling is indeed related to frequency of interaction.

Others have attributed frequency of interaction to various factors. Rosow (1967) reported that frequency of interaction with elderly parents was more strongly related to the degree of parental dependency than to emotional closeness, while Adams (1968a), Blau (1973), and Weishaus (1979) have all stressed the relationship between filial obligation (duty, family loyalty, and so on) and interaction with the parent. Cicirelli (in press a) found that both adult children's feelings of attachment to their elderly mothers and filial obligations were significantly related to the degree of parent-child interaction, although the correlations were low; parental dependency was not significantly related. One can conclude that affectional closeness is not the only factor leading to interaction with the parent, and that filial obligation and parent dependency may also be involved. Nevertheless, affectional closeness represents a purely volitional aspect among those factors associated with parental interaction. Simply put, the adult child makes contact with the parent (at least partially) out of love for the parent and because he or she wants to do so, not just out of a sense of duty or because the parent needs help.

The Helping Relationship

There is much evidence that a mutual helping relationship between parent and child continues throughout life (Bengtson, 1979b; Troll et al., 1979). Such help may be either instrumental (e.g., transportation, housekeeping) or affective (e.g., companionship, sympathy) in nature (Jackson, 1980). Early in life, the balance of help is in favor of the children, while in adulthood it becomes more equal. Parents continue to help their children in many ways even in old age. However, when elderly parents become ill or face loss of other social and economic supports in old age, the balance of help shifts in favor of the parents. We are concerned in this section not with the mutual exchange of help, but with the help proceeding from adult children to elderly parents who are facing the vicissitudes of aging and in the factors that are related to such help and that motivate sustained helping by the child.

The sense of duty has been suggested as a major reason for helping parents. That is, the adult child feels a sense of obligation to help an aging parent that is generally accepted and transmitted by the culture. Blenkner's (1965) concept of filial maturity fits into such a general notion of family obligation. According to Blenkner, at some time in middle age the adult child reaches a greater sense of maturity in the filial role, beginning to look at the parent as an individual with personal needs and goals and taking on a sense of responsibility (or a caretaking role) with regard to the parent. When there is a mismatch between the kind of filial behavior an elderly parent expects of a child and the way the adult child interprets and carries out the filial role in middle age, there is likely be dissatisfaction and difficulty. Seelbach and Sauer (1977) found that parental morale suffered when children failed to meet parental expectations for filial behavior. Clearly, some adult children are motivated by a sense of duty, while others may be more motivated by affection or a combination of affection and obligation (Adams, 1968a). The growth of social programs has done much to relieve adult children of the duty to support and care for elderly parents (Treas, 1977), thus making help to parents more likely to be based on volition than on necessity or social obligation.

Interpersonal conflicts between parent and child (Simos, 1973) can interfere with help to the parent, particularly when the conflict has been of long standing. Rejection, bitter arguments, or alienation may make a child unwilling to provide help to a parent. However, positive and negative feelings can coexist in the same relationship (Troll & Smith, 1976; Troll et al., 1979); thus the existence of conflict would not necessarily interfere with helping behavior.

Life-span attachment theory, as discussed earlier, regards protective behavior toward the parent as developing from the basic attachment bond. Where parental illness, decline in vigor, or lack of material resources would seem to pose a threat to the parent's continued existence, the attached child will seek to provide needed help to protect the parent from the threat and thus prolong the parent's continued existence.

In a recent study (Cicirelli, in press a), we sought to construct a path model based on attachment theory and to test the model with data on adult children's helping relationships to their parents. Attachment theory provides a basis for ordering the variables, with feelings of attachment leading to greater attachment behaviors (proximity and contact) and in turn to greater protective (helping) behaviors. Both present helping behavior and commitment to provide future help were included in the model, since it was felt that any consequences of present helping might have an effect on willingness to help in the future. Also, many elderly subjects had low needs for present help, so it was felt that commitment to provide future help might provide a better test of the model. Other variables included in the model were parental dependency, interpersonal conflict with the parent, and filial obligation. Perception of parental dependency should lead to increased helping behavior according to attachment theory. On the other hand, if filial obligation is an important factor in children's help to parents, it should account for a larger proportion of helping behavior than do the attachment variables. Conflict was predicted to lead to less helping. A full recursive model involving these variables was tested.[1]

The hypothesized causal ordering of the feelings of attachment, attachment behaviors, and present helping behaviors in relation to future commitment to help the parent was supported by the data analysis. The importance of attachment behaviors (proximity and contact) for helping is consonant with the earlier findings of Bengtson, Olander, and Haddad (1976) on the importance of residential proximity for help-giving and the findings of Sussman (1965) on the importance of already existing socialization patterns when help for elderly parents is needed. While feelings of attachment had only an indirect effect on present help to parents (through its effect on attachment behaviors), it both had a direct and an indirect effect on commitment to help in the future. In contrast to the direct role of filial responsibility suggested by earlier research (Bengtson et al., 1976; Blau, 1973), the filial obligation variable had only an indirect effect on help to parents through its effect on attachment behaviors. Interpersonal conflict with the parent had no effect on attachment behaviors or present help and only a weak effect on commitment to help in the future. Parental dependency also influenced adult children's attachment behaviors (Rosow, 1967; Weishaus, 1979) in addition to directly influencing present help to parents. A recent study (Horowitz, 1982) found that the two strongest predictors of adult children's care of elderly parents were parental needs and children's affection, providing further support to the model.

If the causal model is correct, it seems that adult children increase their attachment behaviors toward the parent in later life at the first signs of decline due to aging, and at a point before actual help may be needed. Concerned adult children may thus monitor their parents' aging process, increasing their interactions with parents in order to detect when help may be needed. The model further suggests that appeals to a sense of obligation to persuade an adult child to help a parent may not be particularly fruitful and that it may be better to attempt to induce such attachment behaviors as visiting and telephoning as an indirect means of stimulating help. Our data indicate that adult children do respond by helping when they perceive parental need.

Problems in the Helping Relationship

Childless and One-Child Families

What of those elderly who have only one child, or no children, or who have lost their children? These older people tend to substitute closer relationships with certain other kin and look to them as a source of needed services; they will also tend to turn to nonfamily providers more readily (Cicirelli, 1981b; Cumming & Schneider, 1961). These substitute relationships will help to provide some of the services ordinarily provided by children, but not to a sufficient degree. Those elderly whose adult children had died were less likely to turn to other kin for help than were those elderly who did not originally have children or who had only one child. Presumably these latter groups of elderly had cultivated long-standing relationships with other kin for mutual exchanges of help on occasion and also had developed other styles of coping which persisted into old age. The bereft parents, by contrast, were more likely to have had lifestyles that revolved heavily around their children and involved mutual exchanges of help. When their children were lost, support relationships with other kin were unlikely to be in existence and independent coping patterns were also not well developed. Thus, those elderly who have lost their adult children may be in particular need of help from community service agencies.

Communication on Needs

A potential source of difficulty comes about if adult children help parents in areas in which the parents do not want or need help or fail to give help in areas in which the parents feel they need it. Such a mismatch is likely to leave both parent and child frustrated. The helping relationship may suffer, the parent regarding the child as indifferent or intrusive and the child regarding the parent as unappreciative or unreasonably demanding. We found some evidence of this type of mismatch (Cicirelli, 1981a); parents saw protection, bureaucratic mediation, and reading materials services as more important than did their children, while the adult children saw personal care and home health care as more important than did their parents.

Most elderly parents preferred to remain in their own homes and take care of their own needs for as long as possible, but preferred help from their children to that from any other provider. Therefore it is important for adult children and their parents to learn to communicate effectively about the needs for help that are most important to them, in order to make the most effective use of help that adult children are willing to provide.

Stresses of Helping

The myth that elderly parents are often abandoned or alienated from their children has often been supplanted by the new belief that adult children have unquestioned care and affection for their elderly parents (Rix & Romashko, 1980). Such a helping relationship to an elderly parent can increase the affection of the child caregiver and the emotional satisfaction of the parent receiving the care, thereby bringing parent and child closer together. However, help to an elderly parent can also produce negative side effects. Rosenmayr (1977) has argued that the mere existence of help to the elderly cannot be regarded as an indicator of a positive relationship, since the stress caused by care of the old has negative consequences on those providing the care.

When there was a one-way helping relationship from adult child to parent, there was also a weaker affectional tie (Adams, 1968a). Also, adult children felt less close to a widowed parent than did those who had both parents living. Johnson and Bursk (1977) reported that when elderly parents were no longer healthy and independent, their children felt less positively toward them. Caring for an aging parent can result in stresses on the adult children providing support and care (Robinson & Thurnher, 1979; Troll et al., 1979), particularly when both parent and child reside in an intergenerational household (Brubaker & Brubaker, 1981). In addition, the media and clinical literature on care of the aging abound with anecdotal reports of the personal strains and negative feelings experienced by adult children who carry a heavy load of responsibility for their dependent parents. Such stress can be so severe that the mental or physical health of the child deteriorates; the result can be a complete family breakdown. In some cases, the adult child who is stressed retaliates against the elderly parent with verbal or physical abuse or both (Block & Sinnott, 1979; Steinmetz, 1980). However, most reports of this sort come from families who are in trouble or who are seeking help and do not indicate the prevalence and intensity of stresses of parent-helping among the general population of adult children of elderly parents.

In a recent study (Cicirelli, in press b) some 52 percent of adult children reported experiencing some degree of strain in connection with help to elderly parents on at least one of ten items probing such strain, while 34 percent reported substantial strain. Feeling physically worn out, emotionally exhausted, and that the parent was not satisfied no matter what the child did were the most frequently reported strains. To a lesser degree, adult children felt tied down in their daily schedules by the parents' needs and had to give up their own social and recreational activities. The most frequently experienced strains arose from the caregiving situation itself, and not from secondary effects on home, spouse, children, or job. For most adult children, the total amount of strain experienced was not great. Another possible consequence of helping is that the adult child would experience negative feelings toward the parent or toward helping. Some 73 percent of adult children reported some degree of negative feelings on one or more items, while 51 percent reported substantial negative feelings. Feelings of frustration, impatience, and irritation were most frequently reported, followed by helplessness and guilt.

Those adult children who perceived their parents as more dependent and as having greater needs for services, and who gave their parents more help also experienced more personal strains and negative feelings. Daughters, who typically take on more caretaking burdens (Troll, 1971), also experienced more personal strains connected with helping and were more likely to feel frustrated and resentful. A history of problems, poor attitudes, and a low level of filial maturity may also lead to increased stress (Brubaker & Brubaker, 1981). Personal strains and negative feelings experienced by the adult child thus seem to be a natural if not inevitable accompaniment to a situation in which an aging parent becomes increasingly dependent and where increased helping behaviors are elicited. Thus, it is important to find ways of minimizing such stresses.

In the study (Cicirelli, 1981a), personal strains and negative feelings seemed to be more strongly related to perceived parental dependency than to actual amount of help provided to the parents. Indeed, some adult children reported feeling stressed when they were providing little or no help. This suggests a phenomenon that we term "filial anxiety," the experience of anxiety when contemplating or anticipating the possibility of providing help to parents. The adult children may detect the first signs of aging decline and worry about their own capacity to deal with impending burdens. They may feel a need to monitor their parents' well-being more carefully and may become more worried, anxious, and generally stressed in the process.

In a study in progress, we attempted to construct a measure of filial anxiety that reflected such worries about the parent's future and the child's concern about being able to provide the needed help. In preliminary analyses, filial anxiety was found to be related to perceptions of the parent as declining in mobility, cognitive functioning, and general social adjustment, to love of the parent, and to filial obligation, but not to parental illness or amount of help given. One might conceive of filial anxiety as arising when an adult child has difficulty in reaching a tue filial maturity, that is, in defining or assuming a satisfactory filial role in relation to the aging parent. Instead, the concerned child adopts an anxiety as arising when an adult child has difficulty in reaching a true standing with the parent about the kinds of help needed and how the child can best contribute.

Marital Disruption and the Relationship to Parents

Incidence of Disruption

One of the more important of the social changes that may limit adult children's interpersonal and helping relationships to their elderly parents (Treas, 1977; Ward, 1978) is the increasing incidence of marital disruption in the lives of the children of the elderly. However, we do not well understand how this affects their elderly parents.

By marital disruption, we mean the breaking of the original marriage bond by divorce or widowhood, whether or not there has been subsequent remarriage. Although there are obvious differences, the divorced, widowed, and remarried are similar in that all have lost the original spouse and all share certain problems.

Although leveling off at present, the divorce rate has been rising throughout the past several decades (Norton, 1980; Stevens-Long, 1979; Furstenberg, Spanier, & Rothschild, 1982). The highest proportion of divorced persons in the population is found in the 30-44 age range, with about two-thirds as many in the 45-64 age range (U.S. Bureau of the Census, 1979). Thus, effects of divorce are now likely to be felt by a sizable proportion of adult children of the elderly. Overall, the proportion of widows in the female population is about 14 percent, with about one-fifth below 45 years of age (Berardo, 1968; Lopata, 1979), and the proportion of men about one-fourth that of women (U.S. Bureau of the Census, 1979). Although the number is much smaller than for divorced persons, many adult children become widowed at an age when they have elderly parents needing their care and support.

Many of those who are divorced or widowed will remarry, although remarriage is less likely as age increases and among women who are widowed. Among divorced persons, some 75 percent of women and 80 percent of men eventually remarry (Furstenberg et al., 1982). Among a smaller group, "serial monogamy" or "serial polygamy" occurs, with an individual proceeding through several marriages in turn (Tiger, 1978). At a given point in time, each marital partner may have children of earlier marriages along with children of the current union. Families of this sort have been called step-families, blended families, or reconstituted families (Duberman, 1975; Furstenberg et al., 1982). While good data on the number of people in such marriages are not available, it has been estimated that as many as one in five children may be in a reconstituted family. Sussman (1977) has estimated that 42 percent of all family types in the United States in 1976 were composed of remarried, widowed, separated, or divorced adults, or singles. It is clear that the percentage of adult children with intact marriages has diminished considerably in comparison to earlier times.

Marital disruption involves numerous problems of adjustment, as the individual faces new social, financial, physical, and psychological circumstances; there is also an adjustment in ties to the disrupted marriage, which will always remain in some form (Barkas, 1980). Such adjustments may alter the adult child's resources and lifestyle to such an extent that the capability and willingness to help elderly parents may be significantly reduced. While there has been much research on adjustment problems of those with marital disruption, there has been little interest in the impact on the relationships with elderly parents.

The Trauma to Parents

Whenever an adult child suffers a marital disruption, the parent is also affected, although the nature of the parent's reaction depends to some degree on the type of marital disruption and the marital relationship. When there is a divorce, elderly parents may have a strong emotional reaction to the event (Johnson & Vinick, 1982; Mueller & Pope, 1977; Spanier & Hanson, 1982). If they have been close to the departing spouse, there is a sharp sense of loss (although if the marriage has been a bad one, there may be a sense of relief). They may also feel distressed at the emotional pain the child is experiencing and may feel confused or perplexed by the events leading to the disruption. Similar loss and distress can occur following widowhood of a child. When there is remarriage, the new spouse may not be well accepted, particularly if the first spouse was well liked. Awkward feelings may make it difficult for the adult child to spend time with the parent.

Interpersonal Relationships with Parents

In a recently completed study of parent-child relationships of divorced, widowed, and remarried adult children (Cicirelli, 1981c), we found that most adult children enjoyed positive interpersonal relationships with their elderly parents in spite of marital disruption. They maintained contact, felt close and compatible with their parents, and had a high positive regard for them. Most reported that their relationships were closer currently than before the marital disruption. These findings are in essential agreement with Ahrons and Bowman (1982), Anspach (1976), and Spicer and Hampe (1975), who found a tendency toward increased contact and greater emotional closeness with parents after divorce. Only a small minority of adult children reported poor relationships with elderly parents, or relationships that had deteriorated since the marital disruption. These findings give little support to those who hold that divorce strains the parent-child relationship (Brown, 1982; Duffy, 1982; Hunt & Hunt, 1976; Johnson & Vinick, 1982), at least from the adult child's point of view. Rather, they indicate that poor relationships with parents are characteristic of only a small portion of the maritally disrupted.

The relationship with parents may not be as good as that of adult children whose marriages are intact, however. Those with marital disruption felt less close to their fathers and had less attachment behaviors (proximity and contact), less feeling of filial obligation, and more conflict with elderly parents than did their peers with intact marriages. Obviously, the same factors may be responsible for both the marital disruption and the poorer relationship with parents. However, if such factors did exist, they would be presumed to be less likely to lead to the death of a spouse than to divorce; yet the widowed subgroup had no better parental relationships than did those who were divorced or remarried, suggesting that the marital disruption itself may be responsible for the poorer relationship with parents.

Help to Parents

Adult children with marital disruption do help their elderly parents, but the amount of help is low. They feel committed to give increased help in the future should the parents need it. However, there is a real question as to how much help they could actually provide. Attachment behavior and present helping behavior are low, and these are the best predictors of future help. Also, adult children with marital disruption may have less money and time to provide help than those children with intact marriages. Some 84 percent felt that there was a point beyond which they could not continue to help their parents if such help threatened their jobs, meant denying their own children, or presented some other difficulty. In a study of caregiving among working daughters of elderly (Sherman, Horowitz, & Durmaskin, 1982), working daughters were found to be able to balance work and caregiving roles when parents' needs were low but had to give up one or the other when needs were greater. The divorced or widowed adult child whose job is needed for survival may not be able to make such a choice.

Psychological support, however, is one area that adult children with marital disruption see as especially important, and is a service that they could readily provide. Perhaps these adult children experienced a great deal of psychological trauma in their own marital losses, thus learning the importance of psychological support from others and making them sensitive to their parents' needs for such support in old age and more appreciative of the value of such help.

The type of marital disruption did not appear to result in major differences in helping. In regard to a few types of service, remarried daughters were more likely to give help then were divorced or widowed daughters, while the opposite was true for remarried sons; remarriage may act to increase the resources of women but to decrease the resources of men, who often support two households.

Conclusions

Based on the research we have reviewed and presented, we conclude that most adult children and their elderly parents do maintain a relationship that is based on the affectional bond between them. While the relationship is not one of day-to-day contact or close personal intimacy, neither is it one of mere obligation, pseudo-intimacy, and estrangement, as Blau (1981) suggests. Instead it is characterized by closeness of feeling between parent and child, an easy compatibility between them, a low degree of conflict, and a good deal of satisfaction.

The weight of evidence indicates that the amount of interaction between parent and child does depend on the closeness of the affectional bond, although other factors may also have an effect (duty, parent dependency, other responsibilities). This indicates that attachment to the parent motivates contact with the parent to some degree throughout the life of the parent.

The importance of the parent-child bond is also attested to by responses in those situations in which it is threatened. When adult children have died, elderly parents do not readily substiture other relationships, as they do if they were originally childless. Also, marital disruption appears to have only a slight effect on the parent-child relationship, although it creates severe upheavals in other aspects of the individual's life.

Most adult children do respond by helping when they perceive their parents to be in need, and do feel a commitment to help in time of future need. Such help, too, is based on the bond between them and not just on a sense of duty, as evidenced by the test of the attachment model of helping.

There are areas, however, in which adult children need support in their relationships with elderly parents. One is in the area of developing better communication with elderly parents in order to reach an understanding on what the parents' most important needs are and how the adult children can best make a contribution. Another is in the area of helping adult children to cope with the stresses that seem to be an inevitable side effect of helping elderly parents. Such measures as provision of supplementary or backup services, including such part-time measures as day-care plans or respite care, can do much to prevent an excessive buildup of strains that could culminate in family breakdown or parent abuse. Self-help groups in which adult children share their strains and feelings and thereby gain emotional support are also important, as are counseling activities that help adult children to develop skills for dealing with elderly parents, helping to meet their needs, and coping with the stresses of helping. Such supportive services are especially important in situations in which the adult child is bearing an unusually heavy burden, as in an intergenerational household, or is limited in resources, as in the case of marital disruption. Elderly parents who have lost their adult children are also at particular risk, since they have not developed means of coping that make use of other available sources of support.

The evidence presented here has affirmed the strength of the parent-child bond throughout life. Although social changes may modify the form in which the protective behaviors stemming from that bond are manifest, it appears unlikely that the relationship between adult child and elderly parent will be abandoned.

NOTE

1. Although a model involving reciprocal causality might be more compatible with family systems theory, the simpler recursive model was used since attachment theory does provide a clear basis for ordering the variables.

4

Siblings and Other Kin

JEAN PEARSON SCOTT

Little is known about sibling relationships in the family support network of older adults. One reason for the paucity of research literature is the assumption that siblings have a greater influence on the development of the young. Consequently, most empirical investigations of sibling relationships have been limited to the child and adolescent years (Irish, 1964; Sutton-Smith & Rosenberg, 1968, 1970). Also, in examinations of family support for older persons the focus has usually been on the role of the adult child as the primary source of assistance (Hill et al., 1970; Streib, 1968). For these reasons, examination of older sibling relationships has been limited and given minor attention in the literature.

There are several distinctive features of the sibling relationship that may have implications for the role of siblings in the support networks of the elderly. Cicirelli (1980, 1982) observes that the sibling relationship can have the longest duration of any kin relationship and may be the most egalitarian of any relationship in the family. These features, along with the fact that siblings usually share a common past and are relatively close in age, make the sibling tie a unique family relationship, one that may contribute to the ability of siblings to provide a unique kind of kin support for each other in later life.

Although the number of living siblings declines with age, most older adults have at least one living sibling. Among adults 65 years of age or older, from 75 to 93 percent report at least one living brother or sister (Clark & Anderson, 1967; Cicirelli, 1980; Harris et al., 1975; Shanas,

---

Author's Note: This study is a revised version of a paper presented at the annual meeting of the National Council on Family Relations, Milwaukee, Wisconsin, 1981. The study was supported by the Institute for the Development of Family Resources and the Institute for University Research, College of Home Economics, Texas Tech University, Lubbock, Texas.

47

Townsend, Wedderburn, Friis, Milhoj, & Stehouwer, 1968; Youmans, 1963). The lack of proximity to siblings, however, limits the degree and type of support that siblings can offer. While there is some information regarding the type of assistance and support that middle-aged and young adults exchange with siblings (Adams, 1968a; Allan, 1977), little information beyond frequency of contact measures is available in regard to older sibling relations. The exchange of help and shared activities have not been a focus of study for older adult sibling relations, yet these functions may take on greater importance in old age (Cicirelli, 1980).

More information regarding the type of psychological, social, and instrumental support that siblings offer each other in late adulthood would aid in better assessing the actual and potential supportive role of families for older persons. Consideration of sibling support in the context of that provided by other key family members would provide a more holistic perspective of kin support.

The central research questions addressed in the present study are:

(a) What types of interaction and helping behavior characterize sibling relationships in later life?
(b) How does sibling interaction in this stage compare with other kinds of kin interaction, specifically, child and grandchild relationships?
(c) Among older siblings, how equitable are exchanges of help, and how does equitability between siblings compare with that of child and grandchild relations?

Literature Review

Evidence regarding the nature of the sibling relationship in the lives of older adults is still speculative (Troll, Miller, & Atchley, 1979). The few studies of sibling relationships in later life have focused on the degree to which ties are maintained. In general, two types of indicators have been used to examine the viability of the sibling relationship: frequency of contact and feelings of closeness or solidarity.

Studies have generally shown that siblings do maintain contact with one another in later life. Approximately 40 percent of the respondents (65 or older) in a cross-national study had seen a sibling within a week prior to the time of the interview (Shanas, 1973). Rosenberg and Anspach (1973) reported that 47 percent of the respondents over the age of 65 who had siblings living nearby had seen one within the week preceding the interview. Of the older respondents in Cicirelli's (1980) study, 17 percent saw the most contacted sibling weekly. Very few respondents actually lost contact with a sibling. In addition, Cicirelli (1980) found that frequencies of telephoning were similar to frequencies of visiting, and when neither occurred, letter writing usually took their place.

Generalizations regarding the viability of the sibling bond and its influence on the older person's well-being have differed when the relationship was examined by using frequency of interaction measures. Data from cross-sectional studies showing a negative association between age and frequency of contact (Cicirelli, 1980) are the basis for Rosenberg and Anspach's (1973) conclusions that older sibling relations are not sustained in preretirement and later life. These conclusions were based on proximity and frequency of contact measures from a white, urban, working-class sample. Unfortunately, these data have not assessed the relative value of sibling contact to older respondents. Other investigators have suggested that as social contacts decrease, siblings become relatively more important members of the social network of the elderly (Cicirelli, 1980).

Sibling interaction has been linked to the adjustment of older adults in one study. Ross and Milgram's (1982) exploratory study of closeness in the adult sibling relationship indicates that regularity and frequency of contact with siblings became more important in old age as a means of self-validation and support. Lee and Ihinger-Tallman (1980), however, found no relationship between sibling interaction and the morale of an older, northwestern sample.

When other dimensions were examined, investigators concluded that siblings provide an important source of social and psychological support in later life (Cicirelli, 1977, 1980; Laverty, 1962; Manney, 1975; Ross & Milgram, 1982; Shanas, 1973). Despite reduced contact with siblings, older adults report greater closeness with siblings than younger cohorts (Cicirelli, 1982). In a midwestern sample, a large proportion of older adults (65 percent) expressed a high degree of closeness for the most contacted sibling (Cicirelli, 1980). A similarly high proportion of respondents felt close or very close to their siblings in two studies of young and middle-aged adults (Adams, 1968a; Cicirelli, 1980). Findings from a qualitative analysis of perceived closeness among adult siblings suggest that closeness between siblings seldom originated in adulthood, but was developed in childhood and maintained over the years (Ross & Milgram, 1982). Although their elderly sample was small, Ross and Milgram (1982) identified several factors that seemed more important in older siblings' relationships than in younger respondents' relationships with siblings. Support to siblings—physical, emotional, psychological, and, if necessary, financial—was greater among the older sample than in the younger group. Communication among older siblings and sharing memories served to validate perceptions of self and of reality and to maintain closeness.

The Cumming and Schneider study (1961), one of the earliest investigations of the sibling relationship among older adults, concluded that sibling solidarity not only existed but was often stronger than nuclear family solidarity. While the study gave recognition to the importance of siblings in older persons' lives, no support has been found for Cumming and Schneider's conclusion that sibling relations are a focal point for kin relations in later life (Rosenberg and Anspach, 1973; Young & Willmott, 1957). Most studies confirm that children are the primary source of support for older persons (Cicirelli, 1981a; Shanas, 1973). Only 7 percent of the older sample in Cicirelli's study (1982a) reported that a sibling was the primary source of psychological support.

Sibling relationships are influenced to a great extent by the existing family structure. The sex composition of the sibling dyad appears to have an influence on the degree of attachment in later life (Cumming & Schneider, 1961; Shanas, 1973), the sister-sister dyad being especially strong. Allan (1977) noted that same-sex siblings who were nearest in birth order tended to form stronger relationships than other sibling combinations. In an exploratory study of the effect of siblings on older adults' feelings and concerns, sisters but not brothers were more salient influences on their siblings' adjustment (Cicirelli, 1977). The findings of the study suggest that older siblings, whether male or female, are influenced to a greater extent by sisters than by brothers.

Other family variables, such as birth order, sex, number, and spacing of siblings, have been examined more thoroughly in the child and adolescent years. Likewise, rivalry between siblings is a topic that has received considerable attention in the childhood years. Investigators generally conclude that while rivalry can persist and even be reactivated when there is close interaction, rivalries subside in later life (Allan, 1977; Cicirelli, 1982).

The presence of parents, a spouse, or children in the family network shapes the interaction of siblings in later life. The data indicate that widowed, single persons and older adults without children have greater contact and express greater closeness with siblings (Rosenberg & Anspach, 1973; Shanas, 1973) than married older adults with children. Rosenberg and Anspach (1973) speculated that sibling contact in later life may substitute in a compensatory fashion for the socioemotional support no longer available from a spouse. Lopata (1973) found that although widows often mentioned siblings as those who helped most following the death of a spouse, contact with siblings was infrequent. Widows, however, viewed siblings as real sources of aid, services, finances, or comfort if they needed it. Several investigators have noted the importance of the role of parents as mediators and as focal points for sibling interaction, but few data are available (Adams, 1968a; Allan, 1977; Cicirelli, 1980; Ross & Milgram, 1982).

In summary, a high proportion of older adults have siblings and describe a relationship with at least one sibling as "close" or "very close." While contact is maintained with siblings, it is usually not as frequent as that with children. Even when contact is minimal, older persons view siblings as kin who would provide assistance if needed. There is evidence that widowed, childless persons and lifelong singles have more frequent contact and report greater closeness with siblings than do older married persons who have children. Sisters maintain the closest ties. While the literature is inconsistent, there is support for the importance of siblings to the psychosocial adjustment of older adults. Frequency of sibling interaction measures, however, have generally not been associated with social and psychological characteristics of older adults. Investigations of the supportive role of siblings in later life have been based primarily on contact measures that have permitted, at best, a sketchy understanding of sibling relations. Generalizations regarding the interaction patterns and the general viability of the sibling relationship remain tentative, since studies usually have not examined the content of the contacts or the salience of the relationship in comparison to that of other kin and significant others. The present study adds to the literature regarding older siblings by examining several dimensions of sibling interaction: forms of assistance, equitability of assistance, joint activities, and the perceived quality of the sibling relationship. Furthermore, the study compares the sibling relationship of older adults to that of other kin.

Methods

Sample

The sample included 199 adults, 65 to 90 years of age, who resided in a southwestern city of nearly 200,000 people. Census block statistics were used to select the sample randomly by means of a proportionate area sampling technique. Race and socioeconomic level were controlled by including only white, middle-class respondents in the study. Respondents were interviewed in their own homes. Only one member of a married couple was included in the sample if both spouses were 65 or older. The spouse to be interviewed was chosen on a random basis.

Approximately 75 percent of the sample are female and 25 are male. Over half the sample (54.8 percent) are married, 39.2 percent are widowed, 4.5 percent are divorced, and 1.5 percent are single. Respondents' average age is 73 and the average educational level is eleven years.

Sibling Characteristics. Respondents report from zero to 6 living brothers and from zero to 6 living sisters who range in age from 54 to 94 years. The sibling who is most often in contact with the respondent is a sister for 35 percent of the sample and a brother for 30 percent. Approximately 7 percent say their contact with brothers and sisters is equally distributed, and 7 percent report that they have no contact with brothers and sisters. The sex composition of the sibling dyad, defined as the relationship with the most-contacted sibling, is 38 percent, sister-sister dyads; 37 percent sister (respondent) -brother dyads; 15 percent brother-brother dyads; and 10 percent brother (respondent) -sister dyads. The average age difference among the dyads according to sex composition is 1.7 years in the sister-sister dyad, 5.5 years in the sister (respondent) -brother dyad, 5.3 years in the brother-brother dyad, and 5.1 years in the brother (respondent) -sister dyad ($F[3,139] = 3.03$, $p < .03$).

Measures

The participants were questioned about each category of kin with regard to the number living, ages, sex, and relatives that were most often contacted. A series of questions was then asked about the person identified as most often contacted for each category of kin. Questions about relatives included demographic information, proximity to respondent, frequency of writing and telephoning, types of assistance exchanged, shared activities, and perceived closeness of the relationship.

Mutual assistance between the respondent and the child, grandchild, and sibling with whom the respondent had the most contact was assessed by the frequency with which ten helping behaviors had occurred in the past year. Helping behaviors included (1) provided transportation, (2) made minor household repairs, (3) helped with housekeeping, (4) helped with shopping, (5) helped with yardwork, (6) helped take care of car, (7) assisted when ill, (8) helped make important decisions, (9) provided legal aid, and (10) provided financial aid. For each category of kin, respondents were asked what kinds of *help they had received* and what kinds of *help they had given.* Responses to both questions were coded on a nine-point scale ranging from (1) never to (9) daily. The responses for each item were summed to form a total help received score and a total help given score.

The *type of equity* existing in the helping behavior of the sibling relationship was determined by the following procedure. The help received score for each of the ten helping behaviors was subtracted from the help given score of each respondent in order to determine the direction in which assistance was given. For example, the respondent who gave help to a sibling by providing transportation monthly would receive a score of 5; if the sibling did not reciprocate by providing transportation a score of 1 was given for help received. The equity score for this helping behavior would be 4 (5 – 1 = 4). Scores for each of the ten helping behaviors were then summed for a total equity score. Positive scores represented the "underbenefited" or those who gave more than they received. Negative scores represented the respondents who received more than they gave, or the "overbenefited." Equitable relationships were those in which assistance was given and received equally, and consequently the scores were zero.

In addition to helping behaviors, *the frequency and type of social activities* in which respondents engaged with kin were assessed by the following question: "During the past year, how often have you done the following activities together with your relatives?" Activities included commercial recreation (movies, sports, and the like), home recreation (picnics, card playing, shared leisure time, and so on), outdoor recreation (fishing, hunting, or camping), brief drop-in visits for conversation, vacation visits, large family reunions, working at same locations, happy occasions (birthdays, holidays), attending church or religious group together, and shopping together. Responses were coded on a scale from (1) never to (9) daily. All responses were summed for a total activity score for each category of kin.

The perceived *closeness of kin* was assessed by the following question: "How close would you say you feel to [name]?" Responses were coded (5) very close, (4) pretty close, (3) a little, (2) not too close, and (1) not close.

Findings

Availability

The majority of respondents had a living child (90.4 percent), a grandchild (78.8 percent), and a living sibling (84.1 percent; see Table 4.1). In regard to proximity of kin, siblings who had the most contact with the respondents were, on the average, within 31 to 60 minutes' distance from the respondent, grandchildren were from 11 to 30 min-

TABLE 4.1   Percentages with Living Kin

Number Living	Children (n = 186)	Grandchildren (n = 187)	Siblings (n = 189)
0	9.6	21.2	15.9
1	23.5	17.0	34.7
2	26.1	22.0	22.6
3	16.6	9.0	12.1
4	10.1	10.0	8.5
5 or more	14.1	19.8	5.2

utes, and children 31 to 60 minutes. The data on proximity to the child are based on the oldest child rather than the most contacted child; consequently, the data for child shown in Table 4.2 may be an underestimate of the actual proximity to the most contacted child.

Contact via Letter and Telephone

The respondents were asked how frequently they kept in touch with their most contacted sibling via writing and telephoning. Two-thirds of the respondents, 66.0 percent, said they never wrote. Approximately one-fifth of the sample wrote monthly or more frequently, and 16.0 percent wrote several times a year or less frequently. Telephoning was more frequent; less than 10.3 percent said they never spoke with the most contacted sibling over the phone. Roughly equal proportions telephoned siblings weekly or several times a week. Approximately 20.0 percent of the respondents talked to the most contacted sibling several times a month or monthly, 16.4 percent telephoned several times a year, and 25.3 percent telephoned yearly or less frequently.

Mutual Assistance

The percentage of respondents receiving help from the child, sibling, or grandchild with whom they most frequently interacted is shown in Table 4.3. Approximately 25.0 percent of the respondents received no help from the most contacted child, over half the respondents received no help from the most contacted grandchild, and nearly three-fourths of the respondents received no assistance from the most contacted sibling. Siblings gave relatively little assistance to the respondents in comparison to that given by children and grandchildren. An exception was "assistance when ill," where approximately the same percentage of help was given by grandchildren and siblings. Also, a greater percentage of

TABLE 4.2   Proximity to Kin with Whom Respondent
Had Most Contact (percentages)

Distance	Child[a] (n = 178)	Grandchild (n = 85)	Sibling (n = 146)
Same household	5.1	4.7	2.1
0-10 mins.	19.1	34.1	16.4
11-30 mins.	14.0	27.1	16.4
31-60 mins.	5.1	5.9	9.6
61 mins.-23 hrs.	52.8	27.1	45.9
Day or more	3.9	1.2	9.6

a. Child is oldest child rather than most contacted child.

TABLE 4.3   Percentages of Respondents Receiving Help
from Relatives During the Past Year

Help Received	Child (n = 161)	Grandchild (n = 74)	Sibling (n = 135)
Transportation	47.5	16.2	10.9
Minor household repairs	37.9	13.7	5.2
Housekeeping	18.7	4.1	2.2
Shopping	29.8	6.8	3.0
Financial aid	8.2	0.0	0.7
Yardwork	17.5	9.3	3.7
Care of car	8.2	1.4	2.2
Assistance when ill	41.6	14.5	14.0
Help in making important decisions	49.4	5.4	13.2
Legal aid	3.8	1.4	0.7
No help received	24.1	60.3	72.4

siblings gave help in making important decisions in comparison to grandchildren.

Since proximity has a strong bearing on the extent to which kin can provide assistance, only those kin who resided within an hour of the respondent were included in the frequency distribution (see Table 4.4). As the data indicate, when siblings were as available as were other kin, a greater percentage of them were involved in helping behaviors. Compared to grandchildren, a greater percentage of siblings provided assistance when ill and help in making important decisions. Approximately equal proportions received help from siblings and grandchildren for transportation and shopping. Children, however, still provide a greater

TABLE 4.4   Percentages of Respondents Receiving Help from Relatives
During the Past Year (controlling on proximity)

Help Received	Child (n = 165)	Grandchild (n = 57)	Sibling (n = 64)
Transportation	47.6	21.6	19.6
Minor household repairs	37.8	15.7	10.0
Housekeeping	18.7	3.9	5.0
Shopping	29.3	7.7	6.7
Yardwork	17.5	13.2	0.0
Care of car	8.1	0.0	5.0
Assistance when ill	41.5	18.9	26.2
Help in making important decisions	90.7	5.8	18.2
Legal aid	3.7	0.0	1.7
Financial aid	8.2	0.0	1.7
No help received	0.0	48.1	61.3

NOTE: All kin lived within an hour of the respondent.

amount of assistance in most areas. A repeated measures analysis of variance indicated that children contributed significantly more (X = 19.1) to the support of older respondents on the ten helping behaviors than either grandchildren (X = 13.4) or siblings (X = 10.7) when proximity was controlled (F [2,146] = 26.28, p < .001).

The percentage of respondents giving help to each category of kin is shown in Table 4.5. For almost all types of helping behavior, a greater percentage of respondents provided assistance to a child. Two exceptions were "care of car" and "financial aid," where more respondents gave help to the grandchild. Assistance when ill and helping in making important decisions were the types of help most frequently given to siblings. Table 4.6 shows the percentage of respondents giving help to kin who lived within an hour of the respondent. When proximity was controlled, the same pattern emerged as with receiving help; the differences between categories were reduced but not eliminated. When differences among the three kin categories on total help given were compared, a significant difference was found (F [2,146] = 4.57, p < .01). A significantly greater amount of help was given to a child (X = 13.5) in comparison to a sibling (X = 10.9) or a grandchild (X = 11.7).

Equity of the Helping Relationship

When helping behaviors received by the respondent were compared with helping behaviors given for each category of kin, more respondents were overbenefited by the child and by the grandchild with whom they

TABLE 4.5   Percentages of Respondents Giving Help
to Relatives During the Past Year

Help Given	Child (n = 162)	Grandchild (n = 76)	Sibling (n = 137)
Transportation	14.2	10.1	9.4
Minor household repairs	9.9	2.6	5.8
Housekeeping	8.6	2.6	4.4
Shopping	8.0	2.6	5.1
Yardwork	4.9	0.0	2.9
Care of car	1.2	2.6	0.7
Assistance when ill	18.5	5.3	13.9
Help in making important decisions	28.6	13.3	11.8
Legal aid	1.2	0.0	0.0
Financial aid	4.1	11.8	2.9
No help given	45.5	66.8	74.2

TABLE 4.6   Percentages of Respondents Giving Help to Relatives
During the Past Year (controlling on proximity)

Help Given	Child (n = 165)	Grandchild (n = 57)	Sibling (n = 64)
Transportation	14.2	11.3	17.2
Minor household repairs	9.9	3.9	11.3
Housekeeping	8.6	3.9	8.1
Shopping	8.0	3.9	9.6
Financial aid	14.1	11.5	4.8
Yardwork	4.8	0.0	0.0
Care of car	1.2	3.9	1.6
Assistance when ill	18.6	7.8	24.1
Help in making important decisions	28.5	15.7	22.9
Legal aid	1.2	0.0	0.0
No help given	0.0	64.2	54.7

NOTE: All kin lived within an hour of the respondent.

had the most contact. Approximately the same percentage of respondents were overbenefited as were under-benefited by the sibling with whom there was the most contact. The large percentage of siblings with equitable relationships (71.0 percent) reflects the large number of respondents who were neither providing nor receiving any assistance from the sibling (Table 4.7).

TABLE 4.7   Equity Among Respondents and Their Kin
on Ten Helping Behaviors (percentages)

Equity of Relationship	Child (n = 56)	Grandchild (n = 74)	Sibling (n = 64)
Overbenefited	55.0	47.3	14.0
Equitable	22.0	32.4	71.0
Underbenefited	21.0	20.3	15.0

NOTE: All kin were within an hour of the respondent. Respondents who neither gave nor received help were included in the equitable group.

TABLE 4.8   Percentages of Respondents Who Participated in
Joint Activities with a Relative During the Past Year

Activity	Child (n = 165)	Grandchild (n = 78)	Sibling (n = 138)
Commercial recreation	68.3	50.0	36.2
Home recreation	53.3	41.6	27.5
Outdoor recreation	16.1	13.3	10.4
Brief visits	62.0	65.3	33.3
Vacation visits	40.6	26.6	29.0
Family reunions	30.3	38.5	26.8
Same occupation	0.6	0.0	0.0
Happy occasions	87.6	82.5	43.9
Same church	29.4	13.0	8.1
Shopping together	51.3	28.8	19.1
No participation	.6	7.1	28.6

Joint Activities

The percentage of respondents who participated with kin during the past year according to ten types of joint activity is reported in Table 4.8. Again, for most items respondents participated more frequently with their children than with grandchildren or with siblings. Frequency distributions for percentage of respondents engaging in activities with kin when proximity to kin was controlled are shown in Table 4.9. With one exception (vacation visits), the percentage of respondents engaged in joint activities with the sibling increased when the sibling was within an hour of the respondent. Nearly one-half of the respondents had enjoyed commercial recreation with a sibling, over two-thirds had shared brief visits, and nearly three-fourths shared happy occasions. When proximity was controlled, the mean total activity scores for siblings ($X = 16.7$) indicated somewhat less involvement than grand-

TABLE 4.9   Percentages of Respondents Who Participated in
Joint Activities with a Relative During the Past Year
(controlling on proximity)

Activity	Child (n = 165)	Grandchild (n = 57)	Sibling (n = 64)
Commercial recreation	68.2	54.5	47.5
Home recreation	53.2	41.5	43.6
Outdoor recreation	16.0	15.1	18.4
Brief visits	61.9	86.5	68.3
Vacation visits	40.6	13.2	21.3
Family reunions	30.3	38.5	36.1
Same occupation	.6	0.0	0.0
Happy occasions	87.7	96.4	70.5
Same church	29.4	13.2	14.7
Shopping together	51.2	29.4	27.4
No participation	0.0	3.6	9.5

NOTE: All kin lived within an hour of the respondent.

children (X = 22.3), but neither mean was as high as the mean total activity score of children (X = 25.5). The mean activity score took into account the frequency with which each activity was undertaken. A repeated measures analysis of variance showed significant differences among the three categories of kin according to activity scores (F [2,146] = 29.20, p < .001). A Scheffé test indicated that the mean activity scores for the child were significantly different from the grandchild and sibling groups.

Affect

When respondents were asked to rate the closeness of their relationships with kin, the mean score was 4.8 for child, 4.7 for grandchild, and 4.5 for sibling (a score of 5.0 was the highest possible). Most respondents perceived child, grandchild, and sibling as very close. The highly skewed responses may be due in part to a social desirability response set.

Discussion and Conclusions

The present study examined social interaction and patterns of assistance between older persons and their siblings and compared sibling relations to relationships with children and grandchildren. A sample of 199 white, urban, middle-class adults aged 65 to 90 years was interviewed about their interaction patterns with the most contacted child, sibling, and grandchild. Siblings and grandchildren were not as deeply involved as children in the social networks of the respondents, but they did have a visible supportive role. When proximity was controlled, there were increases in the frequency and types of interaction and assistance between older respondents and their siblings. Less than half of the respondents who lived close enough to siblings to exchange help on a regular basis actually did so. Assistance when ill, help in making important decisions, and transportation were the types of help most frequently exchanged between siblings. A greater amount of social activity between siblings was found in comparison to assistance. Sharing happy occasions, brief visits, and commercial and home recreation were the kinds of activity in which siblings most frequently engaged.

The study provides new findings regarding sibling relationships of older individuals that are comparable to the results of Adams (1968a) regarding sibling interaction of young adults. Adams found mutual assistance and social interaction consisting primarily of brief visits among his sample. The results of the present study indicate that a greater percentage of older siblings exchanged assistance (38.7 percent) than the younger siblings in Adams's study, where 12.0 percent of the sample reported receiving assistance from a sibling. The difference is perhaps a function of the greater number of questions in the present study regarding various forms of assistance. Adams asked one question about help that was engaged with an age-near sibling. It seems likely, however, that siblings would exchange more help in later life than in earlier periods of life given the greater incidence of chronic disease, greater length of recovery from illness, and a greater likelihood of dependency created through disability or widowhood in later adulthood. Whether the amount of assistance indeed changes over time or is a function of cohort differences is an issue that could be addressed by a future longitudinal study of kin assistance patterns. At any rate, the data show that mutual assistance among siblings is a minor function of the sibling relationship for older, middle-class adults. Older siblings appeared to keep in touch via writing, telephoning, and getting together for special occasions, brief visits, and home and commercial recreation. These activities are the major channels for sibling interaction in late life.

A very clear finding was that children were more deeply involved in the exchange of assistance than grandchildren and siblings. Adams's (1968a) explanation for the differences he observed between parent-child and sibling interaction seems to offer a suitable reason for the differences observed in the present study between the respondent-child, -grandchild, and -sibling relationships:

> In summary, on the one hand, enjoyment of the sibling is quite similar to that expressed toward parents. Obligation, on the other hand, is usually

not felt to be as great, and specifc obligation, or obligation to help, is virtually non-existent. The freedom of the young adult to interact and communicate or not with the sibling, as he so desires, is much greater than in parental relations. This freedom, however, is not absolute. General obligation to keep in touch, while not dominant, is still an important aspect of sibling relations. (p. 114)

Older siblings in the present study tended to exercise more freedom in the extent to which help or activities were shared in comparison to children. Also, obligation to help was not evident in the relationship with grandchildren.

While grandchildren and siblings were similar in the frequency with which they interacted with the older respondents, the type of interaction varied. The assistance exchanged by siblings was similar in kind and somewhat more dissimilar for grandchildren. Siblings gave and received the most help with important decisions, transportation, and illness. Grandchildren helped respondents with yardwork and minor household repairs. However, different forms of help were returned; respondents gave help to grandchildren in the form of financial assistance, help in making important decisions, and transportation.

The results may suggest that when older persons have a child who can provide support and join in social activities, siblings and grandchildren will be of less importance in the kin support system of the older adult. To examine this idea further, the mean helping behavior score and social activities score of respondents who had a sibling but no children living within an hour of the respondent were compared with the findings for the entire sample. Due to the small number (N = 12) of respondents who fell into this category, the results can be only suggestive. Respondents who had a sibling but no children close by had a mean of 17.0 for help received from a sibling, 14.0 for mean help given to siblings, and 27.4 for mean shared activities with siblings. All three scores were considerably higher than the means reported by the entire sample for siblings and were comparable to the means reported for the child by the sample. The data suggest that the sibling relationship becomes a more important source of support when children are not available. The Shanas et al. (1968) study supports a similar finding, as singles were found to have more extensive contact with siblings than the married or widowed.

Contrary to the finding by others (Adams, 1968a; Shanas, 1973) of a stronger sibling bond between sisters, the results of the present study found relations with siblings evenly divided by gender. The sibling that respondents tended to have the most contact with and to feel close to was just as frequently a brother as it was a sister for both sexes. A post hoc analysis according to sex did not show any further sex differences, with the exception of a few types of social activities; for example, sisters tended to do significantly more shopping together than the other dyad compositions. While sisters did not show a greater frequency of contact than other combinations, the age difference between sibling dyads was substantially smaller for sister-sister ties. This might provide some evidence for closer ties among sisters similar in age; however, there was no other evidence to support a strong sister bond.

The findings have implications for those who work with older persons and their families. Family practitioners should not ignore the importance of siblings in the support networks of older adults. Siblings appear to be a natural source of psychological support despite physical distances. Getting together or keeping in touch during the year (because of birthdays, holidays, illness) may have special significance for siblings, reminding them of their unique relationship and common past. The high degree of closeness reported by the subjects in the present study despite limited contact seems to support Ross and Milgram's (1982) observation that closeness is a product of early life, contacts in later life serving to renew good memories and warm feelings for each other. While there may be a tendency to focus solely on the central role that the children play in the support network, older persons can feel a greater sense of support perhaps when other kin are recognized and included in planning and discussions with older persons.

Future research needs to address the impact of the equity of kin relationships on older adults' satisfaction with kin interaction. Equity proponents (Walster, Berscheid, & Walster, 1973; Walster, Walster, & Berscheid, 1978) posit that equitable exchanges in relationships provide the basis for greater relationship satisfaction than relationships in which imbalances in exchanges exist. In the present study, most relationships with children and grandchildren were overbenefited. That is, the older respondents perceived themselves as receiving more than they gave. Sibling relationships were more evenly distributed between the over- and under-benefited (excluding those who neither gave nor received help from siblings). These perceived imbalances may provide insight into the general lack of association between kin interaction and morale that has been reported in the literature (Lee & Ihinger-Tallman, 1980).

In conclusion, sibling relations for older, white, urban, middle-class adults are characterized by high positive affect; sociability consisting of brief visits, getting together for happy occasions, commercial recreation, and telephoning several times a year; and limited mutual assistance. Siblings appear to figure in the support networks of older adults in a way that complements relations with children and grandchildren. Further exploration of the equitability of kin relations may provide clues to the enhancement of kin support networks in later life.

5

Grandparents
The Family Watchdogs

LILLIAN E. TROLL

Four general conclusions can be drawn from recent reviews of the literature on grandparenting—as distinct from that on aged family members. These are:

(1) Grandparents are not absent from central family dynamics, but often play an important part in them, even though they usually play a secondary role to parents.
(2) Grandparental interactions and roles are diverse—much more diverse than parental ones, varying in part with social class, ethnicity, and sex, but largely, it seems, with individual feelings and preferences and life circumstances.
(3) Developmental status of both grandchild and grandparent influence their interactions and their reciprocal feelings.
(4) The most important role of the grandparents may be that of maintaining the family system as a whole.

This chapter contains a review of the research literature relevant to these four points. I will then speculate a bit beyond the data about the systemic role hinted at in the title: "family watchdogs."

Grandparenting versus Parenting

From deeply and heavily involved grandparents at one extreme to apparently uninvolved ones at the other (Kornhaber & Woodward, 1981), the importance of grandparents in family functioning is beginning to be recognized. Their influence is not always seen as beneficial, however. Twenty years ago, psychoanalytically inspired thinking about family functioning included a premise that if young couples, upon their marriage, did not separate themselves effectively from their parents, they would experience disturbed relationships between themselves and also have trouble bringing up healthy children (see Bell & Vogel, 1960). This belief is still held by many of us today. Different conclusions are being drawn by recent reviews of the empirical literature (Tinsley & Parke, 1983, Troll, 1980a; Wood, 1982). This literature includes evidence that grandparents play an important role in promoting well-being of one-parent childrearing units, particularly those of teenage mothers (see review by Tinsley & Parke, 1983).

Are surrogate parenting and supportive parenting by grandparents to be found only in distressed or deviant families, though? Three years ago, when I reviewed the then even more meager literature on grandparenting than now exists, I concluded that the significance of grandparenting may lie more in the clues it provides to the strength of general family functioning than in the actual interactions with children and grandchildren (Troll, 1980a). If grandparents, as "family watchdogs," monitor the state of family functioning and step in only when they are needed, they can often appear uninvolved.

Perspectives on Grandparenting Studies

Both research and theorizing about grandparents fall into several discrete categories. These include:

(1) the benefits or lack of benefits grandparents themselves derive (see Neugarten & Weinstein, 1964; Robertson, 1977; Kivnick, 1981; Hill, Foote, Aldous, Carlson, & Macdonald, 1970);
(2) the effect of having grandparents upon the well-being and attitudes of young children (see Tinsley & Parke, 1983; Baranowski, 1982a, 1982b; Hartshorne & Manaster, 1982; Kornhaber & Kornhaber, 1982; Kahana & Kahana, 1970; Wood & Robertson, 1976; Gilford & Black, 1972);
(3) the qualities of grandparents that children of different ages like (see Kahana & Kahana, 1970);
(4) the connecting linkages between grandparents and grandchildren through the middle generation (see Hill et al., 1970: "lineage bridges"; Gilford & Black, 1972);
(5) the styles and meanings of grandparenting in the eyes of the grandparents (see Neugarten & Weinstein, 1964; Wood & Robertson, 1976; Kivnick, 1981); and
(6) the role of grandparents in family systems (Hader, 1965; Troll, 1980a, 1980b; Wood, 1982).

Because a large part of the research from all these perspectives derives from assumptions of grandparents as aged, essentially infirm, and otherwise unoccupied individuals, whose grandchildren and other family members fill a vacuum, we can only conjecture about the full range of grandparental interactions.

In the present chapter, little attention will be given to the literature on what grandparents do for grandchildren per se, unless this falls within the domain of larger family support. Nor are we interested in the views grandchildren—as young children or adolescents—have of their grandparents as "old" people.

Hagestad (1982) calls our attention to the increased probability of grandparental influence upon other family members because the increases in life expectancy produce greater "life overlaps" betweeen younger and older generations in the family. In our culture, the modal age of becoming a grandparent is around 49-51 years for women and 51-53 years for men. Teenage pregnancies, furthermore, produce many grandparents in their thirties. With life expectancy now around the age of 76 years for women and 68 years for men, most Americans can get to know their grandchildren and even their great-grandchildren. Grandmothers, in particular, can see their grandchildren develop well into their adult years. Reciprocally, most young children can get to know their grandparents and even great-grandparents. The complexities of family life have shifted from the horizontal dimension: sibling constellations to the vertical dimension. Horizontal interactions are replaced by a potentially confusing array of parent-child units that Hagestad has labeled graphically the "alpha-omega chain."

When Harris and his associates (1975) surveyed Americans over the age of 65, he found that three-fourths of them had living grandchildren and three-fourths of those saw them at least once every week. Since only about 5 percent of American households include both grandparents and grandchildren, not only must this contact be voluntary but the motivation for it has to be strong enough to induce members of one generation to go out of the home to visit members of the other generation.

Not only is contact constant in most families, but reciprocity of help and services is too, as attested by Hill and his colleagues (1970) for three generations of adult couples and by Kornhaber and Woodward (1981) for a somewhat wider age range of grandchildren. The spate of recent studies on the family situations of teenage mothers (for example, Mogey, 1976-1977; Tinsley & Parke, 1983; Smith, 1975; Badger, Burns, & Vietze, 1981; Field, Widmayer, Stringer, & Ignatoff, 1980; Hardy, King, Shipp, & Welcher, 1981; Mills & Cairns, 1981; Kellam, Adams, Brown, & Ensminger, 1982) consistently report the presence of the maternal grandmother as critical to the successful functioning of the mother-child unit and to the positive development of the infant. Similarly, Hetherington's important study of divorce (Hetherington, Cox, & Cox, 1982) found that the contributions of grandparents were highly related to the quality of the mother-child relationship in that majority of cases in which mothers were the primary child rearers.

While statistics of visiting and helping suggest that grandparents are important persons in family systems, one common finding is paradoxical. There seems to be no relationship between amount of contact with children and grandchildren and older people's morale or life satisfaction (see Wood & Robertson, 1976; Troll, Miller & Atchley, 1979). In fact, some reseach suggests an inverse relationship: The more older people's social life is exclusively with their children, the lower their morale. Socializing with friends is much better for them (see discussion in Troll, et al., 1979).

How can we reconcile these discrepancies? Bengtson and Kuypers (1971) provide us with the heuristic concept of "generational stake." They describe the different emphasis placed by middle-aged parents and their young-adult children upon the amount of similarity in their outlook on life, or values. Youth in their late teens or early twenties tend to exaggerate the "generation gap," disclaiming similarity of values between themselves and their parents. Their parents, on the other hand, tend to exaggerate the similarities. A parallel phenomenon has been suggested by both Bengtson and Troll for the "gap" between middle-aged children and *their* parents (see Troll & Bengtson, 1979).

The intent of this differential emphasis on separation of attitudes is to stress the uniqueness and independence of the younger generation vis-à-vis its parents. This process could be present at any time of life. At the same time, the parents want to believe in the continuity of the effects of their efforts to instill their values in their children. Again, this could hold at all ages. This may not stop with one generation of offspring, furthermore. Grandparents can be as concerned that their children continue to transmit essential values to *their* children as that their children themselves hold them.

Probably few grandparents wish to return to parenting with their grandchildren (see Lopata, 1973; Cohler & Grunebaum, 1981), but they do remain alert to what goes on. If they think all is well, they prefer to remain formal and distant or indulgent grandparents, visiting their children and grandchildren as one part of their regular life activities but otherwise enjoying their own life. It is more interesting to be with their peers, who are likely to share more recreational interests, than helping out with needy children who remind them of their lack of success in parenting. It is nice to be free of worry about the adequacy of the socialization of their descendants and the "carrying on of the torch." If there is trouble, however, they have to give up much of their personal, nonfamily life to meet the needs of the family. This means double suffering for them: deprivation as well as concern (see Mogey, 1976-1977; Tinsley & Parke, 1983).

In my ongoing three-generational research, I have found that grandparents refer spontaneously to their grandchildren 27 percent of the time, but grandchildren refer to their grandparents only 10 percent of the time. One interpretation of this difference may be that grandparents monitor the status of their grandchildren more than grandchildren monitor their grandparents.

That grandparenting is not a renewal of parenting undertaken by empty and possessive elders is seen in the contingent nature of the relationship. Both Cumming and Henry (1961) and Lopata (1973) have stressed this point: Grandparents do not want to start over as parents of young children. Gilford and Black (1972), analyzing the University of Southern California's three-generation sample, found that the grandparent-grandchild interactions and feelings depended upon the attitudes of the parents toward their own parents. Hagestad and Speicher (1981) found that the middle generation of parents remain as mediators of the older and younger generations' interactions even when the grandchildren are adults. In other words, there is replication of the "lineage bridge" phenomenon seen by Hill and his colleagues in their Minneapolis study (Hill et al., 1970). This is interesting because the youngest generation in the Los Angeles study were younger than those in the Minneapolis study. Services by grandparents are rendered when, and usually only when, their children indicate that they are needed.

French, Rogers, and Cobb (1974) see a curvilinear relationship between grandparent contact and general satisfaction of the grandparents. Hess and Waring (1978) use the apt metaphor of the "Goldlilocks effect"; too much grandparenting is as bad as too little. In one respect, too much may indicate lots of family trouble and thus be even worse.

Diversity

It is often assumed that grandparenting is a roleless role because there are no overtly prescribed functions. Parents of young children generally know what is expected of them in raising the children. Grandparents do not, at least not in the same way. The diffuseness of their script can be seen in the wide diversity of grandparenting styles reported by most observers since the now classic study of Neugarten and Weinstein (1964). Efforts to categorize this wide array of styles and behaviors are reflected in the five styles noted by Neugarten and Weinstein; formal, fun-seekers, surrogate parents, reservoirs of family wisdom, and distant figures. A four-part typology is used by Wood and Robertson (1976), based on the two dimensions of personal orientation toward grandparenting and conception of the social or normative meanings attached to grandparenthood. Their four resultant types are: remote, symbolic, individualized, and apportioned. More recently, Kivnick (1981) developed a third typology, using five categories: centrality, valued elder, immortality through clan, reinvolvement with personal past, and indulgence. Rather than assume that different people fall into different categories, Kivnick found it useful to rate everybody on all five dimensions; most of the grandparents she studied fit into all five to some extent. Like other researchers before her, Kivnick found no direct relationship between grandparenthood behavior or meaning and the mental health of the grandparents.

The similarity among the three typologies is noticeable. Each ranges from heavy involvement at one extreme to remoteness at the other. So far, no systematic study has been made of the relationship between amount of involvement and such external variables as social class or ethnicity. In general, of course, family studies have found that poverty or cultural deviance are associated with clumping of relatives, either under one roof or in close geographic proximity. The increase in number of independent households over the past couple of decades, which has so frequently been interpreted as evidence for the breakdown and decline of the family, is probably more a sign of economic affluence. When money is available for multiple rents or buying of houses, not to mention quick and easy transportation among these separate dwellings, family units can spread out.

Multigenerational residences may thus be considered a sign of hard times and trouble. They may also be effective solutions to many social ills. Teenage mothers are best off living in the maternal grandmother's household (Tinsley & Parke, 1983), for example. Aged parents move in with their children (usually a daughter) when they are too poor or too frail to live alone. Grandparents are not the only relatives who jump in when the skies get stormy. Capable grandparents may be the first and foremost to do so, though. The influence of the extended family was easier to overlook when our focus was on the needs of the frail aged, who today are more likely to be great-grandparents than grandparents of young children.

Recent research on working mothers of young children shows the often overwhelming burdens of these women, particularly if they are single parents. So far, there is little study of employed grandmothers and their added household and family responsibilities and burdens.

Developmental Issues

When we consider that the ages of grandparents may be anywhere between 30 and 120 years and of grandchildren anywhere from birth to 80 years, we realize that the respective ages of members of the two generations must be significant in their relationship. Although chronological age per se is a teacherous and inadequate index of developmental status, there can be no question but that there are wide variations in development in both generations. Some grandparents are vigorous, youthful adults, but some are feeble and badly in need of help themselves. Some seek lots of excitement and stimulation in their lives; others want a quiet, predictable routine. Conversely, some grandchildren need infinite nurturance and protection, while others are ready to move out into heady encounters with the world outside the family. Still others may be settled into the responsibilities and restrictions of raising their own young.

These gross developmental differences are reflected in wide differences in styles of grandparenting as well as the kind of grandparents grandchildren want. Neugarten and Weinstein (1964), for example, found that younger grandparents had more diverse styles than older. Some young grandparents were fun-seekers and some were distant figures. That is, some enjoyed playing with their grandchildren and some sought enjoyment in other spheres. Older grandparents, though, were almost always formal and distant, perhaps absorbed in their own failing health.

In the ongoing three-generational study I mentioned earlier, grandparents in their fifties, sixties, and seventies were more likely to say good things about their grandchildren, whereas those in their forties and eighties were more likely to be critical. It could be the 50-, 60-, and 70-year-olds were much more comfortable about being grandparents than those who felt they were too young or too old (see Neugarten,

Moore, & Lowe, 1965, who found clear age designations for when it was appropriate for different life events to occur). At the other end, both Kahana and Kahana (1970) and Clark (1969) report that younger grandchildren are more appealing to older grandparents. There may be an upper limit to this effect, however, with very old grandparents finding highly active preschoolers a trial. Cumming and Henry's (1961) respondents said that they were glad to see their grandchildren come and glad to see them go.

Children change rapidly and dramatically throughout the first two decades of life. According to Kahana and Kahana (1970), in the only systematic study so far on age differences of grandchildren and their attitudes toward grandparents, children under 10 feel closer to their grandparents than do older children. their 4- and 5-year-old respondents said they liked their grandparents to be indulgent, the 8- and 9-year-olds liked them to be fun, and children older than that preferred that they keep their distance. The wish for distancing, if true, may be temporary, because several studies of young adult grandchildren (see Hagestad, 1978; Gilford & Black, 1972; Robertson, 1977) found that all these grandchildren said their grandparents were important to them.

A poignant and, I think, relevant anecdote comes to us from the cross-species research of the anthropologist Hrdy (1981). In a troop of langurs she was observing in India, the coming to power of a new dominant male was often accompanied by his killing all the infants born to his predecessor. No animal in the troop was seen to oppose him in this infanticidal action, with one exception: an old female dubbed Sol. While the younger females—the mothers of the infants but also the future mothers of the infants to be fathered by this new leader—remained passive, it was the no-longer-fertile female who had the nerve to rescue what infants she could. Perhaps they were her grandchildren. I leave the reader to draw a possible parallel to human grandparental involvement in family crises today. Do grandparents sometimes step in where parents fear to tread?

Sex Differences

Early research on grandparenting led investigators and theorists to conclude that it was primarily a nurturant, and thus a woman's, function—that grandfathers became "feminized" in their approach if they were highly involved with their grandchildren. This kind of conclusion parallels that about retirement. In the early 1970s, men were supposed to find retiring more stressful than women because it involved a move into the "woman's sphere"—the home and family—and would thus be a sharp and abrupt transition for men as well as a demeaning one. Accompanying these beliefs was another, that grandfathers had once possessed relevant information to transmit to their grandchildren: skills and observations on life that would still be useful. Further, they were able to continue in "man's work" to the end of their lives. The accelerated social change of modern times, it was further believed, made the skills of the old irrelevant and not only drove them from the workplace but also gave them nothing to hand down to their grandsons.

More recent views about sex differences in job and family spheres see the situation quite differently. Instead of men finding retirement difficult, that is, it is women who do (Atchley & Corbett, 1977). In part, perhaps, this may be because it was a lack of fulfillment at home that led them to seek work outside. This is not to deny that most women seek employment in order to contribute to family income or because they are the sole support of themselves and their children—and even parents. What is not always remembered, furthermore, is that in the "golden age" of grandparenting, when grandparents were still relevant as teachers of the culture to their grandchildren, few grandfathers survived long enough to do so.

In spite of supposed changes in sex distribution of work, traditional differences do seem to be maintained in grandparenting, as they are in parenting. Hagestad (1978, 1982) found that grandmothers are more likely to have warm relationships with their grandchildren—and their children—than are grandfathers. Further, most of these warm relationships are down the maternal line, the mother-daughter tie being a particularly strong one. Influence of grandparents is not, however, restricted to grandmothers. Neugarten and Weinstein (1964) note that although grandmothers are more likely to be surrogate parents, grandfathers are more likely to be the reservoirs of family wisdom. Hagestad's (1978) respondents, on the other hand, indicated that both grandmothers and grandfathers are reservoirs of family wisdom, but operate differently and in different domains. The grandmothers were more generalized in their advice giving, making much less distinction than the grandfathers between whether they were influencing their granddaughters or their grandsons. The grandfathers usually confined their influencing to grandsons. The topics discussed were also differentiated according to sex. Grandmothers tended to discuss interpersonal and intrapersonal topics: how to relate to the family, dating, and the relative

TABLE 5.1   Percentage Distribution of Family Themes in All-Male
and All-Female Three-Generation Lineage Units

	All Male Units	All Female Units
Views on social issues	32	9
Work, education, money	59	9
Health and appearance	9	15
Daily living	–	14
Interpersonal relations	–	53
Total	100	100

NOTE: Percentage distribution of *themes*, not families. Most families had more than one theme.
SOURCE: Reprinted from Hagestad, 1982.

importance of family and friends. Grandfathers concentrated on areas outside the family/personality domain: work, education, money, the management of time, and wider social issues.

When she analyzed family themes in all-male and all-female three-generational lines, furthermore, Hagestad found, as shown in Table 5.1, that male lines (grandfathers, sons, and grandsons) talked to each other about work, education, and money more than half the time and about their views on social issues one-third of the time. All female lines talked about interpersonal relations more than half the time, while the rest was divided relatively equally among the other four areas.

The possibility of cohort or period changes in sex differences is suggested by the fact that the grandchildren said they did not restrict their influencing attempts to their advice-seeking by either subject matter or sex of grandparent. Whether this less traditional sex stereotyping by the grandchildren will stay with them when they become parents and grandparents is yet to be seen.

Family Systems

Little by little, the concept of families as systems is filtering into mainline family theory and research. It is noteworthy that the impressive volume, *Contemporary Theories about the Family,* edited by Burr, Hill, Nye, and Reiss (1979), contains two chapters utilizing a systems point of view: "Communication in Couples and Families," by Raush, Greif, and Nugent, and "Family Process and Child Outcomes," by Broderick and Pulliam-Krager. Even these two excellent reviews restrict their focus largely to couples and young children. An early paper by Hader (1965), titled "The Importance of Grandparents in Family Life," is, from my rapid inspection, the only—or at least one of a few— treatments of the family-system domain that includes grandparents specifically.

Laboratory observations of family interactions that include grandparents are also scarce. Twenty years ago, Scott (1962) watched an interaction sequence between both parents, a teenager, and a grandmother. She reported that the grandmother was not an active participant in the interaction. Field and her colleagues (see Field et al., 1980) have been videotaping interaction sequences in participants' homes. Their subjects are black teenage mothers in Florida, their infants, and their mothers. Like Scott, Field found that the grandmothers mostly sat back and watched the young mother with her baby. Unger (1979) did not measure interaction in life, but did assess the amount of interaction between white low-income mothers and their infants. She was interested in the effect of friends' and relatives' contact with the mothers on the mother-infant interactions. The more supportive adult contacts the mothers had, she found, the greater the amount of interaction they had with their children. We might conclude that while the grandmothers observed by Scott and Field were not interacting directly with their grandchildren, they may have promoted greater or better parent-child interactions by indirect support.

A different kind of information about the involvement of grandparents comes from the ingenious research of Feldman and Nash and their colleagues at Stanford University (for example, Abrahams, Feldman, & Nash, 1978; Feldman & Nash, 1979; Feldman, Biringen, & Nash, 1981; Feldman, Nash, & Cutrona, 1977). By staging a scene in a waiting room that included the presence of an infant, they observed the attraction of the infant for various categories of people. Thus, mothers of infants were more responsive to this "stranger" infant than were pregnant women, cohabitating women, married childless women, mothers of adolescent children, "empty-nest" women, and grandmothers of infants. On the other hand, the grandmothers of infants were more responsive than the mothers of adolescent children or "empty-nest" mothers. Grandfathers of infants were more responsive than men in any category other than fathers of infants.

Tinsley and Parke (1983) are currently pursuing an even more systematic line of research that involves varying the amount of grandparental inclusion in family interactions that take place in otherwise naturally occurring settings. As they point out, it is now time to look at more specific kinds of questions and to use more controlled or at least varied situations.

Conclusion

What is the present state of the art? First, I think we can conclude that grandmothers and grandfathers are definitely not removed from the family picture. On the other hand, we must also conclude that they take a back seat to parents. Unfortunately, this kind of statement is of a low order of scientific specificity. It describes average situations. We need to know a lot more about the effect of demographic factors, about developmental factors, or of family system factors on the incidence and significance of grandparental interactions. What characteristics of the grandparents, of their children, of their grandchildren, or of the family system are associated with greater contact and significance of that contact, and what characteristics are associated with less contact and significance?

Families probably vary widely in their integration: in the strength of their boundaries (see Handel, 1968; Troll, 1980b) and in the sharing of family themes or value systems. If grandparents are really family watchdogs, they would not have to work hard at their mission in highly integrated families, even though they might or might not partake of social interactions. Where family boundaries are permeable and there is little distinction between kin and nonkin, grandparents could share the task of watching that all goes well. We could predict from this premise that only when boundaries are weakening would the grandparents' task be strenuous and active, not only as watchdogs but in filling the holes in the dyke. Divorce is a case in point. Hagestad, Smyer, and Stierman (1982) and the ongoing work of Colleen Johnson (personal communication, 1982) in San Francisco find that grandparents often have greater involvement in the lives of their grandchildren after the parents divorce. Hagestad (1982) uses the term, the "family ripple effect" of divorce. While the number of grandparents who themselves divorce in later life is low, they are very much involved in the divorces of their children.

PART II

Social Issues

A number of issues concerning the family relationships of older persons are examined in this section. Each contribution seeks to provide a cogent discussion of the primary aspects of the issue addressed. The contributions review previous research on the issue addressed and report new research. The issues are couple relationships, marital sexual interaction, family involvement with widows, divorce, violence, sex-role expectations, and minority families.

Robert C. Atchley and Sheila J. Miller examine the effects different types of later-life changes have on the husband-wife relationship. How does retirement affect the couple relationship? Do changes in health have an impact on couples' life satisfaction? How does a change in residence affect an older husband-wife relationship? Data gathered at two points in time from 208 couples are reported. The findings suggest that the couple relationship of these older persons is vital and changes in employment status, health, and residence do not negatively affect the husband and wife relationship.

Sexuality of older couples is the focus of Joseph M. Garza and Paula Dressel. An in-depth review of research on marital sexuality in later life indicates that little empirical research has been undertaken. Garza and Dressel report declines in sexual activity in later years due to structural changes in the marital relationship. The husband is the primary individual responsible for the decline in marital sexual activity. A critique of the research on sexuality in later life and implications for policy and research are presented.

Expectations for masculine and feminine activities of older couples are the concern of Cynthia Dobson's chapter. This study examines definitions of instrumental and expressive qualities for older husbands and wives. Data gathered from 441 persons are presented. The findings indicate that less sex differentiation of instrumental and expressive qualities is expected in later life. For both husbands and wives, expressive qualities are important and may be more important in later life. Policy and practice implications are discussed.

Widowhood is experienced by many older persons. As reported in Chapter 1, many more women than men are widowed. Gloria D. Heinemann discusses widowhood as experienced by women and men. Her primary concern is the involvement of family with the older widowed individual. Data from widows aged 20-69 years (median age of 69 years) are presented. The findings suggest that family involvement with widowhood may be positive and negative. In some cases, the involvement may be related to stressful, less satisfying relationships between the older widowed person and other family members.

Although few older persons are divorced, the number is expected to increase in the future. Little research has been directed toward divorce in later life. Charles B. Hennon reviews the few studies completed and discusses an exploratory study of twenty divorced and twenty widowed older women. The study focuses on physical, psychological, social, and consumer well-being. Differences and similarities between divorced and widowed elderly are highlighted. Implications for practice and research are discussed.

Suzanne K. Steinmetz and Deborah J. Amsden examine dependency, stress, and abuse in families where an older parent is dependent on an adult child. This study is based on interviews with 104 caregivers who have cared for 118 dependent elders. The data indicate that support is needed for caregivers of dependent elders.

The final chapter in this section focuses on minority families and the elderly. Charles H. Mindel examines the unique family patterns of American Blacks and Mexican Americans in terms of the elderly. It is suggested that the family and kinship network is important to the minority elderly.

6

Types of Elderly Couples

ROBERT C. ATCHLEY
SHEILA J. MILLER

This chapter is concerned with the effects of various types of changes that occur in later life on middle-aged and older couples. We are also concerned with the mediating effects of the couple's type of relationship.

We begin with the premise that aging can bring three important types of changes for couples: retirement, changes in health, and changes in residence. The literature on families in later life suggests that all three types of changes can have important results for the couple's relationship. For example, retirement has been found to have negative impact on working-class couples (Heyman & Jeffers, 1968; Fengler, 1975), whereas it seems to improve relationships among members of middle- and upper-status couples (Kerckhoff, 1966; Maas & Kuypers, 1974).

Health is also a major factor. Not only does it have a direct effect on the couple, but it influences the effects of other factors such as retirement. For example, Miller (1981) found that husbands who were in good health tended to be active and to have high morale, which in turn was very strongly related to their wives' having high morale. Husbands' morale also depended greatly on their wives' health. Preserving good health is a major goal of most couples (Feldman, 1964; Neugarten, Wood, Kraines, & Loomis, 1963).

Residential change has received less attention. Longino (1980) reported that movers to resort communities in the Ozarks tended to be couples, whereas movers to full-service retirement communities and low-rent housing for the elderly tended to be single older people, mainly women. But the effects of residential change on elder couples have not been studied.

Another neglected aspect of the literature on couples in later life is the quality of the relationship. This could be addressed in two ways. First, we are interested in the prevalence of various types of couples. Cuber and Harroff (1965) found that the type of couples was very important for their happiness. To examine this issue we have developed a new typology in this chapter. Second, we are concerned with the degree of sharing within the couple and its effect as a mediator of changes associated with aging. For example, Deutscher (1959, p. 109) hypothesized that couples who engaged in mutual activities would define their relationship more positively than those who did not. Although Deutscher's data did not support this hypothesis in relation to the empty nest, we are interested in shared values and activities and the effect they have on the couple relationship.

Data and Methods

The data we use to examine these issues come from a longitudinal study of adaptation to aging that began in a small Ohio township with a population of about 25,000 in 1975. The community is typical of many small towns in that it is geographically close enough to be socially and economically influenced by a nearby major metropolis, but distant enough to remain independent of serious social problems such as high crime rates. Using voter registrations, a postcard census of all mailing addresses, and reports from longtime community residents, we identified all residents of the town who were age 50 or over as of July 1, 1975. We surveyed 1,560 persons in the fall of 1975, and 1,106 responded for a return of 71 percent. The panel was surveyed again in 1977 and 1978, with returns of 852 and 678 respectively.

Within the overall data set were data from both members of 208 married couples. These are the data used for this chapter. The data set includes measures of employment/retirement status, health, residential stability, social status, personal goals, activities, life satisfaction, and a host of others. The 1975 and 1977 waves of data are used for this report.

The sample is mainly middle-class and white. The median years of education of husbands was 16 and of wives was 15. Only 3 percent of the respondents were black. The median age of the husbands was 63 and of the wives was 61. For over 90 percent of both husbands and wives, their current marriage was their only marriage. About 8 percent of both husbands and wives had been married more than once. Thus, the findings reported here are primarily for middle-class, white couples who have been married only once and whose marriages have lasted many years.

Retirement

We looked at three separate questions in relating retirement to couples. First, did marital status have an impact on the timing of retirement? Second, how did retirement affect the couple's life satisfaction? Third, did retirement affect couples' life satisfaction indirectly through its effect on health?

Marital status definitely had an effect on the timing of retirement. A more complete discussion of this relationship has been reported elsewhere (Atchley & Miller, 1982). The vast majority of married men retired around age 65 (although not in response to mandatory retirement), while nonmarried men retired earlier.[1] On the other hand, married women tended to retire earlier than age 65, while nonmarried women were significantly more likely to retire after age 65. The reasons for these trends seem to revolve around economics. Married men work until age 65 in order to maximize retirement benefits for the couple. Nonmarried men tend to be in poorer health and to see less economic need to work longer, and as a result, retire earlier. Married women retire before age 65 because they tend to retire when their husbands do and they tend to be younger. Nonmarried women have much lower retirement income resources compared to nonmarried men and work longer in order to improve their retirement incomes.

Of 185 couples for whom we had this information for both members, the employment status breakdown is shown in Table 6.1. We considered couples to be retired if at least one member was retired. Of the retired couples, 76 percent had been two-worker couples. Over two-thirds of the retired couples currently had neither member employed. Having one member retired and the other employed was rare and was no more likely to involve the wife's earlier retirement than the husband's. For couples in which the husband was retired and the wife employed, the wives averaged 6 years younger than their husbands, while the average age difference for the other employment/retirement status categories was only 2.6 years. This supports Henretta and O'Rand's (1980) conclusion that husband's retirement influences wife's retirement only if the wife is of retirement age herself.

Thus, while the general data by marital status show a contrast between married and unmarried respondents on the timing of retirement, there are also significant variations within couples.

TABLE 6.1   Employment/Retirement Status of Couples

	N	%
Couple retired	43	23.2
Husband retired/wife housewife	23	12.4
Husband retired/wife employed	15	8.1
Husband employed/wife retired	14	7.6
Husband employed/wife housewife	42	22.7
Couple employed	48	26.0
Total	185	100.0

These data on the timing of retirement have several implications. First, the literature is one-sided in viewing retirement as a cause of family factors. However, our results show that family factors can be an influence on retirement. This influence needs further investigation. Second, these family factors operate to cause husbands and wives to retire together except in cases where the wife is substantially younger than her husband. This implies that information on spouse's retirement needs to be considered in any retirement decision-making model (Atchley, 1979).

We found no evidence that retirement affected the couples' life satisfaction. In order to examine this issue, we summed the individual life satisfaction for the members of each couple. The result was a normally distributed index of couples' life satisfaction that ranged from a low of 45 to a high of 72, with a mean of 64.9. Table 6.2 shows that being retired had no effect on the life satisfaction scores of the couples.

Although the category, husband employed/wife retired, appears to have much higher mean life satisfaction, the number of people in this category is small and the difference is not statistically significant.

We also looked at other criterion variables for the results of retirement. The employed couples were not significantly different from those who had retired on measures of self-confidence, degree of goal orientation, or activity level. In every direction we looked, retirement did not make a difference.

In a last attempt to make sure that we had not overlooked something important, we also looked at the small number of couples who actually retired between 1975 and 1977. Again, retirement made no difference in life satisfaction, self confidence, or goal orientation. Although retirement did bring slightly lower activity level, this was not associated with a decline in life satisfaction.

TABLE 6.2   Mean Life Satisfaction Scores of Couples
by Employment/Retirement Status

Employment/Retirement Status	Mean Life Satisfaction
Couple retired	64.4
Husband retired/wife housewife	64.0
Husband retired/wife employed	63.4
Husband employed/wife retired	68.2
Husband employed/wife housewife	64.9
Couple employed	65.5
Overall	64.9

NOTE: $F = 1.256$; $p = .29$.

For the healthy, middle-class couples in this sample, retirement had none of the negative effects on life satisfaction that earlier work would have led us to expect (Blau, 1981), nor did it have the positive effects that others have found (Kerckhoff, 1966b; Maas & Kuypers, 1974). We want to emphasize that in our sample, *retirement had no effect.*

But what about a negative effect of retirement on couples as a result of retirement's possible negative effects on health? In the first place, few investigators with adequate longitudinal data have found that retirement has a negative effect on health. That was certainly true in our sample. Not a single couple who retired during our study reported a decline in health for either member. This is noteworthy because we have several health measures that will be detailed below.

On the other hand, couples in which one member retires because of poor health could be expected to have more difficulties than healthy couples. Indeed, Parnes and Nestel (1981) found that men who retired for health reasons were dissatisfied with many aspects of their lives, much more so than other categories of retirees. But Ekerdt and Bosse (1982) found that about one-third of their respondents experienced improved health following retirement. We could not investigate this issue because we had too few health-related retirements. More work needs to be done in this area in order to investigate more fully the impact of health-related retirement on couples, particularly those with a spouse who remains in poor health after retirement.

Health: Illness and Disability

Health was a major influence on the life satisfaction of the couples in our study. A number of variables could be used to look at this issue.

Self-reported health was a global health measure asking respondents to rank their health as very good, good, fair, poor, or very poor. *Functional health* was measured by a six-item index of activities such as walking up and down stairs, walking a mile, or doing ordinary work around the house. *Health trend* was the respondents' ratings of whether their health was improving, declining, or staying the same. *Activity limitation* was measured by an item asking if respondents had activity limitations due to ill health or disability and, if so, to what degree. All of these measures were highly intercorrelated, as expected. Because it was the strictest definition of "good health' in a functional sense, we used functional health in our analysis. The results would not be substantially different if we had used the global self-rating of health.

We expected health to be important for several reasons. Because husbands tend to be older than their wives and because men are more likely to have activity limitations at any age compared to women, wives could be expected to be more affected by their husbands' health than vice versa. Troll, Miller, and Atchley (1979) suggest that the main effect of health on marriages in later life is "that of turning wives into at least part-time nurses." Lopata (1973) found that 46 percent of the widows she studied had cared for their husbands at home during their final illnesses and that nearly 20 percent of widows had nursed their husbands for over a year. This kind of health problem severely curtails many kinds of marital interactions, and it can greatly reduce the wife's freedom to continue her participation in activities outside the household. Neugarten et al. (1963) also reported that the middle-aged women they studied were more concerned about their husbands' health than their own. Thus, we expected that husbands' health would have a greater impact on the life satisfaction of wives than vice versa.

Our results did not bear out this expectation. While health was most definitely related to life satisfaction, the patterns within the couples were not as predicted. As Table 6.3 shows, the life satisfaction of wives was significantly related only to husband's life satisfaction and to the wife's own functional health.

However, for the husbands a different pattern emerged. As Table 6.4 shows, wife's functional health was very much related to the life satisfaction of husbands.

Thus, while spouse's functional health has a direct effect on the life satisfaction of husbands, for wives the effect is indirect through the relationship between the husband's functional health and his life satis-

TABLE 6.3   Regression Coefficients Predicting Wife's Life Satisfaction

Independent Variable	R2	Beta
Husband's life satisfaction	.09	.28
Wife's functional health	.15	.25

Not significant:
   Couple's total number of goals
   Couple's employment status (retired/other)
   Couple's activity level
   Husband's functional health
   Wife's activity level

faction. However, a more important point is that spouse's health is very much involved in the life satisfaction of both husbands and wives. The earlier literature probably went astray on this issue because husbands have less often been studied.

The relationship between good health and couple's life satisfaction is enormous. In couples where both members are in good functional health (N = 110), 95 percent have high life satisfaction. However, it would be a mistake to conclude that poor health produces low life satisfaction. Indeed, in our sample, only one of our 210 couples had life satisfaction that could truly be called low. Having modest rather than high life satisfaction was the main effect of poor health.

Residential Change

Residential change would seem to have great potential influence on couples' relationships in later life. For one thing, moving means learning a new household environment and developing new routines and ground rules for dealing with it. As such, moving is a source of discontinuity in the couple's lifestyle. In addition, moving to a new community alters the household's relationship to the external environment, and as a result it can introduce substantial discontinuity in the activities of the couple outside the household. It would also seem that moving to a new community increases the extent to which the members of the couple rely on one another for activities and interaction. For some, this could be expected to produce pressures that might in turn reduce life satisfaction.

To examine these ideas, we compared the couples who had recently moved to the township with those who were long-term residents. We

TABLE 6.4   Regression Coefficients Predicting Husband's Life Satisfaction

Independent Variable	R2	Beta
Husband's functional health	.19	.25
Wife's life satisfaction	.22	.25
Wife's functional health	.27	.19
Not significant:		
Couple's activity level		
Couple's employment status (retired/other)		
Couple's total number of goals		
Husband's activity level		

expected that the recent arrivals would have lower activity levels and would have lower life satisfaction compared to longtime community residents. The results did not bear out these expectations. There was no relationship between recently having moved to the town and activity level or life satisfaction.

We did about twenty in-depth interviews with couples in the sample, several of whom were recent arrivals. In every case, the new arrivals had selected the town for retirement migration because they felt that it was a good, safe place to live in retirement. They also felt that it woud offer them plenty of opportunities for the kinds of activities they liked. Finally, many of them mentioned the ease with which they were accepted into the community. They felt that this was much more likely to happen in a small town than in a large city.

Thus, moving did not have the predicted negative effects because the movers were selecting a destination in tune with their desired lifestyles. This fits with the findings of Bultena and Wood (1969), that movers in later life tend to select the environment that most closely matches their needs. Perhaps couples who have to move to less desirable housing or a less desirable community because of health or financial problems experience the effects we predicted, and that possibility needs to be investigated, but moving did not produce negative effects in our healthy and financially secure sample.

Type of Couples

Spouses can relate to one another in numerous ways. For example, couples differ in their approach to the household division of labor, the extent to which the husband is expected to be the sole economic provider, the individual needs that are met through the relationship, and a host of other dimensions. Those few studies that have looked at the household division of labor have found that the traditional gender-based division of household tasks is diminished somewhat by retirement but that husbands still tend to concentrate on "man's work" at home. What may change is the amount of man's work that actually gets done, accompanied by a feeling on the part of the wife that the husband is finally doing his share. This needs to be studied.

Kerchoff (1966) studied the value orientations of couples in terms of their expectations of interaction with their offspring. He found that middle-class couples tended to have "nucleated" family values that stressed independence between generations. He reported that most middle-class older couples were pleasantly surprised at the fact that their children lived nearer and visited more often than expected. These couples also tended to expect sharing of household tasks and to see change as good.

Cuber and Harroff (1965) studied middle-aged, upper-middle-class couples and identified a number of types. Their most common type was the devitalized marriage, in which the closeness that once existed between the partners was no longer there, but they lived together in unexcited dependency. A second pattern was conflict-habituated, characterized by constant bickering. The passive-congenial marriage was a third type, in which there had never been much closeness or excitement—a marriage of covenience. The vital marriage involved the minds and lives of the partners closely with one another. They tended to think similarly and to be involved in similar types of activities. They were intensely tied to one another emotionally.

Swenson, Eskew, and Kohlhepp (1981) found that as duration of marriage increased, especially after the child-launching stage, the experience of love for one's spouse declined, but so did the incidence of marital problems.

On the basis of these bits and pieces of evidence, most from studies of middle-aged couples, we expected that older couples would neither value intimacy very highly nor see keeping close ties with their family as very important. After all, our sample is also the middle class studied by Cuber and Harroff and by Kerckhoff.

We classified the individual spouses in our sample based on their responses to questions about personal goals they felt were important. The spouses were asked to rate a set of sixteen goal statements as very

TABLE 6.5   Family Orientation Categories for Individuals

Category	Close Family Ties	Intimate Relationship
Integrated	Very important	Very important
Family-centered	Very important	–
Couple-centered	–	Very important
Self-centered	–	–

important, important, unimportant, or very unimportant. The two statements we used were "having close ties with my family" and "having a close, intimate relationship." The resulting classification is shown in Table 6.5. We then matched the couples with respect to their family orientations. Couples were called "divergent" if the spouses did not have the same family orientations. The results are shown in Table 6.6.

These results show a number of things. First, most couples did not share family orientations. Second, integrated and family-centered were the orientations most likely to be shared, contrary to expectations. As expected, the couple-centered orientation was rare. Self-centered was not as common a type in this sample as the literature led us to expect.

Since the divergent category was the largest, we broke it down by separate family orientations of the spouses. The results are shown in Table 6.7.

The first point of note about the divergent couples is that most of them involve an integrated and a family-centered spouse, a relatively strong family orientation for the couple. Second, wives are more likely to be integrated in their orientations, while husbands tend to be family-oriented—a surprise, given the standard literature references to men as less interested in kinship roles. Finally, husbands are much more likely to be self-centered than are wives, which wives have been saying for years.

When we look at Tables 6.6 and 6.7 together, we get a clearer picture. Integrated and family-oriented combinations account for 68 percent of the couples. This is certainly strong evidence that intimacy and family ties are indeed very important to a majority of the middle-class couples in our sample.

Next, we used analysis of variance to examine the effects of the couple's family orientation on their life satisfaction. The integrated, family-centered, and divergent couples with strong family orientations all showed very high life satisfaction. On the other hand, the self-centered couples were significantly less likely to have high life satisfac-

TABLE 6.6   Types of Couples by Family Orientation

Type	N	%
Integrated	30	21
Family-centered	23	16
Couple-centered	1	1
Self-centered	12	8
Divergent	77	54
Total	143	100

tion.[2] In other words, the independence from spouse and family that the literature led us to expect was not common, and when it did occur, the result was significantly lower life satisfaction.

Shared Goals and Activities

Finally, we wanted to look at the extent to which husbands and wives share goals and activities and how important this sharing is for life satisfaction.

Shared values are often presumed to be an important basis for integration in groups. However, value consensus between spouses has received relatively little attention in the gerontology literature. Booth and Welch (1978) found that consensus did not emerge as a unidimensional factor. Indeed, it would be surprising if it did. There are simply too many potential issues and too many potential positions.

Instead of trying to use confirmatory factor analysis to measure consensus as Booth and Welch (1978) did, we took the much simpler approach of measuring the percentage of overlap in husbands' and wives' responses to our personal goals questions. The result is an index of similarity that measures consensus item by item on a sixteen-item goal inventory. This is preferable to simply using the difference between totals for the spouses, because individuals can have the same total score but have felt that different goals were important.

The most remarkable thing about the results is the very high percentage of agreement. The lowest similarity score was 70, and the mean score was 85 percent agreement. Five couples had complete agreement on all sixteen goals. Similarity was related to age and duration of marriage. The older the spouses and the longer the duration of their marriage, the higher was the similarity in their personal goals.

TABLE 6.7   Divergent Couples, by Family Orientation
of the Two Spouses

Husband's Family Orientation	Wife's Family Orientation			
	Integrated	Family-Centered	Couple-Centered	Self-Centered
Integrated	0	18	3	1
Family-centered	26	0	0	3
Couple-centered	4	4	0	2
Self-centered	8	5	3	0

But the correlation between goal similarity and life satisfaction was not statistically significant in our couples. While this may seem surprising, remember that *all* of the couples had substantial agreement on personal goals. There were no cases of substantial disagreement, which is the situation that would be most likely to produce conflict and reduce life satisfaction.

Next we looked at similarity in activities. It is often said that "the family that plays together, stays together." We wanted to know if having shared activities influenced life satisfaction in our couples. We used data from an eighteen-item activity frequency inventory to compute similarity scores. There was less similarity in activities than in personal goals, but not by much. The low score was 64 percent similarity, and the mean was 82 percent. However, none of the couples had complete similarities in activities. This is unsurprising in consideration of the sex-role meanings given to such activities as spectator sports. In fact, it is the high degree of similarity that is remarkable. These findings do not necessarily show that couples who play together stay together, but they do show that couples who stay together definitely play together.

Again, probably because of the lack of dissimilarity, similarity scores on activities were not related to life satisfaction of the couple.

Discussion

In many ways, the couples we studied are aging under optimum conditions. They are middle-class people who live in a congenial small township that is safe and that offers a wide variety of opportunities for involvement. Most have good health and sufficient income.

We found that being in a couple influences the timing of retirement, but that retirement has no measurable effect on the quality of couples' lives. This is at variance with earlier studies showing that retirement had a negative effect on self-esteem of the members of the couple (Blau, 1981) and that retirement improved the quality of middle-class marriages.

There are several possible explanations for the differences. First, as we said, our sample is aging under optimum conditions. Not only is the community environment conducive to enjoyable retirement, but the retirement income picture has improved substantially in the years since some of the earlier studies were done. Second, couples in small towns may be different from couples in large urban areas. Atchley, Pignatiello, and Shaw (1979) found that married women in large urban areas were much more isolated from contact outside their households compared to married women in small towns. Kunkel (1979) suggested that size of community is a major factor in the results showing that widows adjust much better in small towns compared to large urban areas. These various hints point to qualitative differences between life in small towns and life in metropolitan areas. Third, studies in the North-Central region of the United States generally have found retirement to be a more positive experience compared to studies done in the East (Cottrell & Atchley, 1969; Atchley, 1976b; Powers, Keith, & Goudy, 1975; Blau, 1973; Streib & Schneider, 1971). This points to possible regional differences in the effect of retirement on couples.

The couples in our study had very high life satisfaction, and the *only* factor we looked at that altered this picture was health. Husbands' life satisfaction is very much tied to the functional health of their wives, while wives' life satisfaction is indirectly affected by the effect of the husbands' health on their life satisfaction. Contrary to the literature, we found that, if anything, husbands are more dependent for their own life satisfaction on their wives' health than vice versa. We speculated that the reason for this contradiction may lie in the fact that in previous studies husbands were underrepresented.

Residential change did not affect the couples' life satisfaction. This is probably because movers select what they see as an ideal environment to meet their needs. The results also indicate that this selection process is a sound one. Further research could look into the impact of involuntary housing changes on couples.

Again, contrary to the literature, we found that most of the couples we studied placed high value on both intimacy and family ties. The suggestion that devitalized couples are most common was not borne out in our sample. The prevailing pattern of shared values and activities was much nearer to Cuber and Harroff's vital marriage. Likewise, the generational independence found in Kerckhoff's middle-class respondents was not found in our sample. Not only did these couples tend to value close family ties highly, but their interaction with children and grandchildren was quite frequent.

The spouses tended to be quite similar with respect to both values and activities. In fact, similarity was so common that we could not adequately test the notion that dissimilarity might be related to lower life satisfaction.

The positive picture we gained through our survey was confirmed in the depth interviews. It was a genuine pleasure to be around these couples. They accepted one another fully, were often obviously devoted to one another, and were very much enjoying their lives together. They were pleased that their marriages had endured. For these people, aging together was indeed a pleasant experience.

NOTES

1. In this analysis we also used data from 118 men and 151 women who were not members of a couple.

2. Since only one couple was couple-centered, an analysis of variance for this category could not be performed.

7

Sexuality and
Later-Life Marriages

JOSEPH M. GARZA
PAULA L. DRESSEL

Interest in sex and sexuality unquestionably dates to antiquity, but the *scientific study* of these phenomena was begun only in the recent past.[1] Despite historical and cross-cultural variations, the topics of sex and sexuality have largely been confined to that cluster of cultural items conveniently labeled "taboo"; a cultural element so identified thus conveys clear and unequivocal instruction to all members of society not to approach the subject openly. One consequence has been to discourage the accumulation of objective knowledge about the particular taboo element in the lives of societal members, thereby relegating it to the realms of misconception, fantasy, gossip, and folklore.

For some time misconceptions and folklore have pervaded our information about sex and sexuality in general and marital sexual expression in particular. Taboos continue to envelop the forms and meanings of sexual expression between husbands and wives, and we suspect that a sizable proportion of the married American population is involved in relationships based on misinformation and folk wisdom. Even less is known about sexual expression among the elderly married. Social research questions have, in general, been applied belatedly to gerontological concerns; the slow transfer of sex research to the aging is no exception to this pattern. As a consequence, what we know about sex and sexuality in later-life marriages is sketchy at best.

Purpose and Scope

The paragraphs that follow are devoted to a description of the research findings on marital and nonmarital forms of sexual interaction in later-life marriages. "Marital sexual interaction" is defined as the forms of sexual expression engaged in by married couples with each other; "nonmarital sexual interaction" refers to those forms of sexual expression engaged in by married individuals in the absence of the marital partner, such as masturbation and extramarital sex. Our use of the phrase "nonmarital sexual interaction" in this chapter must be distinguished from other forms of sexual expression typically associated with the phrase, such as homosexuality, premarital sexual relations, and sexual relationships of the divorced and widowed populations.

This review of relevant literature is focused on studies of (1) noninstitutionalized populations and (2) married-intact couples in which at least one is 60 years of age or older. Only research publications appearing since 1965 and focusing on U.S. populations are presented.

A computer search for relevant literature convering the time period 1965-1981 was undertaken and included *Psychological Abstracts, Sociological Abstracts,* and the computer package on *MEDLINE.* A sample of citations from *MEDLINE* revealed that the publications in this package were strictly of use to professionals in the medical and natural sciences. Further search of this package was therefore discontinued. In addition to these computer packages a search of the following soures was conducted: *Combined Retrospective Index to Journals in Sociology,* 1895-1974, Volume 2; *Women's Studies Abstracts,* 1972-81; the *Inventory of Marriage and Family Literature,* Volumes 2-7; and available 1982 issues of selected family and gerontology journals.

Upon completion of our search for relevant research studies on marital and nonmarital forms of sexual interaction, we realized that a sizable body of literature existed that was not directly applicable to our central focus. More specifically, a good part of this literature was prescriptive (see Butler & Lewis, 1976; Kurlychek & Trepper, 1979; Rowland & Haynes, 1978; Rubin, 1970), myth-challenging but not data-based (see Peterson & Payne, 1975; Rubenstein, 1978; West, 1975), and overwhelmingly clinically oriented (see Cleveland, 1979; Costello, 1975; Finkle, 1973; Sviland, 1975; Weinberg, 1969). Most of these publications derived from the medical and therapeutic professional communities. This proliferation of repetitious articles suggests that writers might make more effective use of their time and energy by directing their efforts to other matters. Since these types of articles were either summaries of previous studies, polemical arguments, or isolated case studies, they do not constitute a central part of our literature review.

As a body, the literature we uncovered has several shortcomings. First, the published research reports are confined almost exclusively to studies of white populations. Second, the possibility that the married elderly might be interested in, capable of, and engaged in sexual expression outside the boundaries of marriage is practically neglected. Third, we observed that most of the literature reflects a concern with individualized aspects of sexuality (level of interest, incidence of sexual intercourse, and various emotional or psychological correlates of sexual intercourse). By way of contrast, little emphasis was placed on the interactional dimensions of the phenomenon under investigation.

We found several reviews of the literature on sexual expression among the elderly (see Berezin, 1976; Friedeman, 1978; Ludeman, 1981; Rubin, 1965; Streib & Beck, 1980; Sviland, 1975; Wales, 1974), but the focus of these reports was not specifically on *marital* sexual expression in later life. Indeed, these reviews served to highlight the relative inattention to research specifically on marital and nonmarital sexual expression during later married life. Nevertheless, some limited research on sexual expression in married life during the later years exists, and we selected for review only those studies directly applicable to our focus. Invariably sexual expression among the married elderly was conceptualized in terms of (1) frequency of sexual intercourse and (2) level of sexual interest. Findings related to these variables will be summarized first with regard to older individuals and then in terms of the couple relationship.

Marital Sexual Expression and Selected Demographic Variables

As we have already noted, the bulk of sex research on aging focuses not on the sexual *relationship,* but on individual variations in incidence of and interest in sex. This section emphasizes those variations for the married elderly with regard to selected demographic variables.

Age and Gender

Since 1965, the study of marital sexual expression among the elderly has been related more to age and gender than perhaps any other variables. Christenson and Gagnon (1965), utilizing a nonrepresentative cross-sectional sample of 241 white females aged 50-90, documented that as marital partners get older, the incidence of sexual intercourse decreases. More specifically, at age 50, approximately 88 percent of the women reported engaging in sexual intercourse with their husbands, at age 60 only 70 percent were doing so, and by age 65 the incidence had declined to 50 percent. In this study no attention was given to frequency of sexual relations between the marital partners.

The most rigorous research conducted to date on sexuality and aging has been the ongoing Duke University studies. Using a sample of 150 still-married respondents aged 60-93 from these longitudinal studies, Newman and Nichols (1970, p. 278) reported that 54 percent of the respondents were still sexually active, with a frequency ranging from three times per week to once every two months. While the association between advancing age and sexual activity was generally negative, only those people over age 75 showed a significantly lower level of sexual activity. Blacks were reported as more sexually active than whites and males were more active than females. However, since most of the blacks in this sample were of lower socioeconomic standing than the white subjects, the original relationship between race and incidence of sexual intercourse remains dubious.

Analyzing a sample of 257 elderly married males and 170 elderly married females in terms of sexual interest and sexual activity, Pfeiffer, Verwoerdt, and Davis (1974, pp. 245-247) found that current sexual interest among males declined as age increased; however, in the oldest age category there was actually a rise in "sexual interest." Among women a similar pattern was detected, the one exception being that in all age categories the percentage of women expressing "no sexual interest" was greater than that found among men. One interesting observation was that among males a slight increase in sexual interest occurred in the oldest age category, and among females an equivalent increase occurred in the next-to-oldest age category. The authors went on to speculate that individuals surviving into their late sixties and seventies might constitute a sexually elite category. Moving from a concern with "sexual interest" to a concern with "sexual frequency," these same authors found an inverse relationship between age and frequency of sexual intercourse for both sexes, with females in all age categories reporting a lower frequency than that reported by males. For males in particular, the authors noted that the absence of an increase in sexual frequency comparable to the increase found in sexual interest among selected subjects constituted a widening "interest-activity" gap.

Palmore's (1981) summary and analysis of data from the Duke longitudinal studies reported on frequency of and interest in sexual intercourse among elderly married couples. In the first longitudinal study there was a decline over time for both males and females in the percentage engaging in sexual relations. However, almost one-half of the married women remained sexually active through their sixties, and about one-half of the married men remained sexually active through their seventies. Even among those who remained sexually active, there was a decline in frequency of sexual intercourse between each round of reporting. In the second longitudinal study Palmore again observed sexual decline in all of the male cohorts and in most of the female cohorts. Further, all of the sexually active in each cohort declined in terms of frequency of sexual intercourse. However, he noted that a large number of males and females reported increases in frequency of sexual intercourse between intermediate rounds. In the first study only three men reported such increases. Significantly, very few of the respondents reported "no sexual activity," the modal pattern being one of stability. Even in the oldest cohort (70-75), one-third of the men and women reported stable patterns of sexual intercourse, and about one-tenth reported increases in sexual activity. Sexual interest and sexual enjoyment followed roughly the paterns observed for frequency of sexual intercourse. However, sexual interest invariably was reported as higher than that of sexual activity (Palmore, 1981, p. 88).

Additional studies documenting the inverse relationship between age and frequency of sexual intercourse were conducted by Keller, Eakes, Hinkle, and Hughston (1978), and George and Weiler (1981). The latter, consisting of 278 married males and females, was derived from the second Duke longitudinal study and focused on sexual activity in mid- and later life. All of the respondents were financially stable and in good health and ranged in age from 46 to 71. Respondents were tested in 1969, 1971, 1973, and 1975. Over the six-year course of this study, the mean level of sexual activity per week for all respondents remained remarkably stable (1.57, 1.56, 1.49, and 1.47) with males reporting slightly higher levels of sexual activity than females at each testing date. Age again for both sexes was shown to have a depressing effect on rates of sexual intercourse.

A sample of 85 subjects (53 male, 32 female) ranging in age from 62 to 81 was examined by DeNicola and Peruzza (1974). Of these, 45 males and 17 females were still sexually active, with reported frequencies ranging from 1 per month to 5 times each week. The authors noted that none of the respondents in this sample was afflicted with a serious disese, thus suggesting that the presence of adequate physical health is conducive to sexual performance in later life.

In general, the research surveyed here supports relationships reported prior to 1965 between frequency of and interest in sexual intercourse and the variables of age and of gender. It is worth noting that among a sizable number of the elderly, sexual intercourse continued, and among some males a slight increase in "sexual interest" was observed.

What has not been given attention in research on sexual expression among the elderly married is the impact, if any, of declining sexual interest and sexual activity on the stability of marriage. Certainly there is some evidence that the elderly are aware of such declines. For example, Pfeiffer et al. (1974, p. 248) noted that a decrease in sexual activity and sexual interest was correlated with an awareness of this decline. Also, Cameron and Biber (1973, p. 145), while not focusing on "awareness of decline," offered evidence to the effect that thinking about sexual activity is characteristic of all age categories, although the elderly did not think about it as intensely as did the respondents in the younger age categories. Further, for those elders whose activity level is not commensurate with their interest level, the question of impact on marital satisfaction becomes salient.

Religion

The relationship between religion and marital and nonmarital sexual expression among the aged has largely been ignored. In a recent review of the literature on sexual expression among the elderly, Friedeman (1978) found that religion as a factor had not been explored to any significant degree. Insofar as cross-sectional data report increasing importance of religion with advancing age (Harris et al., 1975), this lack of attention is somewhat anomalous.

In their study of 241 married white females, Christenson and Gagnon (1965) concluded that degree of religious devoutness was associated with the incidence of marital coitus, with the less devout respondents reporting higher rates of sexual activity. The degree to which religious devoutness affected sexual enjoyment, however, was not pursued in this study. It was pursued, however, in a related study of couples who were roughly in the "mid-life" stage of marriage. In their report on couples married 13-20 years, Wallin and Clark (1964) found that among wives, the lack of sexual gratification did not affect marital satisfaction for those who were religious; however, this relationship did not hold among the husbands. This finding tends to be consistent with findings on younger populations, but the fact remains that the relationship between religiosity and sexual expression (frequency and enjoyment) and their overall impact on marital satisfaction among the elderly married has yet to be explored systematically.

Income, Education, and Social Class

The impact of income, education, and social class on marital and nonmarital sexual expression has been relatively unexplored. Friedeman's (1978) review of the literature offered this same observation.

Christenson and Gagnon's (1965) study of 241 white females aged 50-90 pursued the issue of differences in level of educational attainment. They found that frequency of sexual intercourse was not related to level of education. This observation contrasted sharply with that of Newman and Nichols (1970, p. 280). In the latter report of 150 married respondents aged 60-93, frequency of sexual intercourse was inversely related to socioeconomic status. However, the sample consisted of both blacks and whites, with no attempt made to control on race. Since this same report revealed that blacks were more active sexually than were whites and that they tended to be lower in socioeconomic status, the observed relationship between socioeconomic status and frequency of sexual intercourse may be suspect.

In later reports using the same data base, Pfeiffer and Davis (1974, p. 255) analyzed data on 261 elderly men (98 percent married) and 241 elderly women (71 percent married), all of whom were white. Focusing on factors that might contribute to variance in sexual behavior, they found that income and social class exhibited positive but low correlations with current sexual functioning. In the second Duke study, Palmore (1981, p. 91) noted that for elderly married men socioeconomic status was among the most important correlates of level of sexual interest and activity, but this was not the case for women.

To date, income, social class, and education have not been rigorously examined as correlates of marital and nonmarital forms of sexual expression among the elderly married. Considering the past and current importance assigned to each of these variables in sociological research, the directions for future research seem obvious. It would also be important to separate the SES effect for elders on the basis of gender and race.

Relational Concerns

Perhaps the most obvious shortcoming of existing research on sexual expression among the elderly married has been the absence of concern with the part played by sexual expression in the stability of and satisfaction with marriage and family life. Much of the prescriptive literature "assumes" that frequent and satisfying sexual intercourse is conducive to overall marital satisfaction and by implication to marital stability. While one must applaud the good intentions of such writers, the admonition inherent in the saying, "People with good intentions often do harm" should serve to prevent the researcher from being blinded by the intentions of well-meaning authors. Later in the chapter we return to this topic.

The research that has been conducted on the quality of sexual functioning in later life and its presumed impact on marital satisfaction is indirect but suggestive. For example, the 150 elderly married respondents in the study by Newman and Nichols (1970, p. 280) reported their present sex drive to be lower than that when they were young, but without exception present level of sex drive was directly related to level of sex drive when young. Among these respondents (mean age = 70), 54 percent were still sexually active, but the impact of such activity on marital satisfaction was not pursued directly. Considering that 46 percent were not sexually active, the impact of sexual activity on marital satisfaction goes begging.

Commenting on data obtained from the Duke longitudinal studies, Pfeiffer (1974) concluded that continued sexual expression during the later years is more likely to be a characteristic of those who during their younger years had possessed high levels of sexual interest and activity. Exploring this question more systematically, Pfeiffer and Davis (1974, p. 255) presented data on a sample of elderly married men and women and concluded that while past sexual activity was positively correlated with present sexual activity and enjoyment, the relationship was significantly stronger among females than among males. Among married females the strongest predictor of present sexual enjoyment was level of sexual enjoyment during the younger years.

In an attempt to identify significant elements in long-lasting marriages, Roberts (1980) interviewed 100 elderly respondents on a nonrandom basis, whose mean length of marriage was 55.5 years. A majority of the respondents rated their marriages as "happy" or "very happy," and most said they would marry the same person again. While most reported having had moderate to strong sexual feelings during the younger years, 37 reported moderate to strong sexual feelings currently. Slightly more than half reported that they had been sexually active during the past five years. Six couples had engaged in sexual intercourse during the month preceding the interview, one couple reported engaging in sexual intercourse three times per week, and fifteen couples had not had sexual intercourse for the past fifteen years. Since all of the couples were "successful" in terms of self-ratings and length of time married, the wide variations in frequency of sexual intercourse suggest that marital stability or satisfaction among the elderly is not as dependent on level of sexual activity as the prescriptive writings would lead us to believe.

As we have seen, in a clear majority of cases frequency of sexual intercourse declines with advancing years. For a smaller number, frequency of sexual activity actually increases; for others, it ceases altogether. The impact of such variations on the level of marital satisfaction is a question that has been raised but pursued only peripherally.

Pfeiffer, Verwoerdt, and Wang (1970, p. 299) analyzed data from the Duke longitudinal studies on 67 married males and 73 married females who had stopped sexual activity before completion of the study. Rather consistently, females assigned the responsibility for the cessation of sexual activity to their husbands, and males correspondingly attributed it to themselves. In a subsequent report (Pfeiffer et al., 1974, p. 249) on 257 married males and 170 married females from the same data base, 14 percent of the husbands and 40 percent of the wives admitted to having stopped sexual activity. Roberts's (1980) analysis of a nonrandom sample of 100 respondents provides support as well for the observation that husbands were the ones most likely to cease sexual activity. However, he noted that the cessation of sexual activity was accompanied by an increased emphasis on such things as "emotional intimacy, sitting and lying close to each other, touching, and holding hands." These observations suggest that *if the halting of sexual intercourse has the potential of lowering overall marital satisfaction, its negation can be accomplished through compensatory forms of sexual expression.* These respondents assigned a high level of priority to "give and take" and "confiding in each other on everything" as facors in their marital success.

Palmore's (1981, p. 92) summary of findings from the first Duke longitudinal study and his analysis of data from the second Duke longitudinal study revealed that very few of the respondents reported complete cessation of sexual activity. Referring marginally to its effect on marital lifestyle, he concluded that results from the first Duke study suggest that life satisfaction and health are significant consequences of sexual activity among men. Results from the second Duke study partially indicated that sexual activity tended to enhance health and happiness among both sexes.

In one study of the relationship between marital and sexual problems, Murphy, Hudson, and Cheung (1980) gathered a purposive sample of 189 couples from multiethnic backgrounds, ranging in age from 40 to 86. They found that while the severity of marital problems was highly correlated with severity of sexual problems, *the impact of sexual discord on the quality of marital relationships was less among the older couples.* A cross-sectional analysis (Lowenthal, Thurnher, Chiriboga, and Associates, 1975, pp. 34-35) of white middle-class men and women spanning four life stages (high school seniors, young newlyweds, middle-aged parents, and preretired couples) revealed that compared to newlyweds, middle-aged men were most likely to report no change in quality of sexual satisfaction, while men facing the retirement years were more likely to report a decline in satisfaction. Reactions to the lack of satisfaction varied by gender: women attributed it to "changed attitudes and feelings," and men spoke of "declining interest." Consistent with subsequent findings from the Duke studies, elderly men attributed declining sexual interest and activity to themselves, and women attributed declining sexual interest and activity to their husbands. On the other hand, about one-third of the elderly couples reported increasing quality of sexual satisfaction, with males attributing the increase to more "emotional involvement" and "compatibility," and females to such things as "better understanding of one another" and a "loss of inhibitions." Consistent with earlier reports,[2] these findings suggest that among elderly marriges, sexual factors (frequency and quality of sexual intercourse) might play a secondary role in marital stability during the later years of marriage.

Nevertheless, the cause-effect relationship between sexual activity and marital satisfaction and stability remains unclear, primarily because this relationship has not been explored. Verwoerdt (1976), addressing himself to the Duke findings, suggested that the married elderly who are still sexually active tend to be physically and emotionally healthy and socially involved. Personality growth and maturation, the desire to avoid boredom and depression, the availability of more leisure time, changes in family composition (the empty nest), and the wife's loss of her procreative ability were cited as factors possibly operating to initiate increases in frequency of sexual activity among some elderly couples (Verwoerdt, 1976). On the other hand, Long (1976) acknowledged that the expression of intimacy by elderly couples tended to be discouraged when their adult children were living with them or they were living with their adult children. Thus, it appears that a number of factors may influence the opportunity for, or level of interest in, sexual activity, which in turn affects a couple's marital stability and satisfaction to some unknown degree. Some of these factors include health (most notably the husband's), living arrangements, competing interests or activities, and one's personal orientation toward sexuality. The available research, however, does not enable us to specify the precise nature of these proposed variable relationships.

Summary and Critique

Summary

Literature published since 1965 on marital and nonmarital sexual expression among the married elderly must be credited with having informed varied professionals of the sparsity of objective knowledge available on this topic and of the stereotypes of which they should be wary. What appears to be the primary merit of this literature is also its limitation, however. This is not to say that further advances have not been made, but rather that more sophisicated research efforts must be initiated if understanding of this stage of the family life cycle with regard to sexuality is to be realized. Permitted such an analogy, if we were to chart the history of research on sexuality and aging as Masters and Johnson (1966) have charted the stages of the sexual response cycle, it could be argued that such research has gone beyond the initial excitement phase. Indeed it seems to have reached a plateau where more effort will be required to generate further scholarly excitement and to bring interest in this topic to an intellectual peak.

For the present, the following generalizations can be made:

(1) Gradual declines in sexual activity, interest, and quality continue into the later years of marriage. This is the case more so for females and for the oldest research subjects. Elderly husbands and wives are generally aware of such declines and assign different interpretations to them. However, there is some evidence that slight increases in sexual activity occur for some older persons, largely resulting from structural changes (such as the empty nest) or redefinitions regarding the marital partner and the meaning of marriage.

(2) Responsibility for declining sexual activity is directed unequivocally to the husbands. Husbands typically blame themselves for declines in sexual activity and wives typically blame the husbands. Compensatory forms of intimacy might emerge as stabilizing factors for some elderly marriages.

(3) The relationship between religion and sexual expression has largely been ignored. However, the few pieces of available research on

the elderly support what is known about sexual expression among younger age groups. Specifically, religious devoutness is inversely related to sexual frequency; further, devoutness mitigates the impact of sexual performance on marital satisfaction.

(4) Income, race, education, and social class have also escaped systematic inquiry. In the research reviewed, no consistent findings were ascertained.

Critique

The limitations of existing research on marital and nonmarital sexual expression in later-life marriages can be grouped under three general categories: (a) design deficiencies, (b) limited focus, and (c) untested or questionable underlying models of sexuality.

Design Deficiencies. With the possible lone exception of the Duke studies, the research reviewed here was characterized by significant design deficiencies. Nonrandom and purposive sampling procedures are certainly useful in exploratory research, but data gathered thereby, although interesting and informative, make generalization impossible. Furthermore, the collection of data in this fashion rules out more sophisticated statistical analyses, thus prohibiting statements about the relative impact of certain variables on levels of sexual interest and activity and the relative impact of sexual satisfaction on marital satisfaction or other relationship variables.

A further design deficiency concerns the subjects of available studies. Virtually all subjects were considered as married *individuals* rather than as part of a married couple. The former orientation precludes the likelihood that a researcher will obtain any interactive, or relationship, data of an observational nature, and it minimizes the possibility that such data will be a major focus of survey or questionnaire strategies. Nor surprisingly, then, many of our available data focus on aging individuals who are of the marital status "married." We know a sizable amount about their individualized levels of activity and interest and their personal perceptions of the quality of their sex lives, but we know virtually nothing about what these data mean in relation to one's spouse. To obtain the latter kinds of data, conjoint interviews or comparison of individual interviews of couples is mandatory. Research to date has been conducted in a way that suggests that the sexuality of married individuals can be understood in isolation from the sexuality of one's spouse.

Limited Focus. A second shortcoming of the available literature is its limited focus. As noted earlier, a sizable body of literature embodying myth-challenging and prescriptive appeals exists, much of which is medically or physiologically focused and written by medical and therapeutic professionals. These reports, many of which rely solely on clinical impressions, have typically been concerned with individualized aspects of sexuality (interest, incidence, and sexual problems such as impotence and orgasmic difficulties). While these reports serve useful educational, polemical, and sensitizing functions, it is now time that writers go beyond such exploratory orientations toward the topic. One particular problem with such reports is that they often seem to imply that high frequency of sexual intercourse is equivalent to high quality of sexual intercourse and successful marital adjustment in later life. We will elaborate on this difficulty shortly.

Perhaps the most glaring deficiency in the foci of the available literature is the lack of concern with the relational dimensions of marital sexual intercourse and nonmarital sexuality among married elderly. Specifically, we should ask about the *meaning* of sexual intercourse and other sexual intimacies for each partner and the ways in which they negotiate disparate meanings. Further, we need to inquire about the extent to which differing meanings and congruent meanings about sex have an impact on marital stability or satisfaction during the later years. Given declining sexual interest and activity, what new elements emerge or what existing ones assume new meaning in order to integrate and stabilize the marital relationship? What variations are to be observed by (a) gender, (b) religion (devoutness, identification, participation), (c) race, (d) socioeconomic status (education, income, occupation), and (e) living arrangements? Further, we must be sure to distinguish between the newly married and long-married aged in all research undertakings.

Finally, while we have a growing knowledge of alternative lifestyles among the nonmarried elderly,[3] we know virtually nothing about nonmarital sexual expression among married elders. What forms of nontraditional sexual expression occur (if any) among elderly married couples? How do these behaviors correlate with levels of sexual interest and marital sexual intercourse? Is cessation of marital sexual activity equivalent to cessation of all sexual activity? Knowledge of variations in incidence, frequency, and forms of nontraditional sexual expression by selected demographic variables would add considerably to our general knowledge of sexual expression among the elderly married.

Untested Models. The neglect of relational issues and the meanings of sexual intercourse that we have just described seem both to be a product of and to contribute to a pervasive attempt to conceptualize and understand marital sexuality among the elderly *in terms of standards or criteria derived from younger marriages.* This is to say, the research reflects a uniform application of a "youth-model of sexual expression" onto elderly populations. The imposition of such a model grossly ignores at least two major differences between the two age categories, *one physiological and the other experiential.* The simple fact is that many elderly do not possess the physical capacity to engage in sexual intercourse as frequently or as vigorously as do younger populations. In terms of longevity, the elderly have the added experience of several decades of marital sexual experience behind them, during which time the meaning of marital sexual intercourse might have undergone drastic redefinition. By utilizing a youth-oriented model of sexual expression to understand the elderly, not only is the discovery of "social reality" sidetracked, but ultimately the populations being studied are provided with unrealistic standards by which to evaluate their own behavior and marriages. What we are suggesting is that any model of marital sexual expression among the elderly should be constructed on the basis of observations derived from representatives of that population rather than from populations significantly different in terms of physical capacity and marital longevity.

Explicitly and implicitly, most of the literature with the youth-oriented focus ignores the long-documented observation that such things as high frequencies of sexual intercourse and/or high levels of orgasmic response are not necessarily important contributors to marital stability or quality of sexual intercourse. Wallin and Clark's (1963) study of middle-aged marriages (16-20 years married) found that a proportion of the women who stated that they achieved orgasm in "few" or "none" of their coital relationships also described themselves as usually enjoying sexual intercourse "very much." Further, Verwoerdt (1976, p. 214) cautions that because of physiological changes, marital sexual expression among the elderly necessarily might be directed away from traditional sexual activity (coitus) toward other modes of activity, including touching, oral manipulation and other forms of stimulation, with the aim being not orgasmic release but instead the achievement of excitation and the satisfaction of the need for affection. Cleveland (1976), discussing problems of sexual interaction in postparental marriages, suggests that possibly our definition of sexual interaction as one of intense passion leads us to conclude erroneously that when passion is absent, sexual interaction is a problem. In her judgment, this definition is incongruent with the realities of the aging process (physiology) and aging marriages (longevity). The essence of her article is that while there is nothing inherently negative about encouraging the elderly to "take second honeymoons" and "learn new techniques" in order to improve their performance levels, such encouragement implies that sexual intercourse can again be as vigorous as it was in youth, and this is not possible. It can only increase "performance anxiety." This insensitivity to the emotional needs and physical abilities of the elderly is also recognized by Kalish (1979, p. 400), who refers to it as a "new ageism." He argues that this orientation posits that "older people who respond to their inner worlds or who enjoy and desire passive entertainment are seen as challenges to be overcome, rather than as individuals who are adapting to a lifelong (or recent) preference that could only be fully realized when retirement and the empty nest made it possible."

A recent publication on marital life among the elderly cites a variety of studies indicating that sound marital adjustment in later life might be independent of sexual factors (Troll et al., 1979), and the earlier cited study by Roberts (1980) of highly successful marriages lends additional support to this observation. Even the findings of the Duke studies, with their focus on levels of sexual activity and interest as indicators of sexual expression (a youth-oriented, genitally focused model), imply that declining sexual interest, activity, and enjoyment need not have negative consequences for marital stability.

It is our judgment that *a more complete understanding of marital sexual expression among the elderly will be achieved when researchers begin to construct proposals designed to discover "what is" rather than utilizing as the basis for research questionable assumptions about "what ought to be."* As Thomas (1982) proposes, a fundamental reorientation of our thinking about sex among the elderly is critically needed. We need to learn about the aged from older people themselves rather than use them to confirm preconceived assumptions about the meaning of sexual intercourse.

Finally, not only has research on marital sexual expression among the elderly married been guided by a "youth-oriented, genitally focused model" of sexual interaction, but it also has not been concerned with some forms of sexual interaction known to occur among married couples in earlier stages of the family life cycle. This inattention to the possible existence of sexual behaviors such as masturbation, homosexual experiences, and extramarital affairs *reflects a highly normative approach to the topic.* Perhaps it has been assumed that since older married couples engage in lower frequencies of sexual intercourse (and in some cases cease sexual intercourse altogether) and report lower levels of sexual interest that they are thereby not interested in or do not engage in any nonnormative sexual behaviors. Such a deduction would logically follow from a view of sexual interaction based upon a monolithic monogamous model of marital sexual relations. Sex research on younger married populations (for example, Cuber & Harroff, 1965; Hunt, 1969, 1974) shows clearly that in many instances the monolithic monogamous model of sexual expression is a myth, something that exists more in people's minds than in their behaviors. No equivalent statement can be advanced about participants in elderly marriages, because such questions have not been included in published research reports. However, one bit of data is highly suggestive that such topics need exploration. This is Kinsey, Pomeroy, and Martin's (1948) finding that the incidence of extramarital sex for males shows only a slight decline in the later years. We might ask, for example, if declining interest in and frequency of marital sexual intercourse result exclusively from loss of youthful vigor, or is it more a function of increasing boredom with the same partner? If the latter, and assuming that physical ability and sexual interest are present, then certainly masturbation and extramarital affairs become at least logical possibilities, if not outcomes.

One study uncovered in our review of the literature dealt with attitudes toward nontraditional sexual behavior. Analyzing cross-sectional data from an NORC national probability sample, Snyder and Spreitzer (1976) found that intolerance of nontraditional sexual behavior (premarital sex, extramarital sex, and homosexuality) was associated with being female, having lower educational and occupational levels, regular church attendance, being married, being parents, and being older. However, within the "old-age" category, there was some attitudinal variation. Indeed, the within-group varibility of tolerance of sexual attitudes increased with successive age cohorts. We suggest here that if attitudes have implications for behavior, then an examination of the nonmarital sexual attitudes and behaviors of the elderly would provide us with a more complete picture of their sexual expression in later life.

Policy and Research Implications

Because service professionals intervene routinely into the private lives of older individuals, couples, and families, it behooves us to give some attention to that intersection where private sexual matters become social issues. Those service personnel who encounter issues of sex and aging most frequently are mental health workers, the clergy, and medical professionals. Therefore, they should be aware of accurate information on sexuality in later life, regardless of the research limitations we have already noted. Such information would serve to challenge whatever biases they may have on this topic (see Pease, 1974) and would help to prevent the application of inappropriate interventions. Miller, Bernstein, and Sharkey (1975), for example, cite evidence of premature institutionalization of some aging individuals on the basis of their exhibition of nonnormative sexual behaviors.

The transmission of accurate information to family members and to aged couples could be useful to them for reducing stereotypes and alleviating anxieties. Knowing that other families experience similar situations or that other couples encounter comparable changes in sexual lifestyles might mitigate whatever apprehensions may accompany these occasions. This educational function, in short, becomes a consciousness-raising experience and may, in fact, reduce the need for persons to seek professional advice or intervention.

Beyond the dissemination of information for professional development and for consciousness-raising, accurate information about sexual lifestyles among married elderly could be a useful secondary source of data when anticipating possible latent functions of social policies for the aging. For example, in the consideration of housing alternatives, it will be noted that some provide greater opportunity for privacy than others. All other factors being equal, the policymaker might opt for the more private arrangement in deference in part to a presumed need for intimacy. We noted earlier that sexual expressiveness among older couples seems to be reduced when adult children are present in the household. Policymakers who support subsidized intergenerational housing arrangements instead of subsidized independent housing may want to consider the expressiveness issue in their evaluation of tradeoffs of alternative policies.

Having stated the most obvious kinds of social policy implications, we must conclude by returning to the implications of this review and critique for research policy. We find the latter implications far more compelling because their implementation will provide the basis for accurate knowledge to the various populations we cited. The research implications are threefold and respond precisely to the limitations we detailed above.

First, in order to obtain a more realistic and generalizable assessment of sexuality in later life marriages, research will require more sophisticated statistical analyses, which in turn demand improved samples and more expansive questions beyond interest and activity levels. Research should also be oriented to couples rather than individuals, utilizing conjoint or complementary interviews.

Second, the scope of issues to be investigated needs to be broadened to relational issues and nonnormative behaviors, for, after all, sexual expression is typically interactive and has demonstrated great variability among other studied populations.

Third, researchers should not assume either a youth-oriented, genitally focused model of sexuality or a monolithic monogamous model of sexual relationships. Rather, we need to understand sexuality among the married aged phenomenologically, suspending all preconceived notions of what sexual expression in later life should mean to persons and how they should behave in this realm of life.

In conclusion, there is no shortage of prescriptive, popular, and clinical literature on the topic of sexuality in later life marriages. However, the availability of insightful empirical research is limited, not only in quantity, but also in terms of conceptualization, sampling, and data analysis. Our understanding of this subject has reached an intellectual plateau that needs to be transcended. We are not unmindful of the research limitations inherent in the sensitivity of the topic we have examined. However, we believe that the frontiers of sex research and aging can be pushed significantly farther before we begin to encounter whatever barriers exist in attempting to understand these issues more completely.

NOTES

1. An overview of the scientific study of sex is available in Sandler, Myerson, and Kinder (1980); a general evaluation of sex research can be found in Gagnon (1977).

2. For a review of related studies see Troll, Miller, and Atchley (1979).

3. See, for example, the entire May 1980 issue of the journal *Alternative Lifestyles,* which adresses this topic.

8

Sex-Role and Marital-Role Expectations

CYNTHIA DOBSON

The definitions of sex roles and marital roles tell older couples what is expected of them. Husbands and wives may follow, adapt, or reject these expectations, but the definitions influence the couples' view of themselves and their relationships. Some investigators have argued strongly that sex-role definitions for men and women converge in old age, and various researchers have discussed the changes in marital-role expectations that result from retirement and the end of parental responsibilities. As they enter their older years, husbands and wives may need to reexamine their own behavior and rebalance their relationships in light of the new definitions they encounter.

This chapter will review the evidence for a redefinition of sex roles and marital roles with advancing age. It will also present data from a study of changes between middle and old age in such areas of role definition as the importance of instrumental and expressive qualities for husbands and wives and the assignment of major marital-role responsibilities and household tasks.

Sex-Role Definitions

The lack of extensive theoretical or empirical work dealing with the development of sex-role definitions in adulthood has recently been noted (Urberg & Labouvie-Vief, 1976; Minnigerode & Lee, 1978). Among the few studies that specifically look at middle and old age, the works of Neugarten and Gutmann are particularly well known. From his examination of cross-cultural ethnographic data, Gutmann (1975, 1977) argued that the demands of parenthood are the primary factors that shape sex-role behavior in younger adults and that the end of parental responsibility is the key to shifts observed in such behavior among older people. During early adulthood each sex lives out through the other those aspects of his or her nature that could interfere with adequate performance of his or her parental role. In later life, according to Gutmann (1977, p. 312), "Men recapture the 'femininity' that was previously repressed in the service of productive instrumentality; and women generally become more domineering and independent."

Earlier, on the basis of research using projective techniques, Neugarten and Gutmann (1958) suggested that as women age they become more accepting of their aggressive and egocentric impulses, while men become more tolerant of their nuturant and affiliative impulses. On the basis of Neugarten and Gutmann's various studies, Brim (1976, p. 6) concluded that "apparently this comprehensive developmental event of middle and later-life acts to reverse or at least equalize the domestic status of the partners, and tends to redistribute the so-called masculine and feminine traits among them, so that through these various sex-role changes there is ushered in the 'normal unisex of later life.'"

Other research also suggests a convergence of sex-role definitions in old age. Minnigerode and Lee (1978) used semantic differential scales to map distinctions by sex across the life cycle. They found that differences between male and female definitions were greatest for the adolescent and young adult targets, intermediate for the child and middle-aged targets, and least for the old targets. Cameron (1968, 1976) also argued that with age the sexes become more convergent in interests and personality. He found (1976) that the middle-aged generation was seen as having the most social pressure to do masculine things, while the older generation was seen as having the least. Social pressure to do feminine things also was seen as least for the older generation, with the younger generation in this case rated as having the most pressure. Looking at the results for beliefs concerning personality style, interests, and skills as well as social pressure, Cameron (1976) suggested that the older generation is seen as almost neuter, whereas the middle-aged is the generation with the strongest claim to both masculinity and femininity.

Sinnott (1982) asked older people to describe themselves using the Bem Sex Role Inventory and compared their responses to those reported for college-aged and general adult groups in other studies. Femininity scores were highest for the older men and women, and masculinity scores were highest for the general adult samples. Sinnott noted the difficulty in interpreting developmental trends from these data, but he suggested that they were in accord with a role shift toward femininity for older men and did not preclude a shift toward masculinity among older women.

Discussions of changes in sex-role definition in adulthood have emphasized various points of view, including developmental processes in personality and cognition, selective reinforcement and imitation/ identification, and responses to shifts in the demands of life situations. Studies in the last area have often stopped short of clearly delineating the process by which such shifts are translated into changed sex-role expectations. The work of Abrahams, Feldman, and Nash (1978) suggests one process that may be at work in the transition from middle to old age. They argue that changes in sex-role self-concept and sex-role attitude are directly related to corresponding changes in life situations through self-attribution. For this young adult sample, life situations were better predictors of modernity and traditionalism in sex-role attitudes than was age. The life situations selected by Abrahams et al. (1978) reflected early stages in the family life cycle, but later stages, including retirement, might be expected to have similar impact on sex-role definitions.

Marital-Role Definitions

Marital-role definitions for older couples have been infrequently examined, although the family life cycle perspective as well as Parsons and Bales's instrumental-expressive family-role dichotomy have led to some discussions of expectations for the older couple. In addition, the impact of retirement on role definition and the assignment of household tasks has interested several researchers.

The instrumental-expressive role perspective was based on Bales's (1958) study of small group interaction. He identified two distinct leadership roles: the task specialist, who was concerned primarily with solving instrumental problems, and the socioemotional specialist, who concentrated on the expressive problems of the group. Different individuals usually assumed these complementary roles within the group, leading to the view that for a single individual these roles are incompatible.

Parsons (1955) argued that leadership within the nuclear family is similarly structured. The wife assumes the expressive role, primarily because she bears and rears the children, and the husband is thus left to specialize in the alternative instrumental role. In contemporary American society, the husband focuses on his occupational role as a major part of his instrumental family role. Although this view of dichotomous marital roles was extensively used to analyze family relationships, it later received severe criticism, and the need to consider instrumental and expressive components for both spousal roles was advocated (see, for example, Crano & Aronoff, 1978; Waxler & Mishler, 1970; Broderick, 1971).

Looking at an earlier segment of the family life cycle, Scanzoni (1975) examined instrumental and expressive dimensions of self-concept among a sample of married couples, ranging in terms of wife's age from 18 to 44 years. He found no significant difference between the younger and middle-aged persons over the instrumental dimension but an increase with age on the expressive dimension. In contrast, Fengler (1973) noted that younger wives were more likely than middle-aged and older wives to endorse an expressive or companionship factor in marriage. Thurnher's (1976) research also supported the view that the expressive aspects of marital relationships are most prominent in early marriage, although these aspects were more stressed by pre-retirees than by middle-aged spouses.

On the basis of his research with older persons, Lipman (1961, 1962) argued that retirement requires a new set of role expectations for husbands and wives. The responses of his sample of older men and women to the question of what they considered to be the most important quality of a "good" wife or husband who is past 60 years of age were divided into three categories: expressive, instrumental, and other. More than half of the qualities assigned to the older husband and nearly three-fourths of the qualities for the older wife fell into the expressive category. Lipman contrasted these findings to the stress on instrumental qualities for nonretired spouses that had been found in other research. He concluded that it is retirement that leads to greater emphasis on expressive qualities for both husbands and wives, a view shared by Cumming (1963), Troll (1971), and Lowenthal and Robinson (1976).

Several writers (Grunebaum, 1979; Chiriboga & Thurnher, 1975; Lowenthal & Chiriboga, 1972; Gutmann, 1975, 1977; Neugarten & Gutmann, 1958; Levinson, 1978) have commented on the tendency for middle-aged wives to become relatively more assertive and middle-aged husbands more affiliative. Family life is seen as a prime area in which men can fulfill their developing expressive potential. This trend may be seen as predating the readjustment of marital roles in retirement and as being compatible with a view of decreasing differentiation by sex in sex-role and marital-role definitions in old age.

The division of household tasks among retired couples has also been an area of interest, with participation in such tasks seen as one way for retired men to adapt to their new life situation (Keith & Brubaker, 1979; Cavan, 1962; Donahue, Orbach, & Pollak, 1960; Friedmann & Havighurst, 1962; Morse & Weiss, 1955; Nimkoff, 1962). The impact of a retired husband's expanded housekeeper role on the wife also has been discussed (Aldous, 1978; Bengtson, Kasschau, & Ragan, 1977; Cavan, 1962; Crawford, 1972; Fengler, 1975). More recently, Szinovacz (1980) and Brubaker and Hennon (1982) have investigated the impact of the wife's retirement from employment outside the home on the division of household tasks.

In an early study of marital roles in retirement, Lipman (1961) asked his sample of older persons whether they agreed with the statement: "Once a man retires a wife has a definite right to expect her husband to share in household activities." He found a majority of both men (58 percent) and women (62 percent) agreed, and he interpreted this as evidence of role redefinition with retirement. Kerckhoff (1964, 1966) also reported on the normative assignment of task responsibilities to husband and wife by older couples. Wives were more likely than husbands to advocate task sharing, and couples in the middle and upper occupational groups were more likely than those in the lower occupational category to support such norms. In terms of actual participation, however, Kerckhoff (1964) found similar levels of participation among the occupational groups as well as some increased participation in household tasks among retired men. Keating and Cole (1980) also noted that older middle-class couples may be more accepting than lower-class couples of male participation, although they found little increase with retirement in the husband's household activities.

In an investigation of the assignment of household tasks among older persons, Ballweg (1967) noted the role redefinition that is necessary to meet the loss of occupational status by the husband. He found that in comparison to older couples with an employed husband, retired couples were more likely to report increased activity on the part of the husband and decreased involvement by the wife in the twelve tasks examined. He stated, however, that the frequency of shared as opposed to nonshared tasks did not increase and that the increased activity by the husbands was largely in tasks traditionally considered to be more masculine, factors that may aid the avoidance of potential conflict between the retired husband and wife. Keith and Brubaker (1979) and Jackson (1972) also noted that although retired men may participate in some feminine tasks, they tend to be most involved in masculine activities.

Using a sample of adolescents, rather than older persons, Keith and Brubaker (1980) asked who should have major responsibility for ten household tasks in four target couples with different age and employment characteristics. Male respondents advocated more shared responsibility for the retired couple than for the other three target couples, but female respondents defined the highest level of shared responsibility for the young couple with both spouses employed.

Focusing on the impact of available time for household activities on task participation, Blood and Wolfe (1960) concluded that in the retirement years the wife continues to have enough time to complete the household tasks and there is little need for a redistribution of activities. Silverman and Hill (1967), however, found that the wife's task participation and acceptance of traditional sex-role definitions are highest in the family with adolescent children and then fall, first in the postparental and again in the retired-couple stage.

The impact of the wife's retirement on the allocation of household tasks has been only recently investigated. Szinovacz (1980) noted a variety of patterns, including increased participation by husband or by wife as well as no change. A key consequence of retirement for these couples was the reduction of stress associated with the end of the wife's dual work and household responsibilities. Formerly employed women, however, were not always able to replace their occupational activities and relationships with an increased involvement in household tasks. In another study, Brubaker and Hennon (1982) found that employed wives anticipated greater sharing of household tasks in retirement than retired wives reported. These retired wives also expected more sharing of responsibility than actually occurred in their marriages. Both Szinovacz (1980) and Brubaker and Hennon (1982) noted little change in the existing traditional division of labor in the home with the wife's retirement.

Looking at the differences among three generations, Hill (1965) examined role specialization—the degree to which tasks were done exclusively by one spouse—and role conventionality—the degree to which the division of labor in the household followed traditional male-female definitions. Specialization was highest for the grandparent generation, moderate for the parent group, and lowest for the married child generation. The results for role conventionality showed the grandparent generation to be characterized by both high conventionality and high unconventionality, with this group having the lowest rank for the intermediate levels of conventionality.

Although Nye and Gekas (1976a, 1976b) did not explore the impact of age on marital-role definitions, four of the eight roles they used to describe the position of spouse and parent are of particular interest in an examination of shifts in marital-role expectations between middle and old age: housekeeper, provider, kinship, and recreational. The responsibility for enacting the roles may be assigned along a continuum of complete role segregation to complete role sharing. The overall direction of the respondents' assignments for the provider role coincided with a traditional division of labor, but only about one-third (37 percent) of the women and one-half (57 percent) of the men in the study believed that the husband should be the sole provider (Slocum & Nye, 1976). For the housekeeper role, a similar sex difference appeared, with women being more likely (42 percent) than men (25 percent) to indicate that the wife alone should play this role. Expectations for the recreational and kinship roles were much different, with assignment to both spouses being predominant. For example, a large group of both husbands (80 percent) and wives (86 percent) indicated that responsibility for the recreational role should be shared equally or should be assigned to either the husband or the wife (Carlson, 1976).

Albrecht, Bahr, and Chadwick (1979) used a similar instrument to analyze the impact of the age and sex of respondents on their role definitions. For the provider role there was a moderately strong trend toward greater acceptance of female involvement among young (29 years and under) people, especially among young women, and in all age categories men were less favorable toward female involvement than women. For the kinship and housekeeper roles, however, the definitions demonstrated neither age nor sex differences. In terms of role enactment, as opposed to the preferred division of labor between husband and wife, Albrecht et al. (1979) noted that the provider role was more likely to be shared among middle-aged and older couples than among those who were less than 45 years of age. There were no age differences in the degree of sharing for the housekeeper and kinship roles. They commented on the large discrepancies between the preferred and actual division of labor among all age groups.

This review of literature has indicated the variety of studies concerned with sex-role and marital-role definitions in old age. Research has been scattered among several theoretical perspectives and has utilized a variety of measures, factors that may explain some of the contradictory findings. Replication studies and longitudinal designs have been lacking. Conclusions drawn from such research are necessarily tentative, but several authors argue that the differentiation between male and female sex-role definitions diminishes in old age. In addition, many researchers have commented on the tendency for men to become more affiliative and expressive and for women to become more aggressive and instrumental in middle and old age.

Discussions of shifts in middle and old age in marital-role definitions have stressed the changes associated with the end of parental responsibilities and with retirement. Several investigators argue that the roles of both husband and wife should emphasize expressive rather than instrumental qualities in old age. Some research concerning the retired husband's participation in household tasks suggests that the husband's marital role is redefined, with greater participation being seen as an obligation. Other studies, however, note that expectations for increased participation by the husband are distinct from expectations that the retired couple will together share responsibility for various tasks, and that expectations for greater sharing may not be met.

The study described in the next section investigates the stability or change in role definitions between middle and old age in three areas. First, it examines the degree of importance placed on instrumental and expressive qualities for husbands and wives at these two ages. The literature suggests that a shift should occur, with expressive qualities being more emphasized for both spouses in old age and instrumental qualities being less emphasized in old age, particularly for men. The study also looks at the assignment of both major marital responsibilities and household tasks to husbands and/or wives. The literature reports that expectations should define the greater task sharing for older couples. Earlier research thus supports a general view of less role differentiation between husbands and wives in old age.

A Study of Changes in
Role Expectations

A questionnaire was mailed in the summer of 1978 to a random sample of 931 persons drawn from the Des Moines, Iowa, telephone directory. After two follow-up mailings, usable questionnaires were received from 441 respondents, providing a return rate of 44 percent. The age distribution of the sample indicated 27 percent aged 18-29, 19 percent aged 30-39, 32 percent aged 40-59, and 22 percent aged 60 and older, with 42 percent of the total sample being male.

TABLE 8.1   Characteristics of the Instrumental Qualities Scale
and the Expressive Qualities Scale by Age and Sex

| | | | Situation | |
Characteristic	Older Husband	Older Wife	Middle-Aged Husband	Middle-Aged Wife
Instrumental Qualities Scale				
Range	6-28	6-30	6-24	6-27
Mean[a]	15.3	15.7	10.8	12.7
Standard deviation	4.6	4.9	3.8	4.5
Alpha	.83	.85	.86	.86
Expressive Qualities Scale				
Range	6-30	6-24	6-24	6-24
Mean[a]	9.2	8.8	8.5	8.1
Standard deviation	3.0	2.9	3.0	2.8
Alpha	.92	.94	.94	.95

a. The lower the mean value, the greater the importance assigned to the qualities for the situation.

The questionnaire required the respondents to rate the importance of twelve instrumental and expressive qualities for each of the four situations: a retired husband in his late sixties, a wife in her late sixties, a husband in his late forties, and a wife in her late forties. A five-part response framework allowed the respondents to judge the importance of the qualities as very important, important, unsure, not very important, and not at all important.

The six instrumental qualities included being competitive, enterprising, ambitious, aggressive, industrious, and decisive, and the six expressive qualities included being affectionate, tender, kind, warm, sympathetic, and comforting. The six qualities in each area were summed to create two scales. The reliability, as measured by coefficient alpha, of the Instrumental Qualities Scale ranged between .83 and .86, depending on the situation, and that of the Expressive Qualities Scale ranged between .92 and .95. The values for range, mean, standard deviation, and alpha are presented in Table 8.1. Paired t-tests of means were used in the comparisons of the importance assigned to the qualities for the four situations. A statistical significance level of .05 was selected.

The questionnaire also required the respondents to assign responsibility to the husband and/or wife for four major marital-role responsibilities: providing income, doing the housekeeping, keeping in touch with relatives, and arranging family recreation. These activities were selected from those suggested by Nye and Gekas (1976a). In addition, the respondents were asked who should be responsible for each of twelve houshold tasks: shopping for groceries, cleaning the house, shoveling the sidewalk, preparing the meals, mowing the lawn, doing the dishes, repairing things, keeping track of money and bills, telephoning relatives, writing to relatives, planning a vacation, and inviting friends over. The first eight questions were based on the tasks examined by Blood and Wolfe (1960), the next two on the kinship-role tasks measured by Bahr (1976), and the last two were suggested by the recreational role described by Carlson (1976). For each item the respondents had to provide their expectations for a middle-aged couple (in their late forties) and for an older couple (in their late sixties).

The responses for the major role responsibilities included husband entirely, husband more than wife, husband and wife the same, wife more than husband, wife entirely, husband or wife—doesn't matter, and neither one. The responses for the household tasks were composed of husband entirely, husband more, husband and wife equally, wife more, wife entirely, and neither one. Distributions for these expectations appear in Tables 8.2 and 8.3. Paired t-tests of means were again used to determine whether the role definitions for middle-aged and older husbands and wives differed from one another. In the t-test analysis of the assignment of major responsibilities, the "husband and wife the same" and "husband or wife—doesn't matter" responses were combined, and the "neither one" responses for assignment of both major responsibilities and household tasks were dropped from the t-test analysis because of the low number of answers in this category for most items.

Findings

The means of the Expressive Qualities Scale displayed in Table 8.1, reflected the high level of importance assigned to these qualities in all four situations. The highest level occurred for the middle-aged wife (8.1) and the lowest for the older husband (9.2). The Instrumental Qualities Scale means indicated lower levels of perceived importance, ranging from 10.8 for the middle-aged husband and 12.7 for the middle-aged wife situations to 15.3 for the older husband and 15.7 for the older wife situations.

TABLE 8.2   Assignment of Four Major Marital-Role Responsibilities by Age (percentages)

	Assignment						
Responsibility	Husband Entirely	Husband More than Wife	Husband and Wife	Wife More than Husband	Wife Entirely	Either One	Neither One[c]
Middle-Aged Couple[a]							
Income	11	61	15	0	0	13	0
Housekeeping	0	0	17	65	9	8	0
Relatives	0	0	56	26	1	17	0
Recreation	0	3	74	5	0	17	0
Older Couple[b]							
Income	8	40	15	0	0	33	4
Housekeeping	0	0	22	52	3	23	0
Relatives	0	0	53	19	1	27	0
Recreation	1	3	64	3	1	28	1

a. Number varies between 398 and 399.
b. Number varies between 402 and 403.
c. Omitted from analysis by paired t-tests.

TABLE 8.3 Assignment of Household Tasks by Age (percentages)

| | Assignment | | | | | |
Task	Husband Entirely	Husband More	Husband-Wife Equally	Wife More	Wife Entirely	Neither One[c]
Middle-Aged Couple[a]						
Shop for groceries	0	1	42	53	3	1
Clean the house	0	0	26	66	8	0
Shovel the sidewalk	16	61	18	1	0	3
Prepare the meals	0	0	17	71	12	0
Mow the lawn	16	62	20	1	0	1
Do the dishes	0	1	30	61	8	0
Repair things around the house	14	72	14	0	0	0
Keep track of money and bills	3	14	70	11	2	0
Telephone relatives	0	1	76	21	1	1
Write letters to relatives	0	1	59	35	3	1
Plan a vacation	0	4	95	1	0	0
Invite friends over	0	1	90	8	0	1

Older Couple[b]

Shop for groceries	0	1	66	31	1	1
Clean the house	0	0	42	55	3	0
Shovel the sidewalk	10	52	18	2	0	17
Prepare the meals	0	0	24	68	7	1
Mow the lawn	13	53	21	1	0	12
Do the dishes	0	0	46	49	4	1
Repair things around the house	13	70	16	1	0	1
Keep track of money and bills	4	12	73	10	1	0
Telephone relatives	0	0	81	17	1	2
Write letters to relatives	0	1	59	36	3	1
Plan a vacation	1	5	93	1	0	1
Invite friends over	0	1	90	8	0	1

a. Number varies between 383 and 384.
b. Number varies between 390 and 392.
c. Omitted from analysis by paired t-tests.

121

TABLE 8.4   Evaluation of Importance of Instrumental and
             Expressive Qualities Scales by Age

Scale	$\bar{x}^a$	SD	$\bar{x}$	SD	r	T	df	p
	Older Husband		M-A Husband			Analysis		
IQ Scale	15.275	4.604	10.757	3.786	.51	19.91	345	.000*
	Older Wife		M-A Wife					
IQ Scale	15.776	4.863	12.667	4.530	.70	15.89	347	.000*
	Older Husband		M-A Husband					
EQ Scale	9.143	3.060	8.425	2.933	.77	6.61	357	.000*
	Older Wife		M-A Wife					
EQ Scale	8.822	2.876	8.065	2.764	.74	6.96	353	.000*

*$p < .05$
a. The lower the mean value, the greater the importance.

The comparisons by age of the importance of instrumental and
expressive qualities indicated greater emphasis on these qualities in
middle as opposed to old age. As noted in Table 8.4, instrumental
qualities were rated substantially more important for middle-aged men
as compared to older men, and for middle-aged women as compared to
older women. Examination of the Expressive Qualities Scale scores
indicated more limited decreases in the importance placed on these
qualities for older as opposed to middle-aged men, and for older as
opposed to middle-aged women.

The assignment of major marital-role responsibilities, as presented in
Table 8.2, followed traditional lines, with husbands assigned more
responsibility for providing income and wives assigned more responsibility for housekeeping and keeping in touch with relatives. Differentiation by sex was much more extreme for the provider and housekeeping
roles than for the kinship role. An expectation for shared responsibility
for planning family recreation was evident, and the distribution of
responses for this responsibility differed greatly from the other three.

The comparisons by age of the couple for the four major marital-role
responsibilities are given in Table 8.5. Sex differentiation was less
extreme for the older couple than for the middle-aged couple in the case
of the three responsibilities that were primarily assigned to one spouse:

TABLE 8.5   Assignment of Major Marital-Role Responsibilities by Age

Role	Older Couple		Middle-Aged Couple		Analysis			
	$\bar{x}^a$	SD	$\bar{x}$	SD	r	T	df	p
Income	2.440	.643	2.173	.593	.50	8.34	374	.000*
Housekeeping	3.575	.549	3.820	.569	.47	−8.33	387	.000*
Relatives	3.203	.427	3.261	.468	.59	−2.88	389	.004*
Recreation	3.008	.333	3.023	.316	.29	−.79	388	.431

*p < .05

a. The closer the mean value to 1.0, the greater the assignment to the husband; the closer the mean value to 5.0, the greater the assignment to the wife. A value of 3.0 indicates joint assignment.

providing income, housekeeping, and keeping in touch with relatives. Arranging family recreation was seen to be a responsibility of both spouses for the older as well as the middle-aged couples and showed no shift with age of couples.

The distribution for the assignment of household tasks, given in Table 8.3, also followed a traditional division of labor. Wives of both ages were expected to take more responsibility for shopping for groceries, cleaning the house, preparing meals, doing the dishes, and telephoning and writing letters to relatives, while husbands were expected to assume greater responsibility for shoveling the sidewalks, mowing the lawn, and repairing things. The remaining three tasks were less characterized by sex differentiation: keeping track of money and bills, planning a vacation, and inviting friends over. More than half of the respondents assigned the category of "husband and wife equally" for the kinship and recreation items and for keeping track of money and bills. A substantial number indicated that among older couples neither should be expected to be responsible for shoveling the sidewalk or mowing the lawn.

The comparisons by age of the couples for the twelve household tasks are given in Table 8.6. Changes in task assignment by age were related to the degree of differentiation by sex. None of the three jointly assigned tasks revealed a difference in assignment by age. Five of the six tasks assigned to women and two of the three tasks assigned to men, however, showed a tendency toward less extreme differentiation for the older as compared to the middle-aged couple. Although the tasks remained

TABLE 8.6   Assignment of Household Tasks by Age

Task	Older Couple		Middle-Aged Couple		Analysis			
	$\bar{x}$[a]	SD	$\bar{x}$	SD	r	T	df	p
Prepare the meals	3.829	.555	3.945	.538	.61	−4.55	362	.000*
Clean the house	3.602	.538	3.813	.559	.50	−7.37	363	.000*
Do the dishes	3.565	.584	3.753	.589	.56	−6.50	360	.000*
Shop for groceries	3.309	.503	3.583	.572	.43	−9.03	361	.000*
Keep track of money	2.942	.626	2.950	.646	.77	−.37	362	.715
Shovel the sidewalk	2.168	.662	2.046	.649	.71	4.22	302	.000*
Mow the lawn	2.130	.657	2.068	.618	.72	2.34	321	.020*
Repair things	2.055	.569	2.017	.531	.67	1.65	361	.099
Telephone relatives	3.168	.410	3.213	.443	.58	−2.15	356	.032*
Write to Relatives	3.422	.563	3.397	.554	.67	1.04	359	.299
Invite friends over	3.072	.298	3.077	.306	.51	−.35	361	.724
Plan a vacation	2.951	.273	2.964	.238	.57	−1.09	363	.276

*$p < .05$

a. The closer the mean value to 1.0, the greater the assignment to the husband; the closer the mean value to 5.0, the greater the assignment to the wife. A value of 3.0 equals assignment equally to both spouses.

assigned to the traditional spouse in old age, there was a shift toward expectations of greater shared responsibility for older spouses.

Discussion

This study of changes in marital-role expectations between middle and old age revealed various shifts, including some toward less extreme differentiation by sex in old age. Both expressive and instrumental qualities were assigned less importance for the older as opposed to middle-aged husbands and wives, although the drop for instrumental was much greater than for expressive qualities. Expressive qualities became relatively more important than instrumental qualities for the older couple, but the evaluation of expressive traits in absolute terms was lower than it was for middle-aged husbands and wives. Aging spouses thus meet more stable evaluations regarding expressive attributes while they cope with sharply declining evaluations of instrumental characteristics.

Role expectations regarding the division of labor for household tasks changed in the direction of less sex differentiation in old age. Tasks assigned to both spouses in middle age remained shared in old age. Those activities defined as more the obligation of one spouse in middle age were likely to be characterized by less extreme assignment in old age. Role segregation along traditional lines in the area of household tasks continued to be part of marital-role definitions for older spouses, but to a somewhat lesser degree than for middle-aged spouses. There was also some evidence that the expectations for the male household role may contract in old age, with a large percentage of persons replying that neither older spouse should be responsible for the male-assigned tasks of shoveling the sidewalk and mowing the lawn.

The assignment of major marital-role responsibilities followed the same pattern found for household tasks: Definitions of shared responsibility did not change between middle and old age, while assignments to a single spouse became somewhat less likely in old age. Again marital-role definitions for the older couple were characterized by less extreme differentiation by sex rather than by a convergence of role definitions.

Policy and Practice Implications

Older spouses coping with changes in marital-role definitions and with discrepancies between expectations for and actual behavior may benefit from assistance as they adjust their behaviors and rebalance their relationships. In the move from middle to old age, the roles and adaptations of both spouses need to be jointly considered. Husbands and wives meet expectations of decreasing importance for instrumental qualities. Inclusion of wives as well as husbands in discussions of how to deal with such role redefinition and directions for both spouses on the need to appreciate the changes in emphasis for the other should be explored. Expressive qualities remain important for both husbands and wives and, because of the drop in importance of instrumental qualities, become relatively more important in old age. Spouses who view expressivity as the special responsibility of wives may find themselves at odds with general expectations.

The household division of labor may be a source of role strain for older husbands and wives. Expectations for shared responsibility may not be met, and discussion in the preretirement stage of such expectations might encourage more compatible role definitions between spouses. Greater participation in household tasks may aid the adjustment to retirement, but such participation for women or men rarely succeeds in substituting for lost occupational activities. The views that an expanded household role has been defined for retired husbands and that working wives easily cope with retirement by returning to a housewife identity have not been supported by research. Retirement and family counselors may need to suggest avenues for role replacement beyond the household.

Role expectations do not determine behavior, but, as Block (1973) states, such conceptions influence both behavior and self-evaluation in important ways. Marital-role definitions provide the background for the marital relationships of older couples. To the extent that their definitions are compatible and fulfilled, the couples' level of marital satisfaction should be high. Marital satisfaction is of concern in itself and, additionally, the impact of the marital relationship of older couples on their life satisfaction has been noted (Streib & Beck, 1980).

Current changes in general sex-role and marital-role definitions need to be explored in terms of their impact on possible role redefinitions for older persons. Research in the past has been limited, and the need for further study, particularly of longitudinal design, is evident. Investigation of the process of self-attribution may be a fruitful approach in the search for an explanation of role changes with age in sex-role and marital-role definitions.

9

Family Involvement and Support for Widowed Persons

GLORIA D. HEINEMANN

Widowhood is often viewed as an elderly persons' problem and more often as a woman's problem. While slightly over half (52 percent) of persons age 65 and over are married and living with spouse, over a third (37 percent) are widowed. The proportion of widowed persons among the elderly has remained constant over the thirteen-year period from 1962 to 1975 (Shanas & Heinemann, 1978). The median age at widowhood is 68 for women and 71 for men (Lopata, 1979). Furthermore, with advancing age, the chances of becoming widowed increase, and the disparity in extent of widowhood between men and women increases as well. By age 75, 70 percent of women are widows, whereas 69 percent of men are still married (U.S. Bureau of the Census, 1980). The much greater proportion of women among the widowed population is due to women outliving men by some seven to eight years and women marrying men older than themselves. These factors also explain (1) why remarriage is a much more likely possibility for widowers than for widows, especially among the elderly, and (2) why widows are studied so much more frequently than widowers (see Heinemann, 1982). Thus, published research about widowed men is extremely sparse, and as a consequence, this chapter is heavily biased toward the experiences of widowed women and their family relationships. I attempt, however, to present information for both widowers and widows when such information is available. In places throughout the chapter, I present information for young and middle-aged widowed persons as well, to compare and contrast their family involvements with those of elderly widowed persons.

Author's Note: I would like to thank Ms. Gloria Newberry for typing the manuscript.

Much of the research in the areas of aging, widowhood, and family is based on assumptions underlying the conception of family as the modified extended family. Briefly, the modified extended family is made up of persons related by blood and/or marriage who function, indirectly and noncoercively, in a system of support across households and generations. The modified extended family facilitates the achievement and mobility of its members and complements those tasks of other social systems (Litwak, 1960a, 1960b; Sussman & Burchinal, 1962; Shanas & Sussman, 1977). The major activities carried out by family members are mutual aid and social contact (such as visiting, phoning, communicating by mail, and celebrating holidays and special events together). Exchanges tend to be based on reciprocity, opportunity, and choice; and social interactions are most often affectionate (Sussman & Burchinal, 1962). Individuals and nuclear units are more likely to achieve social goals as a part of the modified extended family than they would be isolated from it because "such relationships provide maximum resources without adding any major burdens" (Litwak, 1968, p. 83). Modern communication and transportation facilitate these contacts and exchanges among family members in westernized societies.

Research has also demonstrated that elderly persons are neither isolated from nor ignored by their families. Findings from Shanas's 1962 and 1975 national surveys of the elderly have shown that the elderly have family resources available to them, that the elderly are in regular contact with family members (especially adult children and, in their absence, siblings), and that exchanging services and visiting are common practices among the elderly and their kin (Shanas, Townsend, Wedderburn, Friis, Milhoj, & Stehouwer, 1968; Shanas & Heinemann, 1978).

However, some concerns have been raised with regard to an overstatement of the significance of the modified extended family in our society, at least for some subgroups of the population (Gibson, 1972; Lopata, 1978). In her 1974 study of Chicago-area widowed and previously widowed women, Lopata found that most involvement and exchanges of support with kin occur through the parent-child line and siblings, and other relatives, even grandchildren, are not strongly involved in the social support systems—economic, service, social, and emotional—of these women. That is, relatives most likely to give support to and/or receive support from widows are parents and dependent children for younger widows and adult children for older widows.

Given these findings about the role and importance of the modified extended family for widowed persons, a review of family involvement and support among the widowed is in order, and such a review is the intent of this chapter. The first part of the chapter includes material related to family involvement and support among widowed persons during the period of becoming widowed (that is, when bereavement and adaptation to the loss of spouse are paramount). The second part of the chapter is concerned with family relationships during the period of being widowed (when adaptation to a single life style has become relatively well established). The third part of the chapter is devoted to reporting findings from my own research about family supports among urban, widowed women. The chapters ends with a summary, conclusions, and suggestions for future research in the area of the widowed and their families.

Family Involvement and Support: Becoming Widowed

The period of widowhood in which one *becomes* a widowed person begins with the death of the spouse and lasts through the reintegration of the individual into the social system with a new sense of identity, a new lifestyle, and often an altered value system. This period includes both mourning and adaptation phases. Varying considerably from individual to individual, it usually lasts from one to three years. The death of the spouse results in a negative self-definition on the part of the individual experiencing the loss. The "grief work" and "reality testing" in this phase serve as beginning attempts to come to terms with the loss and to reestablish a positive identity (Gorer, 1965; Glick, Weiss, & Parkes, 1974). Grief work involves not only the emotional expression of grief, but also talking with others about the loss and attempting to understand it and its ramifications. Grief work is believed to be important if successful adaptation is to take place, since it forces the acceptance of the loss. Reality testing involves attempts to function more independently and to see other persons in the environment as potential resources. The individual begins to develop skills and abilities or to use previously dormant ones to repattern life. New goals are set, and life begins to have meaning and purpose again. Gradually, the individual negotiates and reestablishes salient reference groups and social roles into systems of support among family, friends, and community.

Early Help from and Involvement with Kin

Bereavement tends to bring families closer together. During the early bereavement period, when the ceremonies associated with death must be arranged and carried out, kin—both the widowed person's own relatives and those of the late husband or wife—rally around the surviving spouse and provide a variety of services and supports. Most often relatives insist that the widowed person give up usual daily routines to be free to grieve for the lost partner. Some kin discourage expressions of grief, while others provide an atmosphere for its expression. In their study of widowed persons age 45 and younger, Glick and associates (1974) found that some widows are able to cry and express their grief in front of parents or the late husband's brother.

Female relatives tend to provide most of the services to the widowed (Marris, 1958; Lopata, 1973, 1979). They take over responsibilities for serving as a companion to the widowed person, welcoming and screening visitors, cooking, housekeeping, and caring for children. Mothers and mothers-in-law are especially helpful to young and middle-aged widows, while adult daughters serve similar functions for their elderly widowed mothers. Sisters and sisters-in-law also contribute these services regardless of the age or sex of the widowed person (Marris, 1958; Glick et al., 1974; Kohn & Kohn, 1978).

In contrast, male relatives assist the widowed, especially widowed women, with decisions and arrangements regarding the funeral, financial matters, and insurance benefits. The late husband's brother for young and middle-aged widows and adult sons for elderly widows are most helpful with these matters. Glick and associates (1974) found that, in addition to this help, the late husband's brother sometimes assists the widow with informing other relatives of the death and paying funeral expenses.

Not always do the services provided by relatives coincide so closely with traditionally defined sex-role behavior. Kohn and Kohn (1978) reported an occasion where teenage and young adult daughters helped their widowed father make funeral arrangements according to the wishes of the deceased wife/mother. Gorer (1965), too, noted that sons often take a more general responsibility (that is, beyond mere instrumental assistance) for their widowed fathers.

After the leave-taking ceremonies, many widowed person fear being alone. Siblings and adult children sometimes stay with the widowed person for several days or have the widowed person stay with them and their families for the first week or so after the funeral. Rarely do these arrangements become permanent. Alternatively, widowed persons with teenage children at home often take comfort from them during this time (Glick et al., 1974; Peterson & Briley, 1977).

Gradually, relatives return to their own family obligations, and many widowed persons are left very much on their own (Lopata, 1973; Glick et al., 1974; Peterson & Briley, 1977). Widowers, especially, tend to become socially isolated from relatives. Glick and associates (1974) observed that among younger widowed persons, widowers ask for help from relatives less frequently than do widows during the first year of bereavement. Townsend (1957) and Marris (1958) have noted that when a wife/mother dies, the family loses its common meeting place for family gatherings, but the ties between mothers and their adult children remain strong regardless of the presence or absence of the husband/father.

Marris (1958) found that widows with young children are supported by their families even more so than are other widows. Ties with in-laws, too, sometimes continue over a longer period of time when grandchildren are a part of the scenerio or when the widow's own mother is no longer living; otherwise, contact with in-laws declines considerably over the first year after the spouse's death (Glick et al., 1974). Marris (1958) also found that widows with the closest ties to their own families are most likely to lose touch with the late husband's family.

Lopata (1979) asked widows to recall retrospectively the problems that confronted them early in widowhood. She found that making funeral arrangements, handling financial matters, and dealing with loneliness were problems most often cited. Slightly over a third of the widows in her study remembered children and their spouses as helping solve these problems; another 11 percent mentioned that siblings were helpful; and 13 percent said they took care of the problems themselves. Adult children, parents, and siblings were mentioned most often as persons who helped the widows establish a new life. In-laws and other relatives played less significant roles in this regard.

Sources of Strain in Family Relationships

The family also functions more subtly to remind widowed persons of their changed status and to set norms for them with regard to when they have grieved long enough (Marris 1958; Glick et al., 1974). These functions help the widowed accept the reality of their loss and provide guidelines for mourning which are ambiguous in westernized societies (Marris, 1958; Gorer, 1965). These functions, too, have the potential for creating strained family relations, especially in the case of widows. Women tend to take much of their identity from the role of wife (Gorer, 1965; Lopata, 1973); therefore, widows are reluctant to give up this role and resent pressure from relatives to do so. Additionally, widows take a relatively long time to grieve for their dead husbands and to resume normal daily life patterns. Relatives who return to their own families and become less accessible to widows or who encourage social participation on their part are perceived by some of them as noncaring and insensitive. Widowers, on the other hand, have fewer difficulties with relatives in these matters because their identities are more broadly defined than those of widows and because they return to their jobs or normal routines soon after the funeral and begin to date and make social contacts much earlier than do widows (Glick et al., 1974).

Friction with family members can also result when relatives try to do too much for the widowed person and are perceived as interfering or hindering their movement toward independence and a more autonomous lifestyle. Conversely, relationships become strained if adult children redefine their widowed parent as a burden or potential burden to them. Becoming too dependent on relatives results in loss of standing within the family. Because of this, widows, especially, feel caught between needing help from kin and having to demonstrate their competence to manage on their own (Glick et al., 1974). To avoid this kind of strain, some widows limit their requests for help and underutilize relatives as sources of support (Powell, 1981).

Much of the advice given to widowed persons comes from the family (Peterson & Briley, 1977). While much of it is well-intentioned, poor advice or too much advice can lead to strained relationships between the widowed and their family members. Lopata (1973, 1979) found that much of the advice to widows is more of a burden than a help because it comes from the perspective of the relative with little thought given to the widow's needs, desires, special situation, or personality. Often, too, advice coming from different sources is contradictory. Younger widows tend to be subjected to more outside advice and pressure to make changes in their lives than are elderly widows (Lopata, 1979). Presure to make changes comes mostly in the areas of the widows' relations with their children and men.

For young and middle-aged widows, conflict with their mothers often arises over differing child-rearing philosophies and differing perspectives on management of and priority given to children. Elderly widows, too, find these areas particularly sensitive in dealing with adult children and grandchildren. Anticipated conflict in these areas is cited by elderly widows as a reason for not wanting to live with adult children (Lopata, 1973).

Finally, Glick and associates (1974) have emphasized that the majority of widows move toward establishing independent lives and satisfactory relationships with relatives; conflicts and tensions with family members are experienced by a minority of widows. Conflicts with the late husband's family are more frequent than with the widow's own family, since anger and disappointment are more openly expressed among widows and their in-laws.

Renegotiating Roles with Children

Widowed persons must renegotiate previous roles from the perspective of a single person rather than that of a couple (Peterson & Briley, 1977). The renegotiation of the role of mother has special significance for widows because (1) they place so much importance on this role and (2) their closest family ties are with their children (Lopata, 1973, 1979). Marris (1958) found that widows hold special claims to the loyalties of their children. Widows tend to feel emotionally closer to and rely more on daughters as opposed to sons; this may be the result of more mutual reciprocation in their relationships with daughters (Troll, Miller, & Atchley, 1979). Sons, too, see more of their widowed mothers than they did previously, although they perceive the relationship more in terms of obligation and duty than satisfaction and enjoyment (Hiltz, 1981). According to Marris (1958), the actual nature of exchanges between mothers and their adult children does not change drastically in widowhood; however, mothers do become more dependent on these exchanges with the death of the husband.

Widows' relationships with their adult children are also important because they influence the quality and type of relationships that widows develop with grandchildren. Involvement with grandchildren varies considerably among widows. Those who feel particularly close to grandchildren usually live close to, have frequent contact with, and/or participate in caring for them. Other widows become occupied with their own personal interests and resist requests from their children to babysit or become otherwise involved with grandchildren (Lopata, 1973).

Having dependent children in the home is often a mixed blessing for widowed persons (Caine, 1974; Glick et al., 1974; Peterson & Briley, 1977; Lopata, 1979). Widows, themselves, report that were it not for their children they could not have "gone on" or that keeping busy caring for the children prevented their having nervous breakdowns. Certainly, the role of mother or father can contribute to a positive identity for widowed persons as well as provide them a way to express continuing devotion to the dead spouse; however, some widowed experience anxiety and guilt because their own grieving or the demands of their jobs prevent them from helping their children grieve. They become irritable and quick-tempered with their children, while the children become moody or withdrawn, do poorly in school, or exhibit behavioral problems. Adolescent children can be either an asset or a liability during the early widowhood period, depending on stage of development, level of maturity, and previous relationship with the surviving parent.

The widower may be forced to rely on a relative (usually his mother or sister) or a paid helper to rear his children. The widow may find that the price she pays for becoming emotionally closer to her children is an inability to discipline them (Glick et al., 1974). Furthermore, some widows become overly involved in the role of mother to avoid grieving. They experience depression or delayed grief reactions years later, find themselves lonely and isolated from sources of support and satisfaction, or become disenchanted with their lives as their children grow up and require less of them. Many widows with dependent children resign themselves to a lonelier life with fewer social contacts as they try to be both mother and father to their children (Marris, 1958).

Continued Ties to the Deceased Spouse

Movement from an identity and lifestyle as a part of a couple to those of a single person is a gradual and often painful process, especially for widows. Some of them experience symptoms of the late husband's disease or illness; others wear pieces of his clothing in an attempt to feel comforted by and close to him; and still others continue to set the table and cook for two at meal time. Many widows report experiencing a visual, auditory, or less well-defined sense of the late husband's presence on numerous occasions, especially during the year following his death. During these times, they converse with him, become angry with him for deserting them, and seek his advice on a variety of personal and family matters (Parkes, 1970; Caine, 1974). Widows also report that they try to conduct themselves and rear their children as they believe their late husbands would have wanted.

In the process of becoming reconciled to the loss of the partner, widowed persons selectively remember only the positive aspects of the marriage and positive traits of the deceased spouse. This idealizing or sanctifying behavior is especially characteristic of widows (Lopata, 1973, 1979, 1981). According to Lopata, idealization helps the widow cope with low morale and depression and helps break the tie to the late husband by placing him in a more distant and purified position. Other researchers, however, have reported more dysfunctional aspects of this behavior. For Marris (1958), idealization among widows is an attempt to compensate for or expiate the anger and guilt they feel toward the late husband; it provides a way to deny the satisfactions that life can offer. Additionally, Peterson and Briley (1977) have noted that widows who praise their mates excessively and make their lives monuments to them severely limit their abilities to love other persons again. Such idealization makes it almost impossible for a new male friend to "measure up" to the late husband; therefore, remarriage is not a likely possibility for the widow who continues to remember her late husband in this way.

Glick and associates (1974) found that women whose husbands helped them plan and prepare for the coming changes in widowhood seem to adapt more easily than others; however, such planning was observed infrequently and then only among the better-educated widows.

Family Involvement and Support: Being Widowed

The period of widowhood in which one is characterized as *being* widowed refers to a relatively routinized lifestyle as a single person. For most widowed persons, the loss of the spouse has been accepted, family roles have been negotiated successfully, and friendships have blossomed and are strongest among other single persons. Often, too, new roles have been developed as widowed persons become employed, return to school, join and participate in the activities of social clubs and organizations, and engage in volunteer work in the community. Adaptation continues during this time, but it becomes less a resolution of grief and acceptance of loss; rather, it tends to be characterized more by the day-to-day coping strategies required to lead a satisfied single life in a couple-oriented society (Powell, 1981).

Not all widowed persons have single lifestyles, however. Widowers and young persons, both male and female, have more opportunity and are more likely than elderly widows to remarry and return to a lifestyle based upon the married couple (Glick et al., 1974; Cleveland & Gianturco, 1976; Treas & Van Hilst, 1976; Heinemann, 1982). Glick and associates (1974) noted that among widowed persons age 45 and younger, most widowers move toward remarriage; however, widows whose husbands died unexpectedly are less likely to remarry than are those who anticipated the husband's death.

For elderly widows, remarriage is not likely. According to Cleveland and Gianturco (1976), less than 5 percent of the women widowed after age 55 ever remarry. Furthermore, many of the elderly widows do not expect to remarry. Besides lacking the opportunity, they are reluctant to give up their independence, believe they cannot find a man as good as the late husband, fear losing another loved one, don't intend to care for another sick husband, or fear financial exploitation (Lopata, 1973). Often, too, adult children object to the remarriage of a widowed mother for this latter reason or for fear of losing their inheritance (Treas & VanHilst, 1976).

Elderly widowed persons who do remarry do so for companionship and to prevent becoming overly dependent on adult children (McKain, 1969; Lopata, 1973, 1979). Factors such as having known each other for a long time, sharing similar interests, having the support of children, remodeling or setting up a new household, and giving top priority to each other and not to children are related to successful remarriages in late adulthood (McKain, 1969; Peterson & Briley, 1977).

Besides remarriage, Glick and associates (1974) identified four other patterns of life reorganization among the widowed: (1) organization of life around close, supportive relationships with kin; (2) organization of life around a nonmarital relationship with someone of the opposite sex; (3) establishment of life independent of close relationships with anyone other than one's own children; and (4) lack of life organization (disorganization and chaos).

Relatonships with Kin Among the Long-Time Widowed

Inconsistencies in the literature exist with regard to the amount of involvement the widowed elderly have with their kin. Findings from several studies have shown that these widowed persons have less contact with kin than do their married counterparts and that among the widowed, women maintain higher levels of contact with relatives than do men (Townsend, 1957; Berardo, 1967; Philblad & Adams, 1972; Longino & Lipman, 1981). Conversely, Petrowsky (1976) found that elderly widowed persons are no more isolated from kin than are married persons and that widowed men and women have similar rates of social interaction with kin.

Relatives figure prominently in the social supports of elderly, widowed blacks in the rural south (Scott & Kivett, 1980) and among ethnic immigrants in comparison to native-born elderly (Weeks & Cuellar, 1981). Lopata's (1975) findings, however, suggest that nonurban immigrants experience considerable isolation from primary group resources in large, urban areas. Here, dissimilar findings result, in part, from urban-rural differences and whether or not one's past socialization experiences are relevant to one's present living environment.

The widowed are not unlike elderly persons in general with regard to involvement with children. They enjoy living close to and visiting with, but do not want to share the same household as, their adult children. Maintaining their own households permits widowed persons to enjoy freedom, autonomy, privacy, and a sense of control over their own lives. Some loneliness seems to be a price worth paying for independent existence.

The majority of widowed persons have living children, and contact with them is frequent. According to findings from Shanas's national survey, approximately 75 percent of previously married elderly not living with children (mostly widowed persons) had seen a child during the previous week (Shanas & Heinemann, 1978). There is consensus among most researchers that elderly widowed persons, especially widows, are linked to the family and larger society through involvement with their adult children. These relationships are important to widows because they provide moral support not available elsewhere (Matthews, 1979).

Children are the most frequently mentioned relatives in the support systems of urban widows (Lopata, 1979). The mother-daughter bond is especially strong; daughters provide most of the emotional support to widows, and more daughters than sons exchange services with their widowed mothers (Adams, 1968b; Lopata, 1979). Children contribute to the social supports of widows through sharing holidays, visiting, and entertaining, although many other persons are involved in the leisure-time activities of widows as well. Children rarely contribute to widows' economic supports, however (Lopata, 1979). With regard to caregiving, daughters are the mainstay of the family support system (Treas, 1977). According to Treas, daughters take widowed mothers into their homes, run errands for them, and provide them with custodial care; however, the family support system is taxed by the high ratio of elderly to younger family members. Fewer children are available to care for an aging parent, and many of them are becoming less willing and able to do so.

Siblings are the most important source of support for childless, unmarried elderly (Johnson & Catalono, 1981). According to Cumming and Schneider (1961), sibling relations become especially important for persons in the final stages of the family life cycle. Approximately 18 percent of the unmarried elderly with no living children reside with a sibling, and 34 percent of the previously married elderly with surviving siblings had seen a sibling during the previous week (Shanas & Heine-mann, 1978). Sisters tend to have more influence on the elderly than do brothers; sisters provide emotional support to elderly men and challenge and stimulation for elderly women (Cicirelli, 1977). Johnson and Cata-lano (1981) reported that last surviving siblings often turn to their dead siblings' children as sources of support.

Relationships with more distant relatives are less frequent and less intimate in nature. Nephews and nieces who provide help and support to elderly, unmarried relatives do so with some resentment and out of loyalty to their own parents. They are not likely to be involved in actual caregiving, but rather serve as managers and supervisors of such care (Johnson & Catalano, 1981).

Quality of Relationships

Grown children and aged parents are no longer economically dependent on one another; rather, involvement is based on affection, gratitude, guilt, and/or desire for approval (Treas, 1977). These differ-ent motivating factors can result in relationships of varying quality, especially for widowed persons who have precarious identities, a devalued, stigmatized status, and less income and resources with which to reciprocate in relationships. Among the elderly, married couples tend to sustain one another, while the widowed, most specifically women, look to their adult children and their families for similar kinds of support. Many widows view the relationships with adult children, children-in-law, and grandchildren as most important at the time when these family ties are becoming formally prescribed, ritualized, and unbalanced. For example, adult children tend to define the role for the widowed mother in her relationships with them and their families; elderly widows are expected to attend family gatherings, but are seldom included in plans and preparations for them; adult children and grand-children have other sources of rewards, while they may be the primary source of rewards for the elderly widow (Matthews, 1979). Thus inher-ent in the structure of these relationships are reasons for disappointment and dissatisfaction on the part of elderly widows.

Generally, studies have shown that the elderly are hesitant to criticize and voice overt dissatisfaction with their family relationships; yet, signs of such discontent are evident in that the subject of family involvement is sometimes a sensitive one for elderly widowed persons. Matthews (1979) observed "hints of dissatisfaction" as elderly widows made excuses and justifications for relatives not spending time with them. Additionally, she noted subtle acts of noncompliance on the part of the widows in their relationships with family members; she interpreted these as signs of dissatisfaction as well.

The impact of involvement/interaction with relatives on life satisfaction and morale among widowed persons has been the subject of investigation also. Seelbach and Sauer (1977) found that the higher the filial expectations, the lower the morale among aged parents. Among widowed persons, contact with children contributes less to a positive outlook than does contact with other relatives, and involvement with friends and neighbors is even more important than contact with relatives in maintaining morale (Pihlblad & Adams, 1972; Arling, 1976a, 1976b; Wood & Robertson, 1978). Family relationships are often based on a sense of obligation and can result in role reversal and physical and financial dependency on the part of the aged parent (Arling, 1976b). In contrast, friendships tend to be based on shared interests, mutual needs, and reciprocal exchanges, all of which sustain a person's sense of usefulness and self-esteem (Blau, 1973).

The Family as a Support System

In my own research, I have extended Lopata's work on support systems among relatively longtime widows. While she has defined the concept and investigated the persons and agencies contributing to the support systems of widows, I have concentrated on measuring the strength of support systems and identifying the determinants of this strength among widows in different life stages.

A subset of respondents and variables from Lopata's 1974 Widowhood Support System Survey provided the data base for this research (unweighted number of cases, 963). The data were weighted so the number of widows in each of the five Social Security Administration benefit recipient categories corresponded to their proportion in this particular universe of widows. In weighting these data, an attempt was made to approximate the original sample size in order that tests of statistical significance could be utilized in the analysis.[1]

The widows ranged in age from 20 to 96 years with a median age of 69. Almost half of them had been Chicago-area residents all of their lives. They had completed an average of ten years of formal education and had an average yearly income of between $3,000 and $5,000 in 1973.

Approximately 27 percent of the widows were employed at the time of the study. The majority of them were married only once. The average number of years married to the late husband was thirty; the average number of years spent in widowhood was ten.

Lopata (1974, 1979) has defined a support system as the mutual, but not necessarily symmetrical, exchange of economic, service, social, and emotional supports between an individual and the resources of society—any person or group available as a potential contributor or recipient of support. The individual is the organizing agent who, to varying degrees, consciously and overtly selects and develops out of the resources a set of relations contributing to the personal support systems. According to Lopata, support systems must be flexible to meet changing needs and requirements for meeting these needs. They require negotiation with regard to expectations and actions and are heavily utilized in times of crises. I have modified Lopata's definition in two ways. First, I have defined support systems in terms of the meaningful persons or groups (Lopata's resources) rather than in terms of the four areas of support. That is, while Lopata refers to the economic, service, social, and emotional support systems, I focus on the family, friendship, and community support systems. My definition is closer to Shanas's (1979b) conceptualization in this regard. Second, in the area of emotional supports, Lopata included in the support system persons or groups mentioned by widows as making them angry; I have excluded these persons as sources of support.

Findings reported here are concerned with the family support system. The number of active roles widows had among relatives was used to measure the strength of the family support system. For a role to be considered active, the widow had to have engaged in face-to-face interaction with the role partner during the previous year or mentioned the role partner as being a source or recipient of help in one of Lopata's four areas of support.

From the literature and the assumptions underlying the definition of a support system, I identified four groups of variables that appear to be influential in predicting strength of the family support system among widows. These included certain personal characteristics, personal resources, social and community participation, and social psychological attributes (for example, personality traits and internal sentiments). Figure 9.1 shows the variables and their hypothesized relationships with the dependent variable.[2] Additionally, I hypothesized that different determinants of the dependent variable would be identified for widows in three life stages: young and middle-aged widows, less than 60 years of

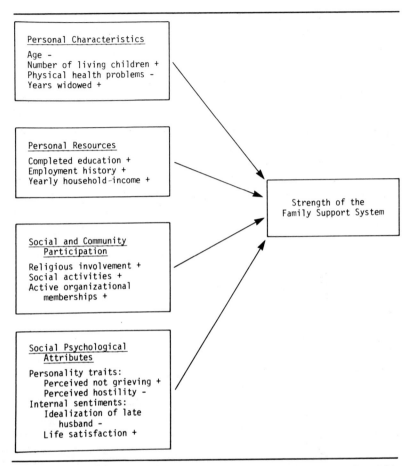

Figure 9.1 Predicting Strength of the Family Support System Among Urban, Widowed Women

age; young-old widows, 60 to 74 years of age; and old-old widows, 75 years of age and over.

The roles that linked the widows with their kin and from which they developed their support system of family members are shown in Table 9.1. For the widows as a whole, the three most prevalent roles were those of mother, sister, and mother-in-law. Seventy percent or more of the widows were involved with children and their spouses and siblings. Additionally, slightly less than a third of the widows were involved with

TABLE 9.1   Percentages of Widows with Specific Family Roles
by Life Stage

Family Roles	Young/ Middle-Aged (less than 60)	Young-Old (60-74)	Old-Old (75+)	Total
Mother	98	91	86	91
Sister	87	81	62	77
Mother-in-law	54	76	74	70
Grandmother	14	38	32	30
Sister-in-law	25	19	9	18
Daughter	48	4	0	14
Aunt	7	12	13	11
Other-in-law	11	10	12	11
Daughter-in-law	34	3	0	10
Cousin	5	7	0	5
Niece	6	2	0	2
Granddaughter	_a	2	0	1
N (weighted) =	(266)	(461)	(311)	(1042)[b]

a. Less than 1% after rounding.
b. Includes four cases in which age is not known.

grandchildren; that is, the fourth most prevalent role for them was
grandmother. The roles of daughter, aunt, and other in-law were less
prevalent among the widows. Approximately 10 to 20 percent of them
were linked to their families through these roles. Roles least likely to be
part of the widows' family scenarios were granddaughter, niece, and
cousin; only 1 to 5 percent of the widows were involved with these role
partners.

The role of mother, the most prevalent role among the widows, was
one of the least influenced by life stage. Although a smaller proportion
of old-old widows was involved with children compared to widows in
the younger two life stages (86 percent compared to 91 percent of the
young-old and 98 percent of the young and middle-aged), mother
remained the most viable role among the very old. The role of sister, the
second most prevalent family role among the widows, was least likely
among the old-old widows, most probably due to the death of their
siblings. Conversely, three-fourths of the young-old and old-old widows
compared to slightly over half of the young and middle-aged widows
were linked to family by the third most prevalent role, that of mother-in-
law. Again, young-old and old-old widows were more likely than young

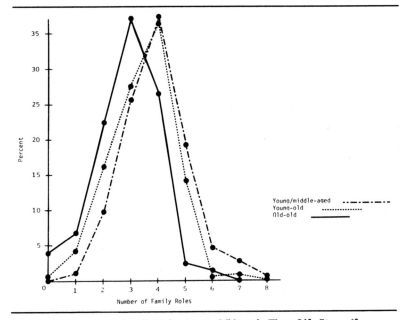

Figure 9.2 **Number of Family Roles Among Widows in Three Life Stages (frequency distribution)**

and middle-aged widows to have grandchildren and be involved with them. Widows in the youngest life-stage group were more likely than other widows to be involved as daughters, daughters-in-law, and sisters-in-law, however.

Figure 9.2 depicts the frequency distributions on the dependent variable, number of active family roles, for the three life-stage groups of widows. None of the young and middle-aged widows was without family roles; the mean number of such roles for this group was 3.9. Less than 1 percent of the young-old widows had no family involvement; their mean number of roles was 3.4. The old-old widows were most likely to be without family involvement, but again, the proportion was small; some 4 percent had no family roles. Their mean number of roles, 2.9, was the lowest of three life-stage groups.

A multiple regression analysis was used to determine the combined effects of all the independent variables on strength of the family support system. Problems of multicollinearity were not an issue, since none of the independent variables was intercorrelated above .45. Table 9.2 shows

TABLE 9.2   Effects of the Independent Variables on Number
of Active Family Roles by Life Stage

Independent Independent Variables	Young/ Middle-Aged (less than 60) Beta Weights	Young-Old (60-74) Beta Weights	Old-Old (75+) Beta Weights	Total Beta Weights
Age	−.120	−.114*	−.381***	−.301***
Number of living children	.084	.125*	.264***	.108***
Physical health problems	.029	−.020	.140**	.028
Years widowed	.020	.012	−.046	.059
Completed education	−.147	−.061	−.062	−.050
Employment history	.107	−.151**	.075	−.006
Yearly household income	.006	−.156**	−.164*	−.127***
Religious involvement	.041	.250***	−.001	.132***
Social activities	.232**	.315***	.371***	.316***
Active organizational memberships	−.006	−.001	.311***	.035
Perceived not grieving	−.028	−.202***	.230***	−.052
Perceived hostility	.007	.090	.260***	.080**
Idealization of late husband	.006	−.159**	.087	−.064
Life satisfaction	.034	.115*	−.301***	−.002
Multiple R	.275	.524	.689	.450
R^2	.075	.274	.475	.250
Overall F	1.212	9.079***	12.877***	18.372***
df	14/208	14/336	14/199	14/773

*$p < .05$; **$p < .01$; ***$p < .001$

NOTE: Standardized beta coefficients from the regression analysis are presented in this table.

the results of the regression analysis for the total sample of widows and for each life-stage group. Taken together, the independent variables explained 25 percent of the variance in the dependent variable. Six of the fourteen independent variables (age, number of living children, yearly household income, religious involvement, social activities, and perceived hostility) were significant predictors of strength of the family support system for the widows as a whole. That is, being younger, having a greater number of living children, being actively engaged in religious and social activities, and being perceived as hostile were related to having a strong family support system.

It is also evident from Table 9.2 that the regression model was not equally predictive of the dependent variable for the three life-stage groups of widows. For the youngest group, the model did not significantly predict strength of the family support system. Only one significant predictor was identified, and only 8 percent of the variance in the dependent variable was explained. In contrast, the model explained 27 percent of the variance in the dependent variable, and nine significant predictors were identified for the young-old widows. The model was most predictive of strength of the family support system for the old-old widows. Forty-eight percent of the variance in the dependent variable was explained and, again, nine significant predictors were identified for the oldest life-stage group.

Finally, Table 9.2 shows that while nine determinants of strength of the family support system were identified for the young-old and old-old widows, only four of them (age, number of living children, yearly household income, and social activities) were identical predictors for both groups. That is, among the young-old and old-old widows, those with strong family support systems tended to be younger, have more living children and less annual income, and engage in more social activities than widows with weak family support systems.

Two other variables (perceived not grieving and life satisfaction) were significant predictors of strength of the family support system for both the young-old and old-old widows; however, the directions of the relationships between the independent variables and the dependent variable were not identical. Of these widows with strong family support systems, the young-old widows tended to be perceived as grieving and scored high on life satisfaction, while the old-old widows tended to be perceived as not grieving and scored low on life satisfaction.

The additional predictors of the dependent variable for the young-old widows included employment history, religious involvement, and idealization of the late husband. Young-old widows with strong family support systems tended to have weak employment histories, strong religious involvement, and low scores for idealization of the late husband. Physical health problems, organizational involvement, and perceived hostility were the additional predictors for the old-old widows. Those with strong family support systems tended to have physical health problems, to have strong organizational involvement, and to be perceived as hostile.

In comparing the findings presented in Table 9.2 with the hypothesized relationships in Figure 9.1, it becomes evident that elderly widows with strong family support systems do not have all of the resources and positive traits and attributes assumed to be necessary for building and maintaining support systems. In fact, the weak employment histories, low incomes, and continued grieving on the part of young-old widows and the poor health, low incomes, hostility, and dissatisfaction with life on the part of old-old widows may be factors that inhibit or limit ability to develop support systems among friends or within a community network. As a result, tearful, bereft, and unhappy widows become heavily dependent on kin for help and support. Family members do not abandon these elderly, vulnerable widows. Instead, relatives accept their frailties, hardships and negative characteristics much more readily than nonrelatives and rally around them in times of need. The norm of reciprocity tends to be relaxed, and the family functions as a succoring, nurturant support system that is both tolerant and flexible.

Summary and Conclusions

The literature concerned with widowed persons and their family involvements shows that relatives rally around widowed persons during the early bereavement period and provide much-needed support, services, and advice. As the widowed person adapts to the loss of the spouse, roles and relationships with relatives are renegotiated from the perspective of a single person. Strained relationships sometimes occur during this time, but for the most part, widowed persons are able to reestablish satisfactory relationships with their kin.

Widowers return relatively soon to their normal day-to-day activities after a wife's death, while widows tend to grieve and withdraw from social activities for a considerable period of time after a husband's death. Widowers, too, along with young widowed persons are more likely to remarry than are elderly widows. Widowers who do not remarry, however, are less involved with relatives than widows. Longtime elderly widows tend to maintain strong ties with their kin through involvement with adult children, especially daughters and, in their absence, siblings.

At times the quality of relationships between elderly widowed persons and their relatives is less than satisfying from the widowed person's perspective. This is often the case when relationships are no longer reciprocal or when expectations on the part of the elderly widowed person tend to be extremely high. The reasons for dissatisfaction with family relationships on the part of some elderly widows and the findings from my own research on the family support system (that widows with few resources and negative traits tend to have strong family supports) suggest that family relations are characterized less by reciprocity than the modified extended family concept would have us believe, and because of this lack of reciprocity, these relationships do not always maximize resources without adding major burdens, especially in four-generation families. It seems that as the structure of the family changes, so do its characteristics and how it functions for its members.

However, those who believe that the functioning of the modified extended family has been overstated seem to have ignored the importance of substituting more distant kin when immediate kin are not available. This substitution mechanism permits elderly widowed persons to maintain their ties to the kinship and the larger social systems.

Certainly more research is necessary before we have a clear understanding of widowed persons' involvement with their family members. Future research should continue to emphasize the changing structure of the family and its impact on family functioning among the widowed. We know very little about the early widowhood period among the elderly, since most of this research has been focused on the young and middle-aged. We also know much less about widowers in comparison to widows and about racial/ethnic subgroups among the widowed in comparison to white widowed persons. More comparative research efforts are required in these areas. Quality of relationships between the widowed persons and their family members is another area requiring additional research and clarification. Finally, we need to extend the work begun by Lopata and others on social support systems among the widowed. We need to compare support systems among family, friends, and bureaucratic agencies; we need to examine support systems over time to determine if certain persons or types of resources are important at different points in the bereavement and adaptation process; and we need to relate family involvement and strength of the family support system to successful outcomes and adaptations among widowed persons.

NOTES

1. More detailed information about sampling procedures can be obtained from the author.

2. All independent variables are continuous, with the exception of physical health problems, which was constructed as a dichotomous variable such that 1 = has at least one physical health problem and 0 = has no physical health problems. Additional information with regard to items used in scale construction are not presented here due to space limitation, but are available from the author.

10

Divorce and the Elderly
A Neglected Area of Research

CHARLES B. HENNON

Little is known about the effects on individuals of becoming divorced in later life or living as a divorced elderly person (Uhlenberg & Meyers, 1981). There is also a paucity of empirical knowledge about the effects of divorce in later life (Uhlenberg & Myers, 1981) or even middle age (Hagestad, Smyer, & Stierman, 1982; Hagestad & Smyer, 1982) on the kinship system and consequent ramifications for support networks. Only slightly more is known about the effects on kinship and the elderly when younger people divorce (Hennon, in press; Anspach, 1976; Smyer & Hofland, 1982; Kalish & Visher, 1981; Ahrons & Bowman, 1981; Johnson, 1981; Johnson & Vinick, 1981). In short, divorce is one of the most neglected areas of gerontological research (Troll, Miller, & Atchley, 1979). In fact, a 1978 conference on older women, held by the National Institute on Aging and the National Institute of Mental Health, concluded that no information could be found on divorce in later life (Hagestad et al., 1982). Since there is a relatively low incidence and prevalence of divorce among the elderly, as will be shown in this chapter, there is probably justification for the lack of research on this topic. However, if people are concerned about the future marital and familial experience of the aged, attention needs to be given to how this situation may change in the future (Uhlenberg & Myers, 1981), as well as how divorce affects the well-being of the elderly (Hennon, 1981; Uhlenberg & Myers, 1981).

Author's Note: The research reported in this chapter was supported by Grant G007604690, Office of Consumer Education, U.S. Department of Health, Education and Welfare, and through the Hilldale Funds, Family Resources and Consumer Sciences, University of Wisconsin—Madison.

The independent variable of concern in this chapter is divorce. This divorce may have occurred previous to old age or after entrance into this stage of life. What these people share is currently living single as a result of divorce. The dependent variables are physical, psychological, social, and consumer well-being. In order to appreciate the magnitude of the effect, a comparison group is needed. If this group is also previously married, it will help to specify whether the way of becoming single has effects over and above just being single and older. The most logical comparison group is a matched sample of elderly widows.

The issue of divorce effects becomes important with the realization that with increased divorce rates (including those in second or subsequent marriages) and an aging population, more people will be spending their later years living as divorced single individuals (for more on this, see Uhlenberg & Myers, 1981). Impacts on individual functioning in the realms of social interaction, economic security, and mental and physical health may be severe and different from those for individuals who are never married or widowed (Hennon, 1981; Kitson, Lopata, Holmes, & Meyerling, 1980; Ward, 1979; Gove, 1979; Uhlenberg & Myers, 1981).

Widowhood and divorce are both conditions under which formerly married people become and may remain single in later life. However, the consequences of divorce may be more severe or different for the following reasons: Widowhood is a more institutionalized status; with death, the spouse is only psychologically present to effect self-concept, while with divorce he or she can be both psychologically and physically present; the social psychological definition of becoming single differs, widowed persons often romanticizing the departed spouse, while divorced may feel anger, guilt, frustration, and the like; desired versus undesired divorce may impinge differently (for example, there may be differences between a woman who desires divorce due to perceived incompetence in her husband and a women who is "dumped" for a younger woman); and divorce may cause a sense of failure after many years of marriage.

Data from an exploratory study of divorced women over the age of 55 are presented in this chapter. Many of these women divorced during middle age. These women will be compared to a matched sample of widowed women on their physical, psychological, social, and consumer well-being as well as their dependency on adult children. The sparse literature will be reviewed after a brief section on divorce rates and projections. Next, the study will be described and findings presented. The chapter concludes with implications for application and future research.

Divorce Rates and Projections

Among the demographic changes of the U.S. population since World War II, the rapid increase in the divorce rate must be considered important. This coincides with the general aging of the population. The postwar era experienced a divorce boom that occurred at the end of the war, when the divorce rate reached a level of 4.3 divorces per 1,000 population. The rates, however, quickly returned to lower prewar rates. More recently, the rate of divorce has grown rapidly, reaching a rate of 5.3 per 1,000 population in 1979 (U.S. Department of Health and Human Services, 1980). This rate has been sustained for a relatively long period of time, and the results have affected many aspects of American life, including school systems, social services, legal services, churches, and the attitudes of the general populations, including expectations for marriage and its duration.

Hypotheses about future trends can be offered, but there is no way to predict what exactly may happen. Demographic projections can be made for offering implications of future incidence of divorce if a given set of rates remain in effect for a period of time (Weed, 1980). With this method, using 1976-1977 rates, the proportion of marriages that will end in divorce increases from 29.5 percent for the 1950 marriage cohort to 49.2 percent for the 1973 cohort (Weed, 1980). Also, 34 percent of the men and 38 percent of the women born between 1945-1949 who marry will end their first marriages by divorce (Census Bureau projection reported by Uhlenberg & Myers, 1981). This confirms other estimates that approximately half the people currently marrying (and entering old age around the year 2020) will divorce (Plateris, 1979). The remarriage rate still remains relatively high, with three out of four divorced persons remarrying within five years and 10 percent of American children under 18 living in stepfamilies in 1978 (Glick, 1979). It is estimated that 44 percent of these remarriages will also end with divorce (Glick & Norton, 1977).

Many people will find themselves faced with living divorced in their later years. There are several reasons for this prediction, including the current rate of divorce in the United States, the rapidly increasing annual rate for those 65 and over (Uhlenberg & Myers, 1981), the lengthening of the age span, and the increasing median age of the population. Another reason is the increase in the proportion of the elderly who will be in second or subsequent marriages that are perhaps more prone to end in divorce than are first marriages. Among those over age 65 who divorced in 1970, 73.5 percent of the males and 78.8 percent of the females had been married more than once (Plateris, 1978). The divorce rate among those over 65 is at least ten times greater for those who have been married more than once than for those in first marriages. It is also likely that cohorts entering old age in the future may be more accepting of divorce as a solution to unpleasant marriages, and the increased economic independence of older women may encourage higher amounts of divorce (Uhlenberg & Myers, 1981).

Living divorced may be especially true of elderly women. It is known that widowers have a higher remarriage rate than widows, resulting from social norms supporting marriage to younger women (and discouraging the opposite), a stonger motivation to remarry, and the demographic advantage of a surplus of women in the marriage market (Siegel, 1976). The same may also be true for older divorced men and women. The likelihood of remarriage is twice as great for women who are under the age of 30 at the time of the divorce as it is for women age 40 or more (Sanders & Spanier, 1979).

Although divorce rates have changed, there is no noteworthy increase in divorce rates after age 40, nor is there a clear-cut trend indicating change in the timing of divorce. Only the frequency of divorce has changed, not the age profile. More people of every age see it as an option. Every year, nearly 10,000 people 65 years of age or older are divorced (Troll et al., 1979). The divorce rate for women over age 65 changed little during the 1960s. However, it nearly doubled from 1.2 per 1,000 married women in this age category in 1970 to 2.2 in 1975 (Carlson, 1979). Only about 1 percent of all divorces during 1975 occurred among people aged 65 or greater (Uhlenberg & Myers, 1981).

As seen in Table 10.1, the percentage of the older population that was divorced (either before age 55 or after) and not remarried grew slightly between 1950 and 1975. In 1975, 2.5 percent of men and 2.6 percent of women age 65 and over were divorced, compared to 13.6 and 52.5 percent who were widowed. In 1979, 3.3 percent of both men and women age 65 and over were divorced.[1] The rate of divorce for the older population in the near future is open to debate. However, as explained above, it is expected that the rate of divorce in later life will increase, as well as the proportion of the older population that is divorced. Since 1970, the percentage of nonremarried divorced older women has been larger for almost each age grouping than has the percentage of nonremarried divorced men.

These current rates and projections of divorce among the elderly and the percentage of the elderly currently single due to divorce[2] point out

TABLE 10.1   Percentages of Population 55 Years Old and Over Who Are Divorced and Widowed, by Gender

	Males				Females			
Age:	55-64	65-74	75+	65+	55-64	65-74	75+	65+
1950								
widowed	7.1	na	na	23.6	25.5	na	na	55.3
divorced	2.1	na	na	2.2	2.2	na	na	0.7
1960								
widowed	6.2	12.7	31.6	18.8	24.5	44.4	68.3	52.9
divorced	3.5	1.7	1.5	1.6	3.2	1.7	1.2	1.5
1970								
widowed	4.1	11.3	27.7	17.1	21.2	44.0	70.3	54.4
divorced	3.0	2.7	1.4	2.3	4.6	3.0	1.3	2.3
1975								
widowed	4.0	8.8	23.3	13.6	20.3	41.9	69.4	52.5
divorced	4.5	3.1	1.2	2.5	5.3	3.3	1.5	2.6
1979								
widowed	na	9.3	24.0	na	na	41.2	69.7	na
divorced	na	3.9	2.2	na	na	4.0	2.2	na

SOURCE: U.S. Bureau of the Census, *Current Population Reports*, Series P-23, No. 59, May 1976, and Series P-20, No. 349, March 1979.

that although being divorced and not remarried among this age group is still a relatively rare experience,[3] it may become more common in the future. That which can be learned now about the well-being of divorced elderly can help in providing support, services, and education to those who will be divorced in the future. Current research can also help in better understanding what research problems need to be addressed so that better empirically based information about divorce and this age group can be provided.

Literature Review

Widowhood, relative to divorce, has better-established norms and self-expectations for behavior as well as uniformity of expectations from others. This provides a form of social support that is lacking for the divorcee. Widowhood is seen as a normative crisis that may affect well-being in later life (Parkes, 1972; Datan & Ginsberg, 1975; Palmore, Cleveland, Nowlin, Ramm, & Siegler, 1979), due in part to adjustment to a single lifestyle and all its concomitant variables such as unhappiness, loss of self-esteem, withdrawal, general decline, desolation, loneliness, and economic insecurity (Butler, 1975; Datan & Ginsberg, 1975; Rosow, 1973). Little similar research has been conducted on the consequences of divorce during the later stages of life (see, for example, Chiriboga, 1979; Kitson et al., 1980; Ward, 1979; Trudgeon, 1978; Hagestad, Smyer, & Stierman, 1982; Hagestad & Smyer, 1982; Deckert & Langelier, 1978), especially for physical, psychological, social, and consumer well-being. In general, there are more physical and mental health problems among the divorced than among the widowed (Gove, 1972, 1973, 1979). Ward (1979) notes that the divorced, especially males, are a vulnerable segment of the older population. Hagestand & Smyer's (1982) data also partially support this; they conclude that mid-life women are better able to work through divorce than are men. They also state, however, that women suffer more financially than men and that starting over may also be more difficult.

Kitson et al. (1980) compared 88 divorced women (average age of 30.7) with a sample of widows weighted to equal an n of 2,807 (average age = 51.0) and another sample of 301 widows (average age = 66.0). They report that when adjustments are made for age, older divorcees feel more restricted in their social relationships, experiencing discrimination and a sense of alienation based on their divorced status. The authors conclude that being divorced is still a stigmatized status. This reinforces the conclusions of Miller (as reported in Troll et al., 1979), that divorced women feel much worse off than widows in terms of financial matters, self-esteem, and relations with others. Widowhood is seen as a sad experience, divorce as a shameful or sinful one. Thus, widows' self-esteem may increase, while that of divorced people may decrease.

The older divorcee, due to her sense of restricted relationships with others, seeks and receives less social support than do widows. Hagestad and Smyer (1982) do report, however, that middle-aged women are more likely than men to seek out social support, especially from their children. Social support eases adjustment to divorce (Raschke, 1977; Weiss, 1975) and widowhood (Clayton, Halikas, & Maurice, 1972). In addition, divorcees are more ambivalent toward their ex-spouses (Kitson et al., 1980). Other research concludes that for both divorced and widowed, ambivalence about the departed spouse can create long-term adjustment difficulties (Weiss, 1975; Parkes, 1972; Greenblatt, 1978). Kitson et al. (1980) suggest that the divorcee's adjustment to her new status is more difficult than that of the widow.

Evidence from national surveys (n = 1366) in 1974, 1975, 1977, and 1978 of those over the age of 60 (reported in Uhlenberg & Myers, 1981) shows that divorced and separated older people have a lower level of satisfaction with some aspects of life. It is interesting to note that divorced and separated males are more dissatisfied than are females. Married people report a higher level of satisfaction that do other people; however, both divorced and separated males and females express less satisfaction than other nonmarried people. It is interesting to note that divorced and separated males are more dissatisfied than females. In fact, for females marital status is apparently unrelated to level of satisfaction with areas of life other than family life. These same surveys discovered few differences between married, widowed, and never-married persons in their subjective levels of financial satisfaction. However, the divorced and separated are much less satisfied. Of the 36 divorced/separated males, 38.9 percent say they are satisfied, 22.2 percent are more or less satisfied, and 38.4 percent are not at all satisfied. The comparative percentages for the 64 divorced/separated women are 28.1, 48.4, and 23.4.

There is an important link between age and impairment. The family (Cicirelli, 1981a; Shanas, 1979b), especially the wife (Silverstone, 1982), provides basic services and support for the impaired elderly. One of the factors that influence the quality of life for the elderly is the type and quality of care and support available to those who are impaired (Smyer & Hofland, 1982). While at this point little is known about how divorce of the older person affects this care and support, some speculation is possible.

About 86 percent of those 65 and older are estimated to have one or more chronic health problems (Butler, 1975), and advanced age is related to more impairment. For example, 35 percent of people 65-74 with chronic illness are subject to significant impairment, while 53 percent of people over 75 are so limited (Brody, 1973). The proportion of people requiring home care is about three times greater for those 75 and older than for people 65-74 (Maddox, 1975). The prevalence of mental disorders also increases with age (Butler & Lewis, 1977).

The extended family, the spouse, and friends are important providers of care and support for all elderly people, especially those who are impaired (Cicirelli, 1981a; Silverstone, 1982; Shanas, 1979b; Smyer & Hofland, 1982). Little is known about how divorce affects the support and care that could possibly be offered. Most probably, the ex-spouse will not provide it. Divorce often reduces and/or changes the friendship system, and older divorcees are often worse off than widows in their relationships with friends (Miller, as reported in Troll et al., 1979; Kitson et al., 1980). Consequently, friends also may not be available to provide this support. Foreseeably, the divorce might negatively affect the relationship between parents and children, and thus children might be less inclined to provide support. Because of the possible effects on support networks and the provision of care and services, divorce might affect the quality of life of older people.

The older divorced person also is at a disadvantage in terms of mortality. Around 1960, death rates for divorced males over age 65 were 33 percent higher than for married males and 7 percent higher for divorced females relative to married females (Kitagawa & Hauser, 1973).

To summarize, there has been little research on the impact that divorcing or being divorced may have on an older person's life; as noted earlier, it is one of the most neglected areas of research in social gerontology (Troll et al., 1979; Smyer & Hofland, 1982). This chapter will add to this sparse data base by comparing divorced to widowed elderly women in terms of their subjective physical, psychological, social, and consumer well-being.

Sample and Methodology

This exploratory analysis is based on data gathered as part of a larger study. The sample was selected to be representative of the population that belongs to senior citizen centers in the United States. A quota sampling procedure was used to select individuals from membership rosters of senior citizen centers in four geographic locations: Salt Lake City and Denver (representing urban areas) and southern Utah and southwestern Montana (representing rural areas). (For more information concerning the sample and its representativeness, see Burton & Hennon, 1980, 1981; Hennon, Mayer, & Burton, 1981). For this analysis, a subsample of divorced and widowed women are matched by age, rural/urban residence, and length of time single since the termination of the marriage.

Matching by age, rural/urban residence, and length of time single after marriage helps specify if the *way* of becoming single and remaining so is a factor determining the state of well-being in previously married elderly women. If statistically significant differences are discovered, this will indicate that the method (divorced or death) of becoming single has effects in later life over and above just the state of becoming single. These results will add to the data base of stressor events and their consequences for life during the later stages of the life cycle.

The face-to-face interview was selected as the method of data collection for this study. Kerlinger (1972) states that although the self-administered questionnaire does have certain advantages (such as uniformity) and that, if anonymous, it encourages honesty and frankness, the face-to-face interview is probably superior to the self-administered questionnaire for gathering information. The flexibility of the interview enables the interviewer to reword questions when necessary. In addition, some persons are more willing to answer questions orally (Craig & Leroy, 1979). Finally, the interview technique seemed especially appropriate for the elderly, some of whom may have had trouble reading and/or writing.

Several forms of the interview instrument used in this study were pilot tested with members of senior citizen centers in Salt Lake City. The interviewers for the final data gathering were gerontology students from four colleges and universities located near the centers where the interviews were conducted. Each interviewer participated in an intensive one-day training program conducted by the project staff and was provided with a twenty-four-page interviewer's guide to provide consistency in the interviewing process. This guide described in detail the purpose of each question in the interview instrument and the manner in which the responses were to be recorded.

The subjects were requested by phone to participate in the interview, and during this call an interview appointment was arranged. The interviews were conducted individually in the subjects' homes or in private rooms at the centers. The interviewees were assured of anonymity. From January to March 1977, 322 usable interviews were obtained, of which 40 (20 each from divorced and widowed women respondents) are use for the analysis reported here.[4]

The samples are composed of both divorced and widowed women with approximate mean age of 69 who have been single postmarriage for an average of approximately twenty years. The divorced were married an average of eighteen years before they divorced; while the widowed were married a significantly longer time ($\bar{X} = 26.5$). The divorced averaged 49 years of age at the time of divorce, while the widowed averaged 55 years of age at the time of husband's death. The range of present age to age at the time of divorce is a 61-year-old divorced at 29 to a 90-year-old divorced at 85. Thirteen were divorced before age 55, and four were divorced after their husbands had retired. The range of present age to age of widowhood is a 68-year-old widowed at 36 to an 88-year-old widowed at 78. Seven were widowed before age 55, and only three had husbands who were retired at the time of death.

Sixty-seven percent of the widowed group lived in rural areas, compared to 43 percent of the divorced. There was a moderate difference in total annual incomes between the divorced and widowed ($\bar{X}s$ = \$4,849 versus \$6,543; p = .09). Eighty-five percent of both groups were retired from a job, while 25 percent were still employed to some extent. Their present or (for those retired) previous occupations ranged from unskilled labor to professional and proprietors of mid-sized businesses.

Both the divorced and the widowed former husbands' occupations and education ranged from unskilled labor to professionals and proprietors of large businesses, and from grade school education to graduate and professional degrees. The respondents' education levels rannged from grade school to graduate degrees. The widowed group had a higher percentage of college degrees than did the divorced group (40 percent in the widowed group versus 25 percent in the divorced group). Forty-five percent of the divorced and 30 percent of the widowed were Protestant, 30 percent of each group were Mormon, 10 percent of the divorced and 35 percent of the widowed were Catholic, one widowed person was Jewish, and 15 percent of the divorced indicated no religious preference. Table 10.2 reports selected characteristics of the sample.

The key variables of physical, psychological, social, and consumer well-being and dependency are indexed as follows:

Physical Well-Being. One self-report item on the respondent's health was included in the interview:

> (1) We would also like you to indicate what you feel is your general state of health. (Excellent to bad on a five-point scale with a higher score indicating better health.)

Psychological Well-Being. The respondents were asked a series of questions about psychological well-being. Each of these will be analyzed separately:

> (1) To what extent do you feel that you can control how happy and satisfying your life is now? (very little, somewhat, a lot)
> (2) To what extent do you feel that no one cares what happens to you? (strongly agrees no one cares to strong disagreement that no one cares, on a five-point scale)

TABLE 10.2   Selected Characteristics of Sample

	Divorced	Widowed
Age		
$\overline{X}$	68.6	68.6
SD	7.48	7.02
range	60-90	60-80
Years postmarriage		
$\overline{X}$	19.8	19.5
SD	10.54	12.02
range	1-36	1-46
Age at divorce/widowhood		
$\overline{X}$	48.8	54.7
SD	13.76	11.32
range	29-85	43-78
Years married		
$\overline{X}$	18.3	26.5
SD	10.07	11.81
range	3-38	9-60
Residence (n)		
Salt Lake City	5	3
Denver	9	9
Southern Utah	4	4
Southwestern Montana	2	4
Annual income		
$\overline{X}$	$4849	$6543
SD	2349	2914
Employed (n)		
Yes	5	5
No	15	15
Retired (n)		
Yes	17	17
No	3	3
Education (n)		
High school	5	3
High school, tech school, some college	10	9
College	3	5
Graduate degree	2	3

(continued)

TABLE 10.2   Continued

	Divorced	Widowed
Husband's Education (n)		
High school	6	3
High school, tech school, some college	8	13
College	0	0
Graduate degree	3	3
na	3	1
Occupation (n)		
White collar	6	8
Blue collar	13	9
na	1	3
Husband's occupation		
White collar	5	9
Blue collar	11	10
na	4	1
Husband retired at time of divorce/widowhood (n)		
Yes	4	3
No	15	17
na	1	0
Religion (n)		
Protestant	9	6
Mormon	6	6
Catholic	2	7
Jewish	0	1
none	3	0

(3) A life review was conducted and the respondents were asked to indicate their satisfaction (very to not very on a five-point scale, higher score indicating more satisfied) with life in five-year increments from age 40 to present age, with projections into the future.

Social Well-Being. The following items were used to indicate kinship interaction/isolation, and will be analyzed separately:

(1) Do you ever help your children or other relatives out financially? (yes, no)
(2) How do you help your children or other relatives?
(3) Do your children or other relatives ever help you out financially? (yes, no)

(4) How do they help?

(5) How often do they help?

(6) Do you ever exchange financial advice with your children or other relatives? (yes, no)

(7) Who gives advice to whom, and under what kinds of conditions?

Consumer Well-Being. Divorced individuals need to establish new management patterns (Buehler & Hogan, 1980), and the elderly have consumer attitudes and procedures that were learned perhaps forty to fifty years ago. The following series of items and measures index the respondents' consumer well-being:

(1) Many people have concerns or worries about money. What are your money concerns or worries?

(2) A series of questions were asked about the respondents' consumer concerns relative to thirty-two consumer areas. These were then rank-ordered as to which areas were of the most pressing concern, using mean scores. A score of 3 indicated major concern, and a score of 1 indicated little or no concern.

(3) The same 32 items were used to obtain an overall measure of Extent of Consumer Concerns. For each consumer item the respondents could respond if it was of major (3), some (2), or little to no (1) concern to them. These scores were then summed and divided by 32.

(4) A life review was conducted and then respondents were instructed to indicate their financial satisfaction (from very satisfied to not very satisfied, on a five-point scale) from age 40 in five-year increments to present age, with projections into the future.

Several other items were included that could tap any of these four dimensions. These items are:

(1) Could you please take a minute to think and tell me what is the single most satisfying thing about your life at the present time?

(2) Now would you tell me about the other side of your life; what single thing is the most unsatisfying part of your present life?

(3) Along these same lines, what are your biggest needs at the present time?

(4) Now let me ask you a question about the future. If worse should come to worst, what is your single greatest worry or fear?

Dependency. The extent to which the respondent reported dependency on adult children was determined according to the following items:

(1) How dependent are you on other people in deciding how to spend your money? 100-76 percent, 75-51 percent, 50-26 percent, or 25-0 percent dependent?

(2) If subject was 26 percent or more dependent on another, she was asked, Exactly who do you depend on for help in making consumer decisions?

(3) Why don't you make these decisions?

Results

Results for each of the four dimensions of well-being will be presented separately.

Physical Well-Being. The divorced individuals report a slightly lower state of general health ($\bar{X}$ = 3.65, SD = .813) than do the widowed ($\bar{X}$ = 3.94, SD = .639), but this difference is not statistically significant (t = 1.23, p = ns).[5]

Psychological Well-Being. The divorced elderly report a lower level of satisfaction with life at the present time ($\bar{X}$ = 3.8, SD = 1.105) than do the widowed ($\bar{X}$ = 4.1, SD = .832). However, this difference is not statistically significant (t = .96, p = ns). Table 10.3 shows the distribution of mean life satisfaction for each subgroup by six age categories. Caution must be exercised when interpreting these findings due to low cell frequencies. It appears that the divorced are less satisfied until the age of 70, although none of the differences approaches statistical significance.

Respondents were asked the extent to which they believed they could control their lives in terms of happiness and satisfaction. The divorced indicate a lower level of control ($\bar{X}$ = 3.42, SD = .838) than do the widowed ($\bar{X}$ = 3.61, SD = .698), but this is not a statistically significant difference (t = .75, p = ns). The divorced indicate a higher level of alienation or isolation in that their mean score for the item, "To what extent do you feel that no one cares what happens to you?" is higher ($\bar{X}$ = 1.47, SD = .772) than the mean score for the widowed group ($\bar{X}$ = 1.37, SD = .761). However, this difference is not statistically significant (t = –.72, p = ns).

Social Well-Being. All of the data for this analysis pertaining to social well-being are measures of kinship interaction, especially exchange of financial advice and wealth.

The divorced women (who have an average income of $4,849 as opposed to $6,543 for the widowed) are less likely to help their children financially than are the widowed (number that help = 10 and 15 respectively, x^2 = 4.73376, df = 1, p = .05) and are less likely to give only money (1 versus 7) or gifts (1 versus 3), but are slightly more likely to provide their houses and money (2 versus 1) or to provide services (1 versus 0). They are equally likely to provide both gifts and money (4). The

TABLE 10.3   Satisfaction with Life and Financial Situation at Current
Age, for Divorced and Widowed (mean scores and n's)

	60-64	65-69	70-74	75-79	80-84	85-94
Divorced	3.42 (7)	3.86 (7)	4.50 (2)	4.67 (3)	–	2.00 (1)
Widowed	4.00 (6)	4.00 (7)	4.00 (4)	4.00 (1)	5.00 (1)	5.00 (1)
			Satisfaction with Financial Situation			
Divorced	2.57 (7)	3.14 (7)	3.50 (2)	4.33 (3)	–	2.00 (1)
Widowed	*3.83 (6)	3.43 (7)	3.75 (4)	5.00 (1)	3.00 (1)	5.00 (1)

*p = .057

children of both groups help out their parents equally (5), but are more likely to give the widowed gifts (3) while giving the divorced gifts and money (2). The children of the widowed help out a little more often (occasionally = 3) than the children of the divorced (rarely = 3).

Widowed respondents are more likely to exchange financial advice with their children (13) than are the divorced (7, x^2 = 5.2347, df = 1, p = .05). Although the flow of exchange is two-way for both groups, it is more so for the divorced group (5 of 7) than the widowed (5 of 12; na = 1). The widowed indicate that they are more likely to have a flow of advice from parent to child (4 versus 1) and from child to adult (3 versus 1) than are the divorced.

Consumer Well-Being. Respondents were asked if they experienced any problems since divorce/widowhood that they had not experienced previously. Of the widowed, 12 answered yes, while only 4 of the divorced answered in the affirmative (x^2 = 7.69044, df = 1, p = .01). The divorced respondents said they had problems in the general areas of home repairs (2), housing, and investments, while the widowed listed public transportation, home repairs, and appliance repairs (3 each), mail orders (2), and clothing (1). However, there is no significant difference observed between the two groups' means on the Extent of Consumer Concerns Scale (divorced $\bar{X}$ = 1.3266, SD = .240; Widowed $\bar{X}$ = 1.3969, SD = .324, t = .78, p = ns).

Table 10.4 shows the rank ordering of thirty-two possible consumer concerns. The divorced and widowed exhibit a similar pattern of ranking of consumer concerns (rho = .637; p = .01). This indicates that although there are some differences in terms of primacy of concerns (for example, the divorcees' top concerns are utilities, dental, housing, leis-

TABLE 10.4   Ranking of Consumer Concerns by Mean Scores, for Divorced and Widowed Elderly

Consumer Concern	$\bar{X}$'s		Ranks	
	Divorced	Widowed	Divorced	Widowed
Utilities	1.95	1.90	1.0	1.0
Dental	1.65	1.40	2.0	16.5
Housing	1.55	1.25	3.5	22.5
Leisure and recreation	1.55	1.30	3.5	20.0
Clothing	1.50	1.50	6.0	12.0
Food	1.50	1.55	6.0	8.0
Telephone	1.50	1.40	6.0	16.5
Home repairs	1.40	1.65	10.5	4.5
Government services	1.40	1.60	10.5	6.0
Medical services	1.40	1.50	10.5	12.0
Eye care	1.40	1.65	10.5	4.5
Automobile	1.40	1.85	10.5	2.0
Taxes	1.40	1.55	10.5	8.0
Appliance repairs	1.35	1.15	16.5	27.0
Public transportation	1.35	1.45	16.5	15.0
Health and hospitalization insurance	1.35	1.75	16.5	3.0
Prescription drugs	1.35	1.50	16.5	12.0
Home security	1.35	1.50	16.5	12.0
Social security	1.35	1.35	16.5	18.0
Legal services	1.30	1.20	20.0	25.0
Auto insurance	1.25	1.50	22.0	12.0
Hearing care	1.25	1.30	22.0	20.0
Estate planning	1.25	1.30	22.0	20.0
Nonprescription drugs	1.20	1.20	24.0	25.0
Homeowner's/renter's insurance	1.15	1.55	25.0	8.0
Mail orders	1.10	1.10	27.0	29.5
Life insurance	1.10	1.25	27.0	22.5
Pets	1.10	1.10	27.0	29.5
Banking services	1.05	1.20	29.0	25.0
Credit	1.00	1.05	31.0	32.0
Investments	1.00	1.10	31.0	29.5
Private pensions	1.00	1.10	31.0	29.5

$r = .637$; $p = .01$.

ure and recreation, clothing, food, and telephone, compared to the widoweds' utilities, automobile, health and hospitalization insurance, home repairs, eye care, and government services), there is a high degree of similarity overall.

The divorced elderly are less satisfied with their current financial situation ($\bar{X}$ = 3.10, SD = .968) than are the widowed ($\bar{X}$ = 3.75, SD = 1.070; t = 2.01, p = .05). Table 10.3 shows the means for both groups across six age groups. Caution must be observed when interpreting this table, due to the low cell frequencies. However, it appears that the divorced are less satisfied than the widowed with their financial situations at each age category, although the difference approaches statistical significance (p = .057) only for the 60-64 age category.

The divorced indicate that their biggest money worries are inflation (6), not enough for emergencies (5), not enough money (2), money will not last long enough (2), and no flexibility in spending (1). The widowed list inflation (4), not enough for emergencies (2), not enough money (2), money will not last long enough (2), and fixed income (1). Four of the divorced and 9 of the widowed say they have no money worries.

The following shows in rank order the responses given to an open ended question about their worst fear of the future.

Divorced	*Widowed*
Dependency (8)	Dependency (11)
Death (3)	General health (3)
General health (2)	Concerns about children (2)
Loneliness (1)	Maintaining a positive attitude (1)
Having a purpose in life (1)	Collapse of the government (1)
Inflation (1)	Automobile problems (1)
No fears (1)	No fears (1)
No answer (1)	

Both groups are most fearful of becoming dependent and declining health. As for current aspects of their life that they find *unsatisfactory*, the divorced say most often their children/family life, loneliness, financial needs, and health, while the widowed mention loneliness, financial needs, and children/family life. The following is the rank ordering of their responses:

Divorced	*Widowed*
Children/family (4)	Loneliness (4)
Loneliness (3)	Financial needs (3)
Financial needs (3)	Children/family (2)
Health (3)	Health (1)
Shopping/housework (1)	Retaining positive attitude (1)
Emotional needs (1)	Possibility of war (1)
Nothing (1)	Death of loved one (1)
No response (4)	Nothing (1)
	No response (6)

Both the divorced and the widowed listed children/family life as the most *satisfying* aspect of their life. Good health, not having to work, and volunteer work were listed next by the divorced, while the widowed listed religion, lack of pressure/time for hobbies, and friends. The rank orderings are as follows:

Divorced	*Widowed*
Children/family (7)	Children/family (6)
Good health (3)	Religion (3)
Volunteer work (2)	Lack of pressure/
Not having to work (2)	time for hobbies (3)
Independence (1)	Friends (2)
Lack of pressure (1)	Independence (1)
Work (1)	Good health (1)
Religion (1)	No response (4)
No response (2)	

Dependency. This exploratory analysis seeks to determine answers to the following questions: (1) Are widowed and divorced elderly women dependent upon others for help in financial management? (2) If so, upon whom are they dependent and what role do adult children play in financial management? (3) Why do these respondents not make their own financial management decisions? (4) Are there differences in 1, 2, and 3 depending upon whether the respondent is divorced rather than widowed?

The results indicate that both the widowed and the divorced are highly *in*dependent. All respondents reported that they were only 0-25 percent dependent on others for help in deciding how to spend their money. Consequently, they were not asked the other two questions concerning dependency. This finding would seem to support the findings reported above that although their incomes were relatively low, few divorced or widowed elderly were likely to receive either direct financial help or financial advice from their adult children, and their worst fear of the future is of becoming dependent.

Summary

As noted by Hagestad and Smyer (1982), the timing of divorce is related to other issues of one's life stage. For some it is a reordering of priorities, a new sense of freedom, and a chance to realize unfulfilled potentials. For others, divorce during the middle or latter stages of life can be a shattering of their lives at a time when they already are feeling vulnerable.

The effects of divorce on well-being in later life is a neglected area of research. This chapter has added a little to this small data base by presenting the results of a study comparing matched samples of twenty divorced and twenty widowed women, all of whom are age 55 or over. The marriages of some of these people ended by death or divorce early on in life and they never remarried; for others, becoming single again has been a relatively recent experience. Results reported are the respondents' subjective satisfaction in the areas of physical, social, psychological, and consumer well-being.

This study indicates that methods of becoming single have some differential impacts on subjective well-being during the later stages of life. Mindful of the limitations of this study, family professionals and gerontologists can use the findings of these similarities and differences in order to promote positive well-being in later life. Educational and social programs for the elderly may need to be developed with the different needs of the divorced and widowed elderly in mind.

This analysis, which has controlled for effects of age, residence, and length of time single, has revealed some differences. Divorced elderly are less likely to help their children financially and are less likely to exchange financial advice with their children, and when they do, it tends to be a two-way flow of communication. These divorced elderly have lower incomes than do their widowed counterparts. This lack of exchange may reflect a lack of integration in an extended kin network or strained relationships between the parents and children. Uhlenberg and Myers (1981) report that elderly divorced women are less satisfied with family life than are elderly widows. Divorce of parents may force children to take sides or they may avoid both parents. However, while four of the divorced women mentioned children/family as the most unsatisfactory aspect of their current lives, seven mentioned children/ family as the most satisfying. This was just about the same for the widowed.

The divorced are less likely to indicate that they have problems that they did not have while married. This may reflect more independence on their part, including more independent decision making and self-reliance. This may be especially true if while they were married they saw their spouses as incompetent and thus developed their own talents.

The divorced are less satisfied with their financial situations. This finding is congruent with the data reported by Uhlenberg and Myers

(1981) and noted by Miller (as reported in Troll et al., 1979). This could well be due to their relatively lower incomes. They also list more money worries than do the widowed, and although the overall ranking of consumer concerns is similar, the top concerns for the divorced are different.

To summarize, these data suggest that, at least for the older widowed and divorced persons who are members of a senior citizen center, some differences exist. Any educational or intervention programs designed for formerly married elderly would have to keep a few distinctions in mind: relative to widowed, divorced have lower incomes, some different consumer concerns, exchange financial advice and assistance less with kin, are less satisfied with their financial situations, have more money worries, are more satisfied with their health, have fewer problems than they had when married, and are perhaps less religious and also less integrated into kinship support systems.

These data also suggest that in many ways divorced elderly are pretty much like their widowed counterparts. Factors such as extent and overall ranking of consumer concerns, current health, degree of alienation, satisfaction with life, financial management dependency, fear of becoming dependent and declining health, concerns about their children, loneliness and financial needs, satisfaction with children and use of their time, and their sense of powerlessness are common to both widowed and divorced elderly. The outcomes experienced by a divorced person may vary over time. The amount of transitional time (Hagestad & Smyer, 1982) is important, especially when the divorce process was not initiated by the individual. It must be remembered that these data are from a select proportion of the older population and that the divorce or death of the spouse was not a recent event. They have been single a relatively long time (about twenty years), and therefore longer-term effects are being tapped.

This exploratory analysis has looked at only one part of the total picture of divorce and elderly. It has focused on only the longer-term effects of being divorced for women. Similar analyses for men are needed. Further analysis is also needed to determine the more immediate consequences of divorce terminating a marriage for an older person. That is, does getting divorced while in the latter stages of life differ from divorcing at a younger age, and does it differ from becoming widowed?

More research on the effects of divorce on kinship systems is also needed. Divorce of younger people may cut off older adults from grandchildren (Hennon, in press) and perhaps the financial and emotional support that otherwise would be available from adult children. Conversely, little is known about the effects of divorce by elderly parents on their children and grandchildren. How do adult children feel about their parents divorcing? Does it affect the types of support offered or social contact? What effects will this have for the well-being of those involved?

Implications

Practice Issues

With the caution in mind that this analysis is exploratory and based on a small sample, it can be suggested that when some important differences are remembered, programs designed to serve the counseling, educational, or support service needs of the "single again" elderly can be general in nature. That is, most programs designed for widowed elderly will also serve those who are divorced.

However, some precautions are necessary to best serve the divorced. The findings concerning sharing of consumer advice across generations might indicate less of a support network for divorced elderly women compared to those widowed. Thus, divorced elderly may not have the resources of a wide kinship system to call upon. And since divorce is still stigmatized, and may especially be so among older cohorts, friendship networks may also be limited. Service programs to supplement these perhaps constricted networks may have to be offered. Educational programs on how to enrich networks (Hennon & Brubaker, in press) to expand what Raley (1982) called the "latent matrix" of kin, quasi-kin, and friends can be offered. Therapy programs to enhance intergenerational relationships (see Williamson, 1982, for example) may need to be different when parents are divorced. Both different issues and different techniques (such as working with one parent and then the other) may be required.

The perhaps weakened kinship support systems may hold implications for both short- and long-term care of the elderly. Wives and other kin appear to be the primary caregivers for elderly frail husbands (Silverstone, 1982; Shanas, 1979b). With divorce, who will provide this care?

There are many programs offered on anticipating or adjusting to widowhood by educational organizations such as the Cooperative Extension Service. Similar programs could be offered for divorced, realizing that a much smaller clientele would currently be involved. This may, however, be an emerging need of the future. One particular issue to be covered in both educational and counseling programs is the social psychological definition of divorcing and being divorced: Does the person accept the new status, experience a sense of failure, blame others for his or her circumstances? Another issue to explore is the sense of loss: Is it similar to or different from that experienced by those losing spouses through death?

The definition of becoming divorced will affect self-concept and perhaps self-esteem. Those who are "dumpees" may have a devalued sense of self-worth compared to "dumpers." This issue needs to be addressed. So will the roles that one will play and the adjustment required to play these new or modified roles (Hennon, 1980; Hagestad & Smyer, 1982).

The financial situation of divorced elderly women must also be addressed. Relative to widowed elderly women, their incomes are lower, as is their satisfaction with their incomes. Societal and kinship system solutions to this problem must be addressed. Inequalities in pension plans for wives of divorced versus widowed husbands need to be corrected. Recently, much national attention has been focused on displaced homemakers and their plight (for example, see Scannell, 1982). Many elderly divorced women fall into this category.

One solution to lowered financial resources of divorced elderly is good-quality consumer education. Consumer education for the elderly is a relatively new idea (Burton & Hennon, 1981; Waddell, 1975), and some research indicates that one program designed for the elderly in general worked well with both singles and marrieds (Hennon, Mayer, & Burton, 1981). As indicated above, widowed and divorced elderly women rank-order their consumer concerns in a highly similar manner. However, the magnitude of the concern differs on various issues and some issues are more salient for the divorced, such as dental, housing, leisure and recreation, clothing, food, and telephone. Programs to address these needs can be developed and delivered at senior citizen centers, nutrition feeding sites, and the like. This effort can enhance feelings of self-worth by helping people take more control over their lives and enhance their quality of life by helping them make informed choices about expenditures (Burton & Hennon, 1981).

Research Issues

Much more needs to be done in all areas of research on divorce and the elderly, including effects on the individuals divorced as well as on the kinship system. More data and theory are necessary on issues of self-concept and self-esteem, health, emotional well-being, social interaction, social support, kinship exchange of goods and services, quality of life, housing, financial well-being, and family care of the frail elderly, to name but a few. Distinctions also need to be made between those who sought divorce and those who were "dumped." Also, the control one has over the divorcing process appears to affect its impact (Hagestad & Smyer, 1982) and should be considered.

Other research problems center on the area of divorce among younger generations and ramifications for the elderly. These include the effects of divorce on the elderly's social support network, including the amount of social interaction, financial support, and health care issues. Also of concern are the questions asked by the elderly concerning understanding their children's or grandchildren's divorces (Kalish & Visher, 1981; Ahrons & Bowman, 1981) and the effects of perhaps making them "ex-grandparents" (Hennon, in press). Clinical observations and demographic and survey studies are needed. Both gerontologists and family scholars should find this a promising new field of inquiry, one in which they can make significant contributions.

Conclusion

Divorce and the elderly is a neglected area of research. This chapter has provided some data on this subject by reporting on the subjective physical, psychological, social, and consumer well-being of divorced relative to widowed women over the age of 55. A few but important differences are reported. To a large extent, the way of becoming single again does not have major effects independent of the fact of singlehood or aging. It appears from this preliminary analysis that divorced elderly women, as a group, are not worse off, except financially and perhaps kin system-wise, than widowed elderly women. Further research with larger samples and more and better measures of physical, psychological, social, and consumer well-being can provide more definitive answers.

NOTES

1. Because of the social stigma associated with being divorced, it is assumed that people misreport their current marital status. It is likely that there is an underreporting of being divorced in census data. Additionally, not all states report divorces to the National Center for Health Statistics. Thus, national divorce rates are estimated. Due to these

weaknesses in the data, the percentages and rate reported here should not be considered to be precise.

2. We are concerned here only with those older people currently living divorced—that is, not remarried. However, some people are concerned about those older people who have ever experienced a divorce. The 1970 census (U.S. Bureau of the Census, 1972) reports that about 16.2 percent of those over 65 have ever divorced, while another estimate is about 25 percent higher (Preston & McDonald, 1979). It is suggested that over 33 percent of those reaching age 65 between 2010 and 2014 will have been divorced (Uhlenberg & Myers, 1981).

3. However, it is not much rarer than is living in a nursing home or some other social, mental, or physical phenomenon affecting older people upon which research is conducted.

4. All respondents who indicated they were divorced were selected from the larger sample (n = 322). There were 20 such respondents (6.2 percent of total sample), all of whom were women. Twenty female respondents of the 132 who indicated they were widowed were then matched as closely as possible on the variables of age, number of years single since divorce/widowhood, and area of resistance.

5. In all cases the correlated t-test procedure was used, since matched samples were studied.

11

Dependent Elders, Family Stress, and Abuse

Suzanne K. Steinmetz
Deborah J. Amsden

When you have small children, who also need your time and attention and a home to manage and you are working out five days a week and you have an older person whose needs are even in excess of those of the children, it is next to impossible to handle it all and do it to any desire of satisfaction. You always feel like you are not cutting the mustard. You are constantly pressured even if it is for meals or cleaning or whatever. You feel like someone behind you is ramming you with a ramrod. You push as hard and as much as you can but it leaves its mark.

This is a description given by a 40-year-old woman who has a full time job, is a mother of two, and is responsible for the care of her 68-year-old mother, who is still able to do a great deal but because of failing eyesight is not able to live alone. This last quarter of the twentieth century can be best described by its shifting age structure. Not only will one of every eight persons be 65 years or older by the close of this century, but the greatest increase will be among the very oldest citizens.

By the end of this century, people under 65 years will have increased by 17 percent, while those 65 to 75 will increase by 14 percent. The greatest increase, 53 percent, will occur among those 75 and older, which has important implications, since this group is most vulnerable to physical, mental, and financial crisis requiring the care of their family and society (U.S. Bureau of the Census, 1977; Brody, 1978).

The increasing number of vulnerable elderly is a distinctive concern of this decade. However, it is not only the increased number of these elderly which is a critical issue. We must also recognize that those in their seventh, eighth, or ninth decade have caregiving children who are themselves elderly. Medical advances that extend life often do so at a considerable financial, physical, and emotional cost to the elderly and their caregivers.

Generationally inverse families, in which the elderly patient is dependent on the child generation for emotional, financial, physical, or mental support, are no longer unique. In these families it is not just a role that is reversed, but a complex set of generationally linked rights, responsibilities, obligations, and ways of viewing oneself and others that is reversed (Steinmetz, 1978).

Today it is not uncommon for one or two brothers or sisters to bear the responsibilites for four or five family members over 75 years of age who are no longer able to live independently. When one adds to this burden the relatives of one's spouse from current as well as previous marriages, the number of potentially dependent elders grows considerably. As the existence of multiple generations featuring generationally inverse families grows, the impact of "parent caring" on these middle-aged offspring must be addressed (Archbold, 1980; Shanas, 1979a; Silverstone & Hyman, 1976). The question of who takes care of the caregivers when the caregivers need taking care of needs to be raised.

For the first time in history, there is a large number of generationally inversed families in which dependent elders must rely on their kin for prolonged physical, emotional, and financial aid. These aging children and their parents are faced with this emerging family form without historical precedents or role models for dealing with these dependent and often disabled elderly family members (Steinmetz, 1978, 1981).

While extending the life expectancy has been a focus of biomedical research, the issue of quality of life, by comparison, has received only minimal attention. The problems created by increased longevity are not confined to the elderly; they encompass the entire family life cycle. The change in the roles from a child being cared for to that of caregiver for one's parent may build feelings of resentment and anxiety in both generations (Hooker, 1976; Knopf, 1975; Silverstone & Hyman, 1976). Feelings of love and respect easily can turn into guilt, hatred, and disappointment as children attempt to function in their next roles of caregiver (Cohen & Gans, 1978; Knopf, 1975). Unresolved conflict between parents and adolescent children often continues throughout the life cycle (Boszormenyi-Nagy & Spark, 1973; Brody, 1966), with the results that communcations may be antagonizing and contact may remain at the level of obligatory vacation or holiday visits during the child's adulthood. When unresolved conflicts exist, it is unlikely that the child will shoulder the responsibility of caring for an elderly parent with open arms and a warm heart. Consequently, the motivation to care for the older kin may be not only out of love and concern but also out a sense of responsibility, duty, or guilt.

Since these middle-aged (or elderly) caregiving "children" are often coping with offsprings' college and wedding plans, their own impending retirement,and age-related physical, social, and emotional changes, the additonal burden of shouldering a parent's problems can become a source of crisis with the potential for abuse and neglect (Kirschner, 1979; Rathbone-McCuan, 1978; Silverstone & Hyman, 1976; Steinmetz, 1978, 1980b, 1981). Surveys of social service professionals and police statistics have consistently shown that victims of assault, rape, homicide, and child abuse are most frequently abused by family members. In fact, it has been frequently observed that you are probably safer from assault in the dark city streets than in the warm and loving family home. Thus it is not surprising that family members predominate as abusers of the elderly.

The goal of this study is to ascertain the relationship between dependency measured by the frequency with which tasks or services need to be provided for the elder, stress as perceived by the caregivers, and the abusive techniques utilized to gain or maintain control.

Stress and Dependency

There are a number of stresses that seem to be related to dependency in generationally inversed families. As the dependency needs of the elderly increase, the stress experienced by the caregiving family can result in abuse of both caregiver and elder unless adequate resources are available (Blenkner, 1965, 1969).

The increased amount of personal time required to care for a dependent elder often absorbs any time available to fulfill the caregiver's own needs. Furthermore, attempts to reserve personal time are likely to be viewed by the elder as an indication of rejection.

Control over one's environment and lack of privacy pose additonal potential conflicts for both generations (Foulke, 1980). To have a smooth-running home, one assumes that all members must function interdependently. However, it is often difficult for an old person who has been transplated from his or her home to find an appropriate role in the new setting. Since this problem is predominantly faced by women (Brody, 1978; Hess, 1979; Morsan, 1969) it takes on an additional dimension; rivalry between mother and daughter over appropriate ways to manage households, husbands, and children (Farrar, 1955; Johnson, 1978).

Economic dependency produces a loss of control, a loss of self-esteem, and thus a loss of power and prestige for the elderly person. Furthermore, the caregiving family experiences economic drain and conflict over competing goals for the utilization of limited resources by the caregiving family. At the very time that one's own family income is leveling off due to retirement and children are depending on financial support for their college and wedding plans, this middle generation often has to assume the cost of caring for their elderly parents (Cohen & Gans, 1978; Silverstone & Hyman; 1976; Steinmetz, 1980b, in press).

Caregivers must also resolve problems resulting from the elder's physical dependency. Physical deterioration, evidenced through a loss of hearing, failing vision, a decrease in strength, and the severe or chronic illness that often accompany aging place additional burdens on the caregiving family.Often the elder resists the physical care provided by the caregiver producing a power struggle that could result in abuse. Families are ill equipped to meet the physical care needs of an elder kin.

Medical costs frequently are not compensated or at best may be undercompensated by public and private health insurance. The stress of meeting the physical needs of the elder is intensified because the caregiver realizes that inadequate care could produce a life threatening situation for the elderly parent (Knopf, 1975). Medical costs, therefore, compete with the other financial demands on the family.

In a study of the effect of elders' dependency on stress, caregivers reported that social/emotional and mental health dependencies were most stressful (Foulke, 1980). Foulke noted that physical dependencies, even when they resulted in increased health care responsibilities, were easier for caregivers to deal with and produced less stress than did social/emotional dependency. Most stressful of these two dependency categories was the "decision making" associated with the mental health dependency. These two dependencies, social/emotional and mental health, were particularity stressful because of the increased amount of personal time spent in social interaction with a dependent elder as well as the decreased time available to fulfill one's own needs. As one grows older, one's social space, the physical areas which defines one's social life, decreases. Thus the caregiver (and family) often became the only social life the elder had. Unfortunately, while the family became the center of the elder's universe, they were resentful that the elder was attempting to become the center of their universe.

A conflict in values also occurs. Where do these middle-aged caregivers place their priorities—in the parents who reared them or in their children, who may still need emotional and financial support? Caught in this dilemma, the caregivers may find that there is no physical, psychic, or financial cushion for themselves.

Finally, the manner in which the decision is made to have the elder move in with an adult child influences the likelihood for abuse. Burstan (1978) has suggested that a hastily made decision to have an aging parent live with an adult child may create conditons for eventual abuse. Because the decision is reached at a time when family emotions run high, family members may feel they are forced into taking the aging parent (Douglas, Hickey, & Noel, 1980). Power conflicts (Renvoize, 1978), increased disability (Lau & Kosberg, 1978), dependencies of the older person, and the existence of a high level of family stress (Blenkner, 1965, 1969; Steinmetz, 1978, 1980c) produce the potential violence.

Thus, one critical aspect of this study is not only to ascertain which of the elder's dependencies were being fulfilled by caregivers, but also to isolate those dependencies that were perceived to be stressful by the caregivers.

Sense of Burden

Neugarten, in an interview with Brubaker and several colleagues (1978) identified the sense of burden expressed by middle-aged children as a critical issue of caregiving. Foulke (1980), in her analysis of the support given by caregiving families, describes the sense of burden as a complex of issues that involves the family, the elder, and the family's situation. When caregivers are asked whether they feel a sense of burden by caring for an elder, they are reflecting their perception of the total effect that this experience has had on them.

Since this perception of being burdened may reflect coping abilities and therefore alternative strategies to violence, this variable may provide important insights. Amsden (1982) found that the degree of elders' dependency, which is an objective measure of additional tasks and responsibilities provided by the caregivers, was not related to a sense of burden, a subjective expression of caregivers' feelings about these tasks and responsibilities. Since we know that a person's perception of a situation is often a better predictor of behavior than objective criteria (Lester, 1968; Neimi, 1974; Steinmetz, 1977), caregivers who report a sense of burden may have a greater potential for using abusive or neglectful behaviors.

Abuse

Although there have been a number of studies of institutional abuse of elders, or their victimization resulting from street crimes, the study of abuse of elders by family members is a new area of research. The initial studies examined abuse perpetrated by "informal caregivers," which included family members as well as friends, distant relatives, and paid caregivers. In one study, 13 percent of service providers who responded to a mail survey reported that they knew of a case of elder abuse. However, 88 percent who responded were aware of the problem even if they had no cases to report (Block & Sinnott, 1979). Douglas, Hickey, and Noel (1980) found that 17 percent of their respondents in a similar survey of professionals reported physical abuse of an elder, and 44 percent reported verbal or emotional abuse. In one of the first studies of elder abuse, a mail survey of over a thousand medical personnel, social service professionals, and paraprofessionals, 183 reports of elder abuse were received. Seventy percent of the reports noted that the abuse occurred twice. Furthermore, 75 percent of the reported victims lived with the abuser, and in over 80 percent of the reports, the abuser was a relative (O'Malley et al., 1979).

During a twelve-month period, Family Service Association of Greater Lawrence, Massachusetts, received 82 referrals of elders suspected of being abused, neglected, or in a potentially threatening situation. Upon investigation, one-fourth of those elders who were living with their family experienced abuse or neglect (Langdon, 1980).

In 1978, the Baltimore City Police Department reported 149 assaults against individuals 60 or older. Nearly two-thirds of these assaults (62.7 percent) were committed by relatives other than spouses (Block & Sinnott, 1979). During the first eight months after passage of Connecticut's elderly protective service law, 87 cases of physical abuse, 314 cases of neglect, 65 cases of exploitation, and 8 cases of abandonment were reported (Block & Sinnott, 1979). By April 1979, the total number of reported cases was 937—651 of neglect, 166 of physical abuse, 127 of exploitation, 32 of abandonment, and 89 needing other kinds of assistance.

The above studies did not focus exclusively on family members as perpetrators of abuse. As the aging population increases, especially among the vulnerable elderly, and the funding for institutional care and support services decreases, it is expected that families will increasingly be called upon to provide care for their elders. We felt it was important to investigate the role of family caregivers in elder abuse.

In a preliminary analysis of a study of the relationship between stress and elder abuse (Steinmetz, 1983), several characteristics were noted. First, the overwhelming majority of the caregivers (90 percent) and vulnerable elderly (over 82 percent) were women, a finding consistent with other studies. Women face a double jeopardy: They bear the stresses and strains of caring for an elderly woman, and they face the high probability of being in the same situation when they became older (Brody, 1978; Block & Sinnot, 1979; O'Malley et al., 1979; Steinmetz, 1980b, 1981). Second, the caregivers are often elderly themselves by the standard Census definition of 60 or older, yet they are caring for an even older dependent (Foulke, 1980; O'Malley et al., 1979; Steinmetz, 1980, 1981).

A third and unexpected finding not considered by most other studies is the double direction of the violence. While violence perpetrated on elders has been sensationalized in the media, violence by elders on their adult children has remained hidden (Steinmetz, 1980c, 1981). The authoritarian father who ruled his children with an iron fist and met a loss of authority or control with a beating apparently still resorts to these techniques at age 90. When the father finds that it is more difficult to maintain control over children, he resorts to temper tantrums and physical outbursts. It is not difficult to understand why these elders would resort to physical violence, as they have no other mechanisms, such as money, prestige, mobility, or independence, with which to assert their will and gain their wishes. They must depend on manipulation or physical control if their children are unwilling to meet their needs or their demands.

The questions to be investigated in this study are:

— Which dependencies were most prevalent? stressful?
— Are "burdened" caregivers more stressed by performing tasks?
— What is the effect of task performance (which indicates dependency), feeling burdened, and feeling stressed on the use of violent methods for resolving conflicts?

Methodology

Sample

A nonrandom sample obtained through a "snowball technique" was used (Bailey, 1980). Announcements of the need for volunteers were mailed to all University of Delaware departments; notices were placed in the university newspaper, the *Review,* and the faculty newsletter; and articles appeared in state and local newspapers and social service news-letters. Participants were contacted by telephone in order to explain the scope of the study and to determine if they met the following criteria:

(1) The family shared a residence, and the elder was not a house guest or a visitor.
(2) The adult child performed some tasks for the elder which indicated that there was some degree of dependency.
(3) The elder was over 55 years of age.
(4) The caregiver was the adult responsible for the household.
(5) If the elder was deceased, death had occurred within the preceding three years.

To safeguard the confidentiality of the participants, many of the interviews were conducted in a mutually agreed upon location at the University of Delaware. For the convenience of some participants, interviews were conducted in the home at a time when the elder was not present. It was suggested that they not discuss their participation in the study with the elder, as it was felt that this might be anxiety-producing and result in the elder's feeling betrayed.

One hundred nineteen individuals were contacted. Of this number, 7 declined to be interviewed; 4 failed to keep their interview appointments; 3 volunteers did not meet the sample criteria; and 1 was unable to take time away from caring for the parent in order to be interviewed. Thus, a total of 104 caregivers were interviewed, resulting in a completion rate of 87.3 percent. Fourteen of the caregivers had cared for more than one elder; thus 118 dependent elders are represented in this study. Because the interaction might differ between the caregivers and each of these elders, as well as different health statuses and levels of dependency, the caregiver/elder information in families caring for two elders is handled as separate cases. For example, a caregiver might report little or no stress and no sense of burden as a result of caring for elder A, yet a lot of stress and a sense of burden by caring for elder B.

Since the focus of this study was on the middle-aged "child" caregiver who lives in a family setting with an elderly relative, our notices for volunteers specified caring for an elderly parent. We discovered that our respondents considered a variety of relationships to represent parent-child and were not just limited to biological or legal mothers and fathers. These relationships included 3 grandmothers, 4 aunts, 1 great aunt, and 2 friends of the family in addition to 74 mothers, 17 mothers-in-law, 12 fathers, and 5 fathers-in-law.

Instrument

Semistructured interviews were taped, and responses to the structured parts of the questionnaires were coded during the interview. The caregivers were asked a series of questions designed to elicit the tasks performed by family members who cared for the elder. The responses were categorized into six dependency categories: household, financial, mobility, social/emotional (which has two components—social/emotional support and social interaction), mental health and grooming/health (which also has two components—personal grooming and health care). (See Table 11. 1).

Responses to the tasks performed were categorized as "never," "almost never," "sometimes," "most of the time," and "all the time." In addition, respondents were asked to assess the stress they experienced as a result of the tasks in each dependency category. For example, the respondents were asked how frequently they had to provide transportation for the elder and then asked to rate, on a five-point scale, how much this bothered them. Finally, caregivers were asked to state how often they and the elder had used a variety of techniques to resolve conflicts to carry out their wishes. At the end of the interviews, caregivers were asked if they felt burdened by their caregiving responsibilities.

Intercoder Reliability. Most of the interviews were taped. These tapes were transcribed, and the data from the interview schedules and transcriptions were coded on computer scan sheets. Ten percent of the interview schedules randomly selected were independently coded by two researchers producing an intercoder reliability of 97.5 percent.

Results

Profile of Sample

Of the elders, 85 percent were women and 95 percent were white. Ninety-one percent were 70 years or older, and 20 percent were in the ninth or tenth decade of life. About 85 percent experienced diminished physical functioning, and 38 percent had been hospitalized during the last year.

Ninety-four percent of the elders were cared for by female caregivers. Three-quarters of the caregivers were married, and more than half of these families still had children living at home. The majority of the caregivers (45 percent) were in their fifties, about a quarter of the caregivers were in their forties, 11 percent were under 40, and nearly 20

TABLE 11.1   Percentages of Elderly Dependent on Task Performance by Caregivers

Tasks	% of Caregivers (N = 118)	Tasks	% of Caregivers (N = 118)
1. Household Management	99.0*	4. Financial Management	89.8*
Grocery shopping	94.9	Help with management of resources	70.3
Cooking	94.0	Write checks or pay bills	69.5
Run errands	93.2	Pay for essential needs	55.9
Laundry	88.1	Pay for luxury needs	50.0
Heavy housekeeping	85.6	Provide financial support	38.9
Light housekeeping	81.4	Other financial tasks	22.8
Provide transportation	90.7	5. Social/Emotional	
Other household tasks	15.3	Social/Emotional Support	98.3*
2. Grooming/Health Care		Provide emotional support	94.9
Personal Grooming	67.0*	Provide a "social life"	87.3
Help with hair care or makeup	57.6	Take visiting	74.5
Dress	50.0	Encourage/help to develop friends	68.6
Bathe	41.5	Social Interaction	72.0*
Health Care	73.7*	Help make phone calls	64.4
Follow doctor's orders	66.1	Write letters for elder	39.8
Give medications	58.4	Read to elder	28.8
Change bedding or diapering if elder		Other social tasks	11.0
incontinent	33.8	6. Mental Health	
Other health/personal grooming tasks	39.8	Help with decision making	94.2*
3. Mobility		Help remember (forgetful)	76.3
Help with walking	61.0*	Help elder not to get lost	85.6
Help up and down stairs	54.2	Deal with nonrational behavior	22.9
Help in and out of chairs	41.5	Deal with explosive behavior	41.5
Help in and out of bed	33.0	Watch, confine, protect	55.9
	27.1	Other	52.5
			20.3

*Family provided at least one of these tasks within each category.

percent were 60 years or older. Thus, nearly two-thirds of the sample were elderly or near elderly.

Dependency

In many of the families, the elders maintained a high degree of independence and autonomy, while in other families almost all tasks had to be performed for them. As the data in Table 11.1 suggest, housekeeping tasks are the most frequently performed tasks. When all household items were considered, 99 percent of the caregivers provided this help. In fact, only one family reported that they did not do any of the housekeeping tasks for their elderly.

Over 98 percent of caregivers provided social/emotional support (two families provided no support) and 92 percent of caregivers helped with mental health tasks (there were six families that were not performing these services). Some form of help with financial management was provided by 90 percent of families; 74 percent provided help with health care tasks; 67 percent helped with personal grooming; and 72 percent of elders were helped to maintain family social interaction. The least frequently observed type of dependency, mobility, was still provided, in some degree, by 61 percent of the families.

Stress

As can be seen by the data in Table 11.2, many of the dependencies were stress-producing. The two least stressful items, "elder's disruptiveness" (disrupt) and "elder's attempt to maintain an authority role" (rolmain) were created because they were repeatedly noted by respondents in the "other" category. Had these two items been on the original questionnaire, more caregivers may have acknowledged these problems. Since 54 percent of the caregivers noted that a lack of room or lack of privacy and 50 percent reported that the elder's excessive demands were stressful, this would suggest that caregiving was viewed as a disruption in about half of the families studied.

Abusive and Nonabusive
Conflict Resolution Techniques

In an attempt to gain or maintain authority, a variety of methods were used by the elderly parents and their adult children. While 85 percent of the adult children reported talking out problems, many noted that this talking was often done with a raised voice or loud tone.

TABLE 11.2 Comparison of Stress as Perceived by Nonburdened and Burdened Caregivers

Caregiving Stressors	Stress Total Sample (N = 118) %	Nonburdened Caregivers (N = 43) x	Burdened Caregivers (N = 75) x
Elder is lonely	64	2.1 (19)*	2.6 (56)*
Lack of room or privacy in household	54	2.2 (14)	2.5 (50)
Household management	54	1.5 (9)	2.4 (54)*
Elder makes excessive demands	50	1.9 (15)	2.8 (44)**
Elder has severe physical disability	45	2.2 (15)	2.5 (38)
Elder has severe emotional/mental disability	42	2.2 (12)	3.0 (37)*
Elder needs help with personal grooming	36	1.1 (8)	1.9 (35)**
Elder needs transportation	35	1.2 (8)	2.0 (33)**
Elder is mobile but senile	25	2.4 (7)	2.7 (23)
Elder will not eat	25	2.6 (10)	2.5 (19)
Elder is financially dependent	23	2.5 (2)	1.7 (25)
Elder has special dietary needs	19	2.3 (3)	2.2 (19)
Elder is disruptive to family's lifestyle	14	4.0 (2)	3.4 (14)
Elder attempts to maintain authority role in the family	8	2.7 (3)	2.8 (7)
Other caregiving stresses	25	2.8 (12)	2.9 (17)

*Significance by t-tests ≤ .05.
**Significance by t-test ≤ .005.
NOTE: Scores ranged from 1 (hardly ever bothered) to 4 (bothered all the time).
SOURCE: Adapted from Amsden, 1982.

TABLE 11.3   Percentages of Adult Children and Elderly Parents
Utilizing Various Conflict Resolution Techniques (N = 118)

Methods	Child to Parent	Parent to Child
Talked	83.0	–
Sought advice	61.9	–
Considered alternative housing	21.7	–
Threatened nursing home	8.6	–
Pout/withdraw	–	59.8
Confined to room	1.7	–
Manipulated others	–	42.6
Imposed Guilt	–	49.6
Used disability to gain sympathy	–	32.5
Forced food	3.5	–
Refused food	–	16.1
Withheld food	3.5	–
Forced medication	13.9	–
Refused medication	–	12.8
Scream and yell	42.7	34.8
Cry	–	37.9
Called police	–	6.3
Physically restrained	7.9	–
Threatened physical force	4.3	–
Slapped, hit with object, shake	.9	18.6
Doesn't respect privacy	–	40.2

Screaming also was frequently used by a sizable number of adult children and their parents (see Table 11.3).

The technique caregivers reported that elders used most frequently as a control mechanism was to pout or withdraw. Sixty percent of the elders used this method as a means of dealing with conflict. Other psychological methods used by elderly included manipulation, especially pitting one family member against another (43 percent), crying (38 percent), using their disabilities to gain sympathy (33 percent), or imposing guilt (50 percent).

Adult children also utilized a variety of methods of problem solving. Sixty-two percent sought the advice of a third party, 22 percent considered alternative housing, and 9 percent threatened to send the elder to a nursing home. Since 16 percent of the elders refused food and 13 percent refused medication, it is not surprising that 4 percent of the children resorted to forcing food and 14 percent used force to medicate an elder. Four percent withheld food, but it tended to be done for dietary reasons (for example, keeping sweets from a diabetic elder).

As a result of conflicting demands, abusive and neglectful methods often become the method of last resort. The data in Table 11.3 reveal a variety of negative methods of control, although many times they were used to keep the elder from danger (physical restraint of the elder, which was used by 8 percent of the caregivers). Physical force was threatened by 4 percent of the caregivers, and physical force was actually used by 1 percent of the caregivers. The data in Table 11.3 also indicate that the violence is not unidirectional. Nineteen percent of the elders slapped, hit with an object, or threw something at their adult child caregiver. Some of the methods used by elders in their attempt to maintain control were perceived by the caregivers as incidents that precipitated the decision to arrange for alternative caregiving.

Burden

One of the final items in the interview schedule asked the caregivers whether they felt a sense of burden as a result of their caregiving role. We felt that while caregivers might state that providing certain tasks was stressful, they still might not perceive the overall responsibility as burdensome. Likewise, some caregivers might not consider providing these tasks stressful, but the overall responsibility or some untapped aspect of caregiving might result in these caregivers feeling a sense of burden as a result of the caregiving role. The data supported this position. While 64 percent of the caregivers reported a sense of burden, this was apparently not related to the performance of tasks for elders (Amsden, 1982). When the 34 tasks performed for elders were examined, burdened and non-burdened caregivers differed significantly only on the items "bathing the elder" and "helping with decision making."

However, when the stress resulting from performing these tasks was compared for burdened and nonburdened caregivers, burdened caregivers tended to report a greater degree of stress as a result of the elder's dependencies (See Table 11.2), and six of the thirteen items compared were significant. Three of the six significant items were in the social/emotional area (elder is lonely, elder makes excessive demands, elder has an emotional/mental disability); the remaining items tapped the stress resulting from additional chores being performed by the caregiver (household management, personal grooming, and transportation).

These findings provide support that neither stress resulting from caregiving tasks nor performing the tasks themselves necessarily produces the overall feeling of being burdened by the responsibility of caring for an elder. In fact, many more families report being stressed by some aspect of caregiving than that they are burdened.

The Relationship Among Dependency, Stress, Burden, and Abuse

Studies reviewed earlier as well as the data reported above suggest that the elder's dependency is often stress producing. Since stress has been closely linked to other areas of family violence (see Steinmetz, 1978, 1980, in press, for reviews of this literature), one might expect a relationship to exist between the stress resulting from the provision of tasks and feelings of burden and abusive forms of interaction between elders and caregivers.

Dependency and Abuse. While one could expect a significant relationship between "forced" the elder to take medication against his or her will and the variable measuring health care tasks (totperth), "force medication" was also significantly correlated with financial dependency (totfin), mobility (totmob), social/emotional dependency (totemot), mental health dependency (totmen) and an overall measure of dependency (totdep). This may indicate that by the time the elder is dependent on the caregiver for basic medication, all other needs are being fulfilled by the caregiver. It is interesting to note that household dependency (tothous) was not correlated with forced medication. Since household tasks are provided by almost all caregivers, the providing of this task may not be affected by the elders' level of dependency in other areas.

One of the most interesting relationships, because it illustrates the importance of educational and support services to caregivers, is that between the elder's level of mental health dependency (totmen) and elder's and caregiver's use of verbal and physical abuse. For caregivers, the correlations were .46 for screaming/yelling and .18 for hitting/slapping; for elders, the correlations were .21 and .49 respectively. In fact, the variable "elder hits/slaps/throws" produced high, significant correlations with all the dependency variables except household management (tothous) and mobility (totmob). This might reflect the elder's loss of other means to gain control (lack of money, loss of ability to maintain social life, dependency on caregiver for health and grooming needs, as well as the mental health variable, which measures nonrational and explosive behavior).

Likewise, when one examines the variable that encompasses all aspects of mental health dependency (see Table 11.1), it appears that this

188

TABLE 11.4 Correlation Matrix

Conflict Resolution Technique	F:indep	C:romdep	E:motdep	Physdep	Mobscn	Noleat	Dietned	Lonely	Demand	Houseman	Transp	Privac	Rolmain	Disrupt	Tothous	Totperh	Totl:in	Totmob	Totmot	Totmen	Totdep	Sense of Burden
						Stress										Dependency						Burdened
CAREGIVER																						
Talked	07	-12	11	22*	-08	12	-07	19*	01	-12	-12	-06	02	08	0	04	-09	11	11	-02	04	-22*
Screamed/yelled	05	25*	34*	24*	44*	18	-03	11	12	19*	20*	18*	-03	-13	10	20*	14	06	12	46*	25*	09
Physical restraint	03	12	24*	20*	32*	06	0	29*	22*	33*	11	05	02	-02	05	13	26*	21*	16*	27*	24*	15
Forced feed	-10	02	11	0	16	36*	-08	07	-05	18*	-04	-13	-05	-07	07	25*	04	28*	-06	16*	17*	13
Withheld food	-10	-05	17	24*	13	-03	-11	10	-04	-07	-06	-14	-05	-07	04	06	11	06	-07	03	05	06
Threat/nursing home	03	17	17	10	20	11	-01	10	16	07	10	04	-08	-11	17*	-03	12	16*	16*	18*	20*	04
Threat physical force	-06	21*	17	03	19	-06	-01	09	20*	07	08	03	04	-01	03	-01	02	05	01	07	03	05
Confine/room	39*	08	07	-02	04	04	–	02	03	01	0	-07	-04	-05	05	12	07	17*	-05	10	07	-08
Hit/slap	–	12	-01	04	04	09	–	–	03	05	11	04	-03	-04	08	03	04	12	12	18*	13	07
Give medication	23*	15	38*	32*	40*	18	-04	08	.17*	08	17*	0	-08	0	04	29*	21*	20*	24*	44*	33*	16*
Seek advice	16	30*	19	16	30*	27*	11	25*	32*	31*	18*	01	11	03	07	20*	11	06	18*	38*	23*	30*
Alternate housing	25*	10	28*	17	29*	05	-10	27*	10	07	01	27*	-05	18*	19*	04	-06	-01	02	33*	12	02
ELDER																						
Screamed/yell	12	21*	28*	04	16	24*	0	34*	37*	21*	18*	14	09	08	-13	-01	12	05	09	21*	06	10
Pout/withdraw	23*	17*	15	18	17	-03	14	26*	40*	04	25*	-05	-05	05	-03	-01	09	12	11	19*	10	05
Refuse to eat	46*	21*	25*	03	37*	50*	01	03	20*	04	20*	06	-07	-02	17*	18*	22*	05	24*	33*	28*	-05
Refuse medical treatment	24*	06	10	14	05	24*	-01	11	12	16*	23*	09	-03	11	03	03	-01	06	15*	24*	11	08
Manipulate	36*	10	28*	17	16	06	51*	17*	54*	23*	42*	29*	11	-07	-11	-14	02	-02	-08	05	-08	20*
Cry	39*	12	14	07	05	07	20*	13	25*	-01	45*	02	0	06	-07	08	16*	10	24*	30*	18*	02
Hit/slap/throw	33*	32*	34*	12	48*	29*	09	21*	21*	19*	29*	33*	05	-07	15	29*	29*	09	30*	49*	38*	11
Use disability	40*	14	10	07	08	13	31*	23*	51*	09	44*	20*	06	18*	-01	08	21*	15*	29*	26*	22*	15
Call police	42*	26*	29*	06	35*	23*	15	11	26*	23*	27*	29*	-06	-09	09	14	19*	-01	25*	33*	24*	16*
Impose guilt	42*	24*	14	07	12	07	22*	27*	54*	19*	27*	26*	09	13	-10	-09	14	-04	24*	22*	07	13
Doesn't respect privacy	24*	15	08	03	08	06	23*	29*	42*	26*	39*	35*	18*	23*								

TABLE 11.4   Continued

Stresses:

Findep—elder financially dependent
Gromdep—elder needs help with personal grooming
Emotdep—elder has severe emotional/mental disability
Physdep—elder has severe physical disability
Mobsen—elder is mobile but senile
Noteat—elder won't eat
Dietned—elder has special dietary needs
Lonely—elder is lonely
Demand—elder makes excessive demands
Housman—household management
Transp—elder needs transportation
Privac—privacy
Rolmain—maintain authority role in family
Disrupt—elder is disruptive to family lifestyle

Dependency:

Tothous—total score for all household tasks
Totperh—total score for all personal grooming/health care tasks
Totfin—total score for all financial tasks
Totmob—total score for all mobility tasks
Totmot—total score for all emotional/social tasks
Totmen—total score for all mental health tasks

*Significant at ⩽ .05.

set of tasks is significantly correlated with abusive techniques of problem solving for both caregivers and elders. In addition to caregivers "yelling and hitting" as noted above, significant correlations were found for the use of physical restraints (.27), forced feeding (.16), threats to send to a nursing home (.18), and giving medication (.44). Furthermore, mental health dependency was highly correlated with seeking advice (.38) and seeking alternative housing for elder (.33). Mental health problems were correlated with pouting or withdrawing to one's room (.19), refusing to eat (.33), refusing medical treatment (.24) crying (.30), using disability as a way to gain attention or sympathy (.26), calling police for imagined problems or to show caregiver that they had some resources (.33), or imposing guilt (.22). Social/emotional dependency revealed similar relationships.

Not only did the interviews reveal that social/emotional and mental health variables were frequently performed (only household management tasks were performed more frequently) and were reported to be the most stressful, but also they differentiated the burdened from nonburdened caregivers and were found to be strongly (and significantly) correlated with abusive caregiver/elder interaction.

Burden. The relationship between a sense of burden and the conflict resolution techniques is weak and nonsignificant, with a few exceptions. For caregivers, a sense of burden was related to talking to elders, giving medication, and seeking advice; only the elder's attempt to manipulate and calling police were related to caregivers reporting a sense of burden.

Stress. The stress produced by performing tasks for elders was found to be related to abusive elder/caregiver interaction. Caregivers were likely to yell and scream when health and grooming tasks, emotional and physical and mobility dependency, household and transportation tasks, and lack of privacy were issues. Threats of physical force were associated with demanding elders, and physical restraints were used for a variety of stress-producing dependencies. However, out of 169 possible relationships, less than one-fourth (23 percent) were significant.

Stronger relationships were found between the caregiver's reports of feeling stressed by performing particular tasks and the caregivers' reports of the methods elders used to gain control. For example, strong significant correlations were found between caregivers' stress resulting from elder's financial dependency and all methods used by elders to gain control except screaming and yelling. However, only "confine to room,' "give medication," and "seek alternative housing" were reported by caregivers as methods of control or conflict resolution. Likewise, being dependent on caregivers for transportation was highly (and significantly) correlated with all methods of conflict resolution for elders, whereas there were only weak (but significant) correlations with "scream/yell," "give medication," and "seek advice" for caregivers.

It appears that being dependent and perhaps being told by the caregiver of how stressful these tasks were was associated with disruptive, abusive behaviors by the elders. Out of 154 possible relationships, 51 percent (n = 78) were significant, and these relationships tended to be stronger than those exhibited between caregivers and conflict resolution techniques. Out of 168 relationships between caregivers and elders, only 36 (21 percent) were significant.

Conclusions

Family members are providing a large number of caregiving tasks for their elders in the generationally inversed families studied. Many of these tasks are perceived as stressful to caregivers; 64 percent considered caregiving to be burdensome. However, there were few differences between the burdened and nonburdened caregivers in their reporting of stress. Only household management, excessive demands, severe emotional/mental disability, personal grooming, and transportation differed significantly. When the relationship between these five variables and the methods of conflict resolution used by elders and caregivers were examined, a greater proportion of these items were significantly related to abusive or disruptive interaction. For example, 33 percent of the items found to produce a greater degree of stress for burdened than nonburdened caregivers were significant; only 19 percent of the other relationships were significant. For elders, 71 percent of the above five items were significantly associated, while only 39 percent of the other relationships were significant.

Doing tasks for the elders, the stress resulting from the dependence of the elder on the caregiver, and an overall feeling of a sense of burden interact to increase the likelihood of abusive and disruptive family interaction.

Not only have few caregivers gained knowledge through coursework in gerontology in a formal setting, but also few have had the opportunity to learn parent-caring through role modeling. This lack of hands-on experience for dealing with an elder who may need to be fed, restrained, or medicated against his or her will can also result in abuse. Families need to understand the developmental characteristics of aging and accurately assess the limits of their ability to provide care.

The data clearly indicate that social/emotional and mental health dependencies are the most stress-and violence-producing. Understanding the aging processes will enable both the adult child and the elderly parent to communicate their needs more effectively instead of denying the aging process.

The interaction in these generationally inversed families becomes a social concern because of the incidence of abuse. There is a point when even the most dedicated, loving child is ill equipped to deal with the personal grooming, physical, social/emotional, and mental health needs of an elderly parent. These familes will need support services to help them cope and, when necessary, to seek alternative arrangements. The use of services such as visiting nurses, geriatric aids, and friendly visitor and respite programs could relieve the family of these tasks, or, even more important, relieve the frustration and stress the caregivers perceive from providing these tasks and thus may enhance the caregiver/elder interaction and provide a positive role model for future generations.

12

The Elderly in Minority Families

CHARLES H. MINDEL

Discussions of ethnicity and family life have often been the subject of numerous myths and mythologies. At times the myths are positive, at times they are negative, and often they are in contradiction. It is sometimes suggested that there is an "American family" that reflects the so-called melting pot theory of racial and ethnic assimilation. At other times there is a notion of American society as a conglomerate of "unmeltable ethics" existing in a somewhat tenuous societal pluralism. Within these two polar extremes various descriptions of ethnic families are often made. Some ethnic groups are attributed to have more superior qualities than others. Thus we often hear about the "strong" families of some ethnic groups, and the disintegrating and "pathological" families of other ethnic groups. The truth, of course, lies somewhere within all of this, though it has been quite difficult at times to discover where the truth actually lies.

The family is an extremely important institution with respect to the continuation of ethnic identities in American society, and within this context the elderly are often important participants. It is within the family that primary socialization occurs, in which the ethnic culture is learned and in which future behavior is often channeled. The family is the institution that transmits the culture, the important beliefs, values, and norms both of the family and the ethnic group. Thus, it is within the family that a whole range of activities, which are often perceived by individuals as distinctively ethnic, are transmitted. Such matters as the size of the family, for example, or husband-wife role relationships, attitudes toward divorce, attitudes toward relatives and other kin, notions of filial responsibility and support for the elderly, and the larger issue of "familism" and the importance of family life in the social world of the individual, are all mediated and learned.

In the paragraphs to follow, the patterns and variations distinctive to ethnic minority families and their relationships with the elderly will be described. These variations can be categorized into three broad areas: (a) the structure and organization of the nuclear family; (b) the relationships between nuclear family units and the nature of their interdependence; (c) the relationship of the family unit, both nuclear and extended, with the wider society.

With regard to the structure of the family, matters that are relevant to the place of the elderly include authority relations, sex-role differences, generational differences, and the relative importance of lineal versus collateral kin. The interdependence of nuclear families is also of tremendous concern to the elderly, for it is in the exchange network and support network between and among nuclear families that much care and service is rendered to elderly members. It is in this area that much of the research on interchanges between nuclear families and their elderly kin has taken place (see Bengtson & Schrader, 1982; Mindel, 1982, for a review of these studies). A significant amount is known about the visiting patterns, mutual aid relationships, and relative proximity to kin that family members have. Last, the interaction of elderly within the family context and the wider society is another area of increasing importance. Families differ and are changing the extent to which they will relate to an external, nonfamily support system and to what extent they insist that care be provided entirely or mostly in their family. What appears to make sense in one cultural context—for example, the willingness of members to accept aid from strangers or agencies—is often seen as abhorent and a sign of failure and weakness in other cultural contexts.

Discussions of the ethnic family and kinship relations typically have not focused centrally on the elderly, inasmuch as they have been generally concerned with kinship activities and mutual aid arrangements. However, when the issue of extended family relationships is being discussed, it is clear on closer examination that, by and large, the relationships being discussed are parent-child relationships. Studies examining visitation with kin are more often than not examining visitation of adult children with their parents and to a much lesser extent visitation with other kin. Mutual aid between kin usually translates as aid between parents and adult children (or perhaps siblings). Numerous studies have made it clear (see Mindel, 1980; Adams, 1968b; Hill, Foote, Aldous, Carlson, & MacDonald, 1970; Sussman, 1953) that, for the most part, aid between more distant kin is minimal and idiosyncratic. Thus, the studies of kinship relations of ethnic and minority groups as well as majority groups tend to be discussions of older parent-adult child relations. It is in this context, then, that the research on elderly and their family relationships can be viewed.

In the discussion to follow, the distinctive family patterns of the two largest ethnic minority groups, American Blacks and Mexican Americans, will be presented. Generally speaking, ethnic groups that still maintain relatively strong ethnic identities among their members tend to have more closely knit and more highly structured extended kinship relationships. An important analytical point to bear in mind is the question of how much a particular family pattern is a culturally defined arrangement, and to what degree it is a functional adaptatation to a particular position in the stratification system. For example, do members of a particular ethnic group maintain close ties to kin because of family tradition passed down through the years, or are close ties maintained as a survival mechanism in a poverty-level existence? Invariably, both of these factors are intertwined, but it is well to keep them analytically distinct.

Mexican Americans and Their Elderly

Structure of the Family

As numerous writers (Alvirez & Bean, 1981; Maldonado, 1975; Gallego, 1980) have noted in recent years, to speak of "the" Mexican American family can be misleading and potentially erroneous. Not only has the Mexican American family changed over time, but it also differs with respect to urban-rural setting, socioeconomic status, and extent of acculturation. Even though these differences exist, it is probably worthwhile to describe the traditional Mexican and Mexican American family as well as some of the changes that have happened to it. It is also useful to describe this family type in a discussion of the elderly, since for many of the elderly their perception of the family is tied to this image of the traditional family. Keep in mind, however, that this family description no longer exists in many cases.

Three structural characteristics or features of the traditional Mexican American familiy that have been widely described in the literature are familism, male dominance, and subordination of younger persons to older persons.

Familism

Grebler, Moore, and Guzman (1970) have stated that, with respect to the importance of familism,

> the major theme dominating the classic portrayal of the traditional Mexican family is the deep importance of the family to all its members. The needs of the family collectively supersede the needs of each individual member. . . . Mutual financial assistance, exchange of work and other skills, and advice and support in solving personal problems are ideally available in the extended kin group. (p. 359)

This statement is typical of many statements regarding the nature and importance of familism and extended familism in the Mexican American family. In recent years there have been a number of challenges to the continuing importance of this factor (see Gallego, 1980; Gilbert, 1978; Grebler et al., 1970). Gallego, for example, in studying Mexican American elderly in Utah, found that "Mexican American family solidarity and reciprocity and friendship support systems are a myth and this need for human interpersonal relationships is absent in the Mexican American elderly population." He suggests that such factors as urbanization, vertical mobility of offspring, and nuclearization of the family possibly have eroded the natural and familial support system of the Mexican American family for the Mexican American elderly. Gilbert (1978) also stresses that "extended family among Mexican Americans is not a unitary and constant configuration nor do norms of obligations unvaryingly extend over the entire universe of kin." Implied here is that distinctions are made among parents, siblings, children, and other, more extended kin, such as aunts, uncles, and cousins. Gallego (1980) concluded that there were no differences between the Mexican American elderly that he studied with regard to family and friendship network support systems, and Anglo elderly, in that "with regard to children there was no difference between the visitation of Anglo children and the Mexican American children to their elderly parents" and that "all of the recent studies suggest that the family and natural support systems that have always been associated with Mexican American families are no longer there."

It should be remembered that Mexican American scholars have for many years stressed the fact that the Mexican American family system and Mexican Americans are extremely heterogeneous with respect to class, status, and generational differences (see Hernandez, 1976; Melville, 1980; Miranda, 1975). Among these different strata, whether social, cultural, or regional, different attitudes toward the elderly and different expectations exist. It is not surprising, then, that we will find discrepancies between cultural values and actually existing behaviors.

Authority Relations

One of the most widely discussed characteristics of the Mexican American family and one that is most emphasized in popular literature is the issue of male dominance and male superiority. Embodied largely in the popularly misunderstood concept of *machismo,* the role of males and the role of females in the family is actually much broader and more important than the currently popular notions about sexual virility, masculine pride, and the like would suggest. In the traditional Mexican American family, the father is seen as the head of the family, with absolute authority over wife and children. His authority and power are delegated primarily through males; women and younger children are expected to carry out his orders. *Machismo* in a broader context implies manliness, but not just with regard to sexual prowess. Alvirez and Bean (1981) state that it "includes the elements of courage, honor, and respect for others, as well as the notion of providing fully for one's family; and maintaining close ties with the extended family." Murillo (1971) argued that one important aspect of *machismo* was the encouragement of the "use of authority within the family in a just and fair manner." Thus, while *machismo* and its meaning of masculinity and manliness might include to some degree extramarital sexual behavior, its important cultural meaning for the family is its requirement of being a good husband and man to the family in providing for its needs.

Along with the notion of male dominance in the traditional Mexican American family is the complementary notion of female submissiveness. As Grebler et al. (1970) note, "the bearing and rearing of children continue to be seen as perhaps the most important function of a woman, symbolizing her maturity." Traditionally her primary role is of a home-maker and mother occupying a place secondary to the husband and other family members. It has been argued that these traditional distinctions between males and females are breaking down. For example, Grebler et al. (1970) suggest that with increasing urbanization and length of stay in the United States, Mexican American family sex-role authority relationships are becoming increasingly egalitarian. With declining sex-role authority, the historical respect that the elderly mother and father had can also be expected to decline.

Generational Differences

One other very important characteristic of the traditional Mexican American family is the subordination of the younger to the older. Alvirez and Bean (1981) argue that "older people receive more respect from youth and children than is characteristic in Anglo homes." Respect is reflected in speech patterns and in manners and behavior. It is clearly part of the Mexican American culture that elderly are deserving of respect from youth. The pattern of subordination of the younger to the older has been traditionally widespread throughout the family. Not only are the elderly supposed to be more highly respected than younger family members but even older siblings have higher authority and greater power in the family than younger children

The issue of the respect and authority of older versus younger has come under considerable analysis in recent years, and it is clear from numerous studies that this pattern is breaking down. For example, Gallego (1980) found that second- and third-generation Mexican American youth who are raised in primarily Anglo areas tend to devalue the worth of the family ties and the worth of the elderly. He suggests that "with the high fertility rates of the Mexican American population and the emphasis on youth, old age is devalued and ofttimes the elderly feel highly threatened and abused verbally and physically by the youth." Sotomayor (1973), in analyzing Chicano grandparents in an urban "barrio," found that grandparents still played an important role in child rearing, that they were often turned to in times of crisis, and that they still maintained a certain amount of influence over family decisions. However, Sotomayor found that there was less of a role for grandparents in the areas of religious upbrining and the transmission of family and ethnic cultural history and heritage. It would appear that a substantial amount of authority and respect still resides in the elderly, but that perhaps with time and increasing modernization these aspects of Mexican American culture are declining.

Marital Status and Living Arrangements

The Hispanic elderly, in terms of marriage patterns, generally follow the trend of the larger white population. However, as can be seen in Table 12.1, there are some noticeable differences.

Most Hispanic as well as Anglo elderly men are married, but slightly less than half of the elderly women are currently married. The major differences occur after age 75, when substantially fewer Hispanics are

TABLE 12.1   Marital Status of Hispanic and Anglo Elderly
by Age, 1978

| | Hispanic | | Anglo | |
Marital Status	65-74	75+	65-74	75+
Females				
Married	47.0	15.8	49.3	23.5
Widowed	37.1	76.3	40.4	68.3
Divorced	6.7	3.3	3.6	2.1
Never married	8.3	4.7	6.8	6.1
Males				
Married	82.8	66.2	82.7	72.2
Widowed	7.1	25.4	8.7	21.8
Divorced	5.6	1.4	3.2	1.4
Never married	4.5	7.0	5.5	4.6

SOURCE: Data are from U.S. Bureau of the Census statistics, appearing in Jackson, 1980, pp. 129-131.

married. There appears to be a marked increase in the number of Hispanic widows and widowers.

A better example of differences between Anglo and Hispanic family characteristics occurs when the living arrangements of the elderly are compared. Table 12.2 indicates clear differences beteween the two groups. Substantially more Hispanic elderly than Anglo elderly live with relatives, and many fewer Hispanic elderly live alone as primary individuals. Fewer Hispanic elders live as heads or wives of heads of their own households than do Anglo elderly.

In an attempt better to understand the phenomenon of shared households, Mindel (1979) examined census data on living arrangements of elderly. He found shared households (with relatives) rarely included the elderly couple; rather, when the living arrangement did occur it most often involved a "single" elderly person (that is, a widowed, divorced, or never-married elder). He found that 6.5 percent of all the male elderly and 16.1 percent of all the female elderly lived with relatives in 1970. However, when the single elderly were viewed separately, it was found that 34.6 percent of the single males and 37.4 percent of the single females were living with relatives. The rates for Hispanics based on the data in Table 12.2, which includes all elderly, married as well as single, suggest a shared household rate substantially higher than that of the Anglo group. If we could examine the rate for single elderly, a figure

TABLE 12.2   Living Arrangements of Hispanics by Sex,
65-74 and 75+, 1970

| | Hispanic | | Anglo | |
	65-74	75+	65-74	75+
Males				
Primary individuals	13.9	16.2	13.0	20.3
Family heads	74.4	59.1	81.1	66.0
With other relatives	10.1	22.4	4.6	13.6
Secondary individuals	1.6	2.3	1.3	0.1
Females				
Primary individuals	21.4	25.0	33.2	41.1
Family heads	12.6	12.2	7.8	9.8
Wives of family heads	38.6	18.4	45.4	21.0
With other relatives	25.6	42.8	12.2	26.3
Secondary individuals	1.6	1.6	1.4	1.8

SOURCE: Data are from U.S. Bureau of the Census statistics, appearing in Jackson, 1980, p. 134.

twice the national figure would probably not be an inaccurate assessment of the shared household rate. Certainly, a majority of the "old-old" single Hispanic elderly could be expected to share households with their relatives.

Sena-Rivera (1979) has argued that multigenerational households have "never been the norm for Mexico or Mexicans in the U.S. or for other Chicanos, except at times of individual extended family or conjugal family stress or periods of general societal disorganization." This assessment of the normative belief is consistent with other studies on attitudes toward multigenerational families and supporting elderly (see, for example Dinkel, 1944; Wake & Sporakowski, 1972); nonetheless, the presence of this family type is more prevalent among Hispanics. Ramirez and Arce (1981) maintain that there is no consensus on whether the Chicano extended family is primarily a cultural holdover or primarily a functional adaptation. Analysis of data on the persistence of multigenerational households at different social class levels is not yet available.

Kinship Relations and Family Support

While elderly sharing residences with kin, either as the primary household heads or as dependents, represent an important component of the family status of Hispanic elderly, another important component concerns mutual aid and informal support implicit in the extended family system. A number of studies have found that Mexican Americans and other Hispanics have a highly integrated kin network providing emotional and financial support. Generally the exchange of aid and services was higher than among Anglos (Mindel, 1980; Wagner & Schaffer, 1980; Keefe, Padilla, & Carlos, 1978, 1979; Gilbert, 1978). Hispanics also tend to live in greater proximity to their kin; and Mindel (1980) found that location and presence of kin in a community was associated with migration to that community. Mindel (1980), in his study of Hispanics, Blacks, and Anglos in Kansas City, found that Mexican Americans have a more highly developed mutual aid network than the other two groups. Numerous other sources have shown that Mexicans prefer to rely on family for support than on friends or other, more formal sources (see Ramirez & Arce, 1981; Keefe et al., 1978, 1979; Saunders, 1954; Clark, 1959).

Recently, writers have been noting the decline of the extended family support system. Maldonado (1975), Penalosa (1968), Moore (1971), and Gallego (1980) have suggested that increasing urbanization, industrialization, and social mobility have caused a breakdown of the extended family, leaving many aged without support. Grebler et al. (1970), in their study of Mexican Americans, cite increased acculturation and assimilation as also contributing to the decline of the functional aid system of the extended family. Other research has found that Hispanics as compared to whites feel that the government was more responsible than the family for meeting certain needs, such as living expenses, housing, medical costs, and transportation (Crouch, 1972; Bengtson, 1979a; Crawford, 1979).

The question of whether or not the extended family system of Hispanic elderly is breaking down is probably not answerable yet, since historical data on the subject are not available. What is clear is that there are discrepancies between what had been believed to be the cultural norms and the actual experience of Hispanic family members. There is no doubt that there has been a decline of extended family aid to the elderly, especially with the growth of institutional and entitlement programs. Whether this signifies a major cultural breakdown or merely a shift in structural arrangements in the society is difficult to tell. Recent research by Mindel and Wright (1982b) on use of government- and agency-provided services vis-a-vis family-provided services for the elderly found a division of labor emerging. The government and agencies were seen as the source of basic maintenance and survival services, financial aid, food, medical care, and the like, whereas the family provided personal care, transportation, and aid that did not have a direct monetary character. Thus, it may be that it is not that the mutual aid system is "breaking down," but rather that it is taking a different character in light of the role of government and other formalized systems of support.

The Black Americans and
Their Elderly

Structure of the Family

Discussions of the Black family over the last fifteen to twenty years have often been stormy and hotly debated. Though the "Moynihan Report" (Moynihan, 1965) was originally the focal point for discussions of the Black family, issues raised in this report go back at least thirty years earlier than its publication. Most discussions until the publication of the Moynihan Report concerned the problems of lower-class Black families and the so-called pathology of the lower-class Black family. The report acted as a lightning rod, and for a number of years research on Black families tended to be confined to either support (see Rainwater, 1966) or rebuttal (see Billingsley, 1968; Hill, 1971; Staples, 1981). However, out of these discussions challenging the arguments of the Moynihan Report—that the Black family was a "sick" version of the middle-class white family—came a larger understanding of the cultural uniquenesses and cultural validity of the Black family. The argument came to be made that the structure of the Black family is grounded in its own cultural heritage and is not merely an inadequate copy of the white family (see Ladner, 1971; Hill, 1971; Staples, 1981). With additional work by anthropologists such as Shimkin, Shimkin, and Frate (1978), who examined Black extended families in Mississippi and Chicago, a greater understanding of the extended family system and the structure of the Black family was reached. In general, it was found that the larger Black extended family system was highly integrated, was not based on female dominance, and provided important resources for the survival and social mobility of its members. In recent years considerable new work has been done examining the nature of the Black extended kin support system and its ability to care for its members. With respect to the elderly, this support system often become crucial, considering that in many cases formal governmental support systems are not always sufficient. A common theme which runs through much of the discussion of the Black family is the important function of the Black family as a social and psychological refuge, for individual members. For example, Stack (1974) found extensive networks of kin and friends supporting and reinforcing each other, devising schemes for self-help "strategies for survival in a Black community of severe economic deprivation."

The elderly tend to be an important element in the structure of this family system. In fact, Wylie (1971) argued that the elderly are more apt

TABLE 12.3   Marital Status of Black and White Elderly, 1978

	Black		White	
Marital Status	*65-74*	*75+*	*65-74*	*75+*
Females				
Married	40.3	17.4	49.3	23.5
Widowed	48.4	78.4	40.4	68.3
Divorced	6.2	2.6	3.6	2.1
Never married	5.1	1.6	6.8	6.1
Males				
Married	68.6	55.9	82.7	72.2
Widowed	18.9	31.2	8.7	21.8
Divorced	5.8	6.0	3.2	1.4
Never married	6.8	6.9	5.5	4.6

SOURCE: Data are from U.S. Bureau of the Census statistics, appearing in Jackson, 1980, pp. 129-131.

to be included in the Black family structure than in white families. Cantor, Rosenthal, and Wilker (1979) found that elderly Black women continued to carry out instrumental and effective familial roles far beyond the period customary among whites. Their argument was that the elderly Black women were more highly involved in a mutual assistance system among and between family members.

Marital and Living Arrangements

Before we begin a more detailed discussion of the family system into which the Black elderly are interested, some statistical and demographical data on the Black elderly relevant to their family life should be examined. In Table 12.3 the marital status of Black as compared to white elderly males and females is presented.

It can be seen clearly that among the Black elderly, whether male or female, a lower percentage are married both in the young-old period and in the old-old period. Substantially more Black elderly are widowed and divorced than are white elderly.

Mindel (1979) examined multigenerational households in the U.S. population and found that a major change had occurred with respect to the multigenerational household. It appears that elderly who might have lived with their kin have gradually shifted to living alone. While it cannot be seen what the historical changes have been, Table 12.4 indicates that in 1970 the Black elderly were rather similar to the whites. It appears that among the Black elderly there is almost as great a tendency for the elderly to live by themselves as there is among the whites. It has been noted elsewhere (Hill, 1971) that four times as many families

TABLE 12.4   Living Arrangements of Black and White Elderly by Sex, 65-74 and 75+, in 1970

| | Black | | White | |
	65-74	75+	65-74	75+
Males				
Primary individuals	21.6	24.5	13.0	20.3
Family heads	66.5	56.0	81.1	66.0
With other relatives	7.0	14.2	4.6	13.6
Secondary individuals	4.9	5.3	1.3	0.1
Females				
Primary individuals	31.8	33.1	33.2	41.1
Family heads	17.8	17.1	7.8	9.8
Wives of family heads	31.9	15.2	45.4	21.0
With other relatives	15.7	31.3	12.2	26.3
Secondary individuals	2.8	3.3	1.4	1.8

SOURCE: Data are from U.S. Bureau of the Census statistics, appearing in Jackson, 1980.

headed by Black elderly couples take younger relatives into their households than do white elderly couples. The lesser probability that the children or other kin will absorb the elderly person into their household is reflected in Table 12.4. The greater likelihood that an elderly female will be a head of a household is also apparent. Cantor et al. (1979) also found that a larger number of Black elderly women were likely to be reporting themselves as household heads than was the case among white families. Cantor contends that this sharing of limited resources "on the part of Hispanic and Black elderly suggests a positively adaptive method of meeting the pressures of poverty and unemployment within a functional family system."

Kinship Relations and Family Support

Discussions of kinship in the United States usually cover three areas, affectional attachments, interaction, and mutual assistance. There is a growing literature on the Black family describing the components of the kinship system. For example, in an earlier section it was shown that the proportion of extended family households among Blacks is slightly higher than among whites, but definitely lower than for Hispanics. There is also a growing literature on the kinship interaction among Black families as well as the system of mutual aid and support that persists and exists within Black families.

Staples (1981) has claimed that it is "generally acknowledged that the Black kinship network is more extensive and cohesive than kinship bonds among the white population." It appears from the research that for Blacks the kinship network serves its members most effectively as a functional mutual aid system. Numerous studies have shown the Black relatives help each other with financial aid, child care, advice, and other supports to a rather extensive degree (Aschenbrenner, 1975; Hill, 1971; Martin & Martin, 1978; Shimkin et al., 1978; Stack, 1974). Mindel (1980), in a study of Anglos, Blacks, and Hispanics in Kansas City, found that both the Blacks and the Hispanics had higher levels of interaction and exchange of aid with kin than Anglos, but that the Blacks actually had a more functional aid system than the Hispanics. Curran (1978) found that elderly Black women as compared to elderly white women had a substantially greater use of both formal and informal support systems and a larger social network.

On the other hand, there have been a number of studies that have found relatively few differences by race among the elderly in participation with family and kin. For example, Cantor (1979) found relatively minor differences between elderly Black women and elderly white women in terms of emotional ties and interaction with relatives. Rubenstein (1971) also found relatively few differences by race in terms of participation. Hays and Mindel (1973) and Mindel (1980) found that Blacks interacted with family members to a greater degree than whites, but differences were not always very large.

Two recent studies by Mindel and Wright (1982a, 1982b) have served to clarify the relationship between the informal support system as represented by the kinship group and the formal support system as represented by the kinship group and the formal support system existing in the community with respect to aid to the elderly. In the first study on a national sample of elderly, Mindel and Wright (1982a) examined the multiple factors that predict the use of formally provided social services by Black and white elderly. Each group was analyzed separately on the same factors. It was found, contrary to some views which suggest that either one receives aid from one's informal kinship system or one receives aid from the formal support system of government and voluntary agencies, that for Black elderly, the two support systems were not alternative systems but rather they were supplements and/or complements to each other. Black elderly who tended to receive aid from family and kin groups were also the ones who needed and used the greatest number of formally supplied social services as well. Rather than serving as an alternative support system, the family appeared to be providing supplemental aid to those in greatest need. Curiously, this relationship between the informal family support system and the use of formally supplied support was not apparent in the white sample.

In the second study by Mindel and Wright (1982b), a closer examination of the types of aid that both the informal, kinship support system and the formal support system provide was examined for both Black and white elderly. In this study, conducted in Cleveland in 1976, the aid and support provided by both informal and formal support groups was measured in terms of dollars of aid, with each type of aid having a cost per unit of service. After controlling for social class, the findings provided some further insight into findings of the earlier study. It appears that formal and informal support are, in fact, complementary to each other for both Black and white elderly. The informal support system provided certain types of support for the elderly and the formal support system provided other types. Table 12.5 summarizes the specialization of support functions of the two systems. For example, for Blacks it was found that the formal support system provided substantially more of what was called basic maintenance services than it did for whites. These services included financial aid, food, and living quarters. The informal support system, on the other hand, tended to provide home and personal care services, which included checking, supervision, meals, nursing care, and homemaker services. In addition, the formal support system provided such services as physical and mental health services about equally for Blacks and whites. In addition to the division of labor between the formal and informal support systems, it was found that the differences between the Black and white elderly, once the effects of social class were removed, were not especially great. The Black informal support system supplied somewhat more home and personal care services, but the white informal support system provided somewhat more basic maintenance services. The Black elderly received more services from the formal support system than did the white elderly, but only in the basic maintenance area.

What appears to be true from the analysis of information concerning the support system of the Black elderly is that to a somewhat greater degree the informal family and kinship group of the Black elderly provides and sees to it that the elderly are helped. In addition, it is also clear that for many Black elderly it is they, the elderly, who are a main source of support for younger members within their families. In this sense, the support system is a mutual system of exchange of aid. This reciprocal nature of the exchange system within the Black family perhaps explains why the support for the Black elderly as measured in the study by Mindel and Wright (1982b) may mask the true nature of the support system within the Black family, since only the one-way exchange of aid from the support system to the elderly was examined in that study. It did not reflect the support of the elderly to other family members.

Conclusion

Much of the research on American kinship relations in past decades, though not explicit, has concentrated on the relationship between older

TABLE 12.5   Mean Dollars Expended on Social Services
by Black and White Elderly Support Systems,
Adjusted for Income (N = 1354)

Services	Formal Support		Informal Support	
	White $	Black $	White $	Black $
Home and Personal Care				
Checking	.2	.1	3.8	4.5
Continuous supervision	1.4	4.9	11.3	13.0
Personal care	122.7	162.7	725.7	593.4
Meals service	15.4	30.6	36.7	45.4
Nursing care	228.8	475.3	291.8	452.1
Homemaker	68.6	113.3	363.1	416.2
Subtotal	$437.1	$786.9	$1432.4	$1524.6
Basic Maintenance				
Financial aid	137.4	435.7	46.5	18.3
Food, groceries	25.0	62.0	16.2	8.6
Living quarters	118.2	198.5	149.5	161.3
Subtotal	$280.6	$696.2	$212.2	$188.2
Physical and Mental Health				
Medical care	806.9	852.4	n/a	n/a
Physical therapy	98.7	101.8	3.8	.0
Mental health	24.1	26.1	n/a	n/a
Psychotropic drugs	15.9	14.1	n/a	n/a
Subtotal	$945.6	$994.4	$ 3.8	$ .0
Social Support				
Transportation	6.5	24.0	195.0	159.2
Social/recreational	114.5	158.0	n/a	n/a
Administrative/legal	3.1	2.2	4.9	8.7
Escort	.7	1.5	n/a	n/a
Evaluation	.9	1.4	n/a	n/a
Relocation	.1	.1	.8	.5
Subtotal	$125.8	$197.2	$200.7	$168.4
Total expenditure	$1789.1	$2664.7	$1849.1	$1881.2

SOURCE: The data utilized in this table were made available by the Inter-University Consortium for Political and Social Research. The data for the Study of Older People in Cleveland, Ohio, 1975-1976, were originally collected by the United States General Accounting Office. Neither the collector of the original data nor the Consortium bears any responsibility for the analyses or interpretations presented here.

parents and their adult children. Early on, the issue of the "isolation" of the nuclear family and by extension the "abandonment" of the elderly was debated. It has become quite clear that neither is the nuclear family "isolated" nor are the elderly "abandoned" by their children. In fact, it was discovered time and again that the American kinship system was alive and functioning and changing. Elderly parents did not live with their children quite as often as they once did, but this appeared to be less a rejection of the elderly than self-determination and greater affluence on the part of the elderly people. Care and support of the elderly in time of need still is a major responsibility of children of all races and ethnic groups.

The debate on the existence and functioning of the kinship group in the general population has had a similar sound in discussions of minority families. The Black family has been criticized as "sick" and "pathological," unable to care for its own and to produce productive, responsible members of society. An enormous amount of data and research in recent years has emerged to challenge this view. The kin group, it has been discovered, functions as a strong support system for its members, providing a whole range of services to family, frequently beyond the narrowly defined nuclear families of orientation and procreation. As a mechanism for survival in an often unfriendly world, the Black extended family, some argue, has done extremely well. Additionally, the Black elderly are, often by necessity, more active participants in the maintenance and support of family members.

For Hispanics as for many traditionally defined American ethnic groups (such as the Poles, Italians, and Japanese), the opposite view is often held concerning the functioning of the kinship system. Hispanics have often been viewed as having strong family ties in which they "take care of their own." In large measure the data, of which there is not a substantial amount, bear this out. But there are a number of warning signs. Mexican Americans are not Mexicans, Cuban Americans are not Cubans, Puerto Ricans on the mainland are not Puerto Ricans living in Puerto Rico. Culture is not static, and social change based on cultural contact and assimilation has occurred. To describe the Mexican American family and its ties to the elderly as if transplanted out of Mexico from some nostalgic time in the past is a serious mistake. However, this is still often seen in descriptions of the Mexican American family. Warnings of the effects of social and geographical mobility, urbanization and industrialization, and acculturation and assimilation on the structure and functioning of the Mexican American family are appearing, and a more accurate picture is emerging.

Certainly what is needed is more information on minority families and their relationships with their elderly members. Each minority group brings its own unique cultural definitions and meanings to its family structure. Change is a constant feature in present-day American life constantly affecting the interplay of traditional cultural values and patterns with the demands of modern life. How minority groups cope and adapt to these forces is the subject of continuing research.

PART III

Practice and Policy

The third and final section focuses on policy and practice issues concerning older persons and their families. Research and theory about older persons' family relationships are important to the development and implementation of policy. Services may enhance family relationships. To do so, an awareness of the complexity and variability of old persons' family networks is necessary.

Joseph A. Kuypers and Vern L. Bengtson discuss the aging process and social transitions that characterize the career of aging families. Issues of coping with these transitions are explicated. The importance of the interrelationship between generation and the need to be aware of the family history are recurrent themes in this chapter. The Family Support Cycle is presented to illustrate that intervention may reverse the Social Breakdown Syndrome.

The other contribution in the section addresses service provision to older persons and their families. Ellie Brubaker discusses the service delivery process in terms of older clients. The aspects discussed include initiation of relationship with older persons and families, information collection, development of priorities, service provision, and evaluation and continuation or termination of relationship. A number of case studies illustrate the stages presented.

13

Toward Competence in the Older Family

JOSEPH A. KUYPERS
VERN L. BENGTSON

Increasing attention is being given in contemporary social science literature to changes in systems as they age. One such system is the older
family.[1] What normal issues and expectable change does the older
family encounter as it ages? What refinements are required in the
practice literature on family therapy to engage and help the older family
adequately? Are alterations needed in the practice literature to account
for the unique dynamics of the older family? This chapter deals with
these broad questions. It focuses on the older family as an aging system
and explores some of the predictable passages, strains, and issues facing
older families. Second, it discusses differences between older and
younger families and in doing so identifies special concerns practitioners
may have as they attempt to engage older families in corrective action.

We discuss the older family with the following bias. Mental health
practitioners are often confronted by specific problems that shake the
foundations of family life. This is especially true in older families. When
a particular individual or family is embroiled in the uncertainty of a
crisis, the unspoken agenda often involves fundamental questions—of
health, belongingness, meaning, and endurance of the known and famil-
iar. To some degree, older families in trouble share a fear that the order,
structure, and style of the family will be dramatically altered.

It seems wise to hold this perspective in mind as the dynamics and
issues of older family life are studied. It is too easy to let apparent
instrumental concerns (money or transportations) cloud the fundamental challenges older families face. Study of the changing older family
must ultimately address questions of what the family is, how it will
remain, and whether it will be recognizable. Who is at center, by what
rules does the family continue to operate, and what expectations does it
exact from its members?

Positions in the family are quite different, and personal agendas are quite varied. Sex and developmental positions intermix and combine as the family system creates its own form. The older family is a highly complex system in constant flux and reaffirmation. In the face of transitions and dislocations, loss, and death, each of which prompts disequilibrium, the meaning members make of family life and their sense of whether that meaning will endure appears to underly all else. It is in this context that we hope to understand and discuss the effect of change on the older family.

Aging as a Career

A number of popular volumes have appeared recently that counsel older families to anticipate and respond to age-related changes (see Ragan, 1979; Schwartz, 1977; Silverstone & Hyman, 1976). Some changes are expectable and affect family structure (as with marriage and the sudden additional of an affinal family, or birth and death). Some expectable changes mark realignment of position relative to the wider society (as with career shifts, retirement, or entering the educational system or labor force in mid-life). Some speak of interior spaces—where body changes and identity intertwine with fundamental questions of purpose and personal agenda. Other changes may be less expectable (as with off-time death, accidents, economic successes, or failure).

While the taxonomy of change may vary from author to author, all emphasize the inevitability of change. In the developing biography of an individual and the family, normal aging involves continual alteration in the body, in sense of self and social roles, in kinds and extent of personal networks available, and in the degree of integration with the broader society. Change is unchanging.

However, this changeability is not so constant or massive that it serves, for most of us, to uproot our sense of balance, predictability, and membership. Adaptations to these changes, sometimes stormy and sometimes subtle, take place in the context of powerful forces leading toward continuity. Age status position ("mother" and "child"), norms and values transmitted from one generation to the next, family traditions and identities within the family, the place of the family within the broader social system—all are factors that promote continuity in the negotiation of change.

What is the process by which individuals and families maintain their sense of continuity in the face of change? Two perspectives may characterize the enormous range of answers to this question: a sociological and a cognitive perspective. In the sociological perspective, the term most often used to characterize adaptation is *socialization:* the learning of new behaviors and orientations appropriate to a new position or role. Social systems and social institutions prepare families for new roles by providing information, support, guidelines, and reference groups. Socialization is properly regarded as a process of continuous negotiation between the social system and the individual as he or she moves into new positions through time. The efforts of the social system and the individual's integration of these new roles assure that the consequences of change are integrated with ones' past and present social agendas. They assure a sense of continuity.

The cognitive view argues for the inherent tendency, in the nature of thought itself, to incorporate new information into existing structures (Piaget, 1952) and to do so without rendering outrageous violence to previously held perspectives (see Frank, 1961; Diekman, 1973). Peter Marris (1975) has applied this observation to the adult life cycle in his integrative work *Loss and Change.* Marris analyzes the conservative force of thought throughout the life cycle. He claims that the task of the person, family, or community is to reestablish a sense of continuity—in meaning and purpose—subsequent to loss. The process of this re-creation is essentially a cognitive one and is the primary business of grief work. Successful grief work assures a sense of continuity.   As we combine the sociological and cognitive views, we might argue that a primary task of the older family concerns its ability to maintain a sense of continuity in the face of fundamental changes in process and structure. The task may not be easy. We have argued elsewhere (Kuypers & Bengtson, 1973) that the two foundations (socialization and cognition) that help assure continuity are often inadequate in regard to the older family. The social context of aging creates vulnerability by withdrawing much of the support provided in earlier years. Normative guidance as to what successful and healthy aging entails is poorly articulated. This is especially true for older families. Established roles are literally lost (through death or ill health) or withdrawn (as with retirement and child launching). Reference groups that provide arenas for activity and identity tend to be youth-oriented or stratified by factors other than age. We would claim that this social context creates vulnerability in the older family. This vulnerability increases, according to our previous argument, the likelihood of social breakdown and incompetence.

In regard to the cognitive perspective, we would argue that the capacity to reestablish a continuity of meaning and purpose is difficult insofar as a person's or family's images of aging and late life are borrowed from cultural stereotypes and myth. We intend to expand on this latter issue throughout the remainder of this chaper. For now, however, we want to underscore that the aging family is placed in a vulnerable position as it encounters change.

The operative question, for clinicians concerned with assisting troubled older families and for theoreticians concerned with sorting out the laws of adaptation to change, is centrally one of vulnerability. What accounts for the relative failure of some individuals facing the inevitable changes in late life? What factors predict personal or family vulnerability? To what degree is the family's own history adequate preparation for successfully dealing with grief work? And how is vulnerability created by the negatively toned or underdeveloped social context of aging? It is to these questions that we now turn our attention as we attempt to give a sensitive focus to the complex issues and processes involved.

Expectable Transitions in Old Age: Four Crises in Well-Being

The career of aging families is frequently marked by four events that involve significant transitions. These events, expectable in the sense that one only has to live long enough and they will probably be encountered, include (a) independence of children, the "empty nest"; (b) retirement from employment; (c) incapacitating illness that may require institutionalization; and (d) disruption of the family unit through death or divorce. Each of these events involves other family members as willing or unwilling participants in the negotiation of change. Obviously, not all persons experience all four events. The single or childless adult may miss the first, while a fatal heart attack may preempt all but the first.

Child Launching

The first transition is the most expectable, if least discussed. Most individuals who have children can expect to see them "launched" and living away from the parental home. It is an expectable transition with often unanticipated consequences in mental health or psychological well-being.

Pauline Bart (1968) has researched the frequency of psychiatric disorder among middle-aged women consequent to the physical and emotional leave-taking of children. In her study of 533 women hospitalized for the first time for mental illness, she found a high incidence of depression among "empty nest" females. Some women may be more vulnerable because their identities had a limited social foundation. Bart notes that women whose sense of self was derived mainly from their roles as mothers rather than from their roles as wives or wage earners were in a difficult position when their children left. Maas and Kuypers (1974) found a similar connection for older women. In their work with elderly people, those women who appeared most depressed and least socially integrated were those whose family roles dominated their middle years. Bart, Maas, and Kuypers concur that in these circumstances, the adoption of a "sick role" may serve to provide some centrality to one's identity. A narrow range of roles may create vulnerability.

These negative reactions describe only a few. In many cases, perhaps most, leave-taking of children can be a welcome opportunity for new freedom, as is documented by Hagestad (1980), or it may be unrelated to dimensions of happiness (Bremer & Ragan, 1977). In fact, though the empty nest portends negative psychological outcomes for some women with intense investments in mothering, the majority of women face no such crisis when their children leave home. Evidence from a large national survey (Glenn, 1975) suggests that, if anything, women in the postparental stage experience higher morale than do those with children still at home.

Retirement

A man's self-esteem has traditionally been tied to the work world, and retirement presents the special case for concern in late life. Women's growing work force involvement may point to more problematic labour force transitions for them as well.

It should be noted that studies of adaptation to retirement have not documented a high incidence of trauma associated with leaving work. Few mental disorders are attributable to retirement (Atchley, 1975), and successful negotiation of this role change appears to be the rule, not the exception (Streib & Schneider, 1971). However, although the consequences of retirement may not be directly linked to mental health disorders (Nadelson, 1975), it is obvious that retirement represents a significant transformation in the ordering of schedules, interpersonal contact networks, and sense of self, in addition to changing consumption patterns. Certainly, the older family is center stage in negotiating these changes.

Widowhood

A third expectable transition with old age is the loss of spouse through death. Increasingly this end of marriage has been preempted by divorce. Though the two events are obviously different, they share common features in terms of bereavement and adaptation. Each involves loss, adaptation to living alone, psychological processes of bereavement, and an altered sense of self. Living alone is an increasingly likely condition in old age. By age 65, three out of five women in America are without spouses, and by age 75 the figure is more than four out of five. About one in three men over age 75 is a widower (Lopata, 1973).

The normal process of bereavement includes anger, guilt, depression, anxiety, and obsession (Parkes, 1972). Bereavement may represent a relatively short-term decline in feelings of well-being, or it may linger. Lopata (1973) found in her study of widows that 48 percent said they were "adjusted" to their husband's death by the end of the first year, while 20 percent reported they had not gotten over it and did not expect to. A longitudinal study of bereavement found that those who reacted by becoming depressed were more likely than others to report poor health a year later (Bornstein, Clayton, Halikas, Maurice, & Robins, 1973).

Dealing with bereavement is a family process. Having lost a parent, it may be equally painful for the middle-aged child to witness the surviving parent's continuing preoccupation with the death of her spouse. The relations among surviving family members may be altered by the loss of one of their own. Lifelong relationships with in-laws may fade with the loss of the living link between families. Without parental intervention, sibling rivalries may escalate into bitter breaches. A surviving parent may turn to children in place of the spouse, calling upon them as confidantes, helpers, or beneficiaries of well-meaning administrations. In short, death demands both personal adjustment and interpersonal adaptation, and the family is central in the process.

Physical Incapacity

Chronic health disabilities are a fourth normal and expectable transition in the aging process. A 1972 national survey compared the lives of the disabled and nondisabled (Franklin, 1977). Not only did this study document the greater disability of the older population, but also it pointed out the unfortunate correlates of poor health. The disabled reported that their participation in household activities (shopping, chores, and money) had declined, along with their participation in the work force. Similarly, they reported that they devoted less time to hobbies and to social activities inside and outside the house than they had done before their health problems developed. Day-to-day activities of the disabled were altered markedly by their changing health, a situation with potentially serious ramifications for mental health and well-being. There was little evidence, furthermore, that the families of the disabled were able to compensate for their loss of good health. Although respondents tended to report spending more time with the spouse than in the past, there is no indication that the extended families of the disabled provided more money, household services, or companionship than did families of those in good health.

Incapacitating illness, resulting in hospitalization and then institutionalization, is one aspect of this expectable transition in the career of growing old. At a given point in time, half of Americans over the age of sixty-five have a major health incapacity, although less than 5 percent are institutionalized (Shanas & Maddox, 1976). The longer one lives, however, the greater the likelihood of serious illness and institutionalization.

Taking an aging parent into one's home continues to be an alternative solution for some families, but it is clear that this arrangement poses problems along with benefits. A national study surveyed grown children who had parents living with them and grown children who had parents living in an institution (Newman, 1976). One-third of each group identified at least one problem with the parent's living arrangement. Those with parents in their home mentioned interpersonal conflicts and restrictions on privacy and freedom, while those with institutionalized kin mentioned that the distance between family home and nursing home discouraged visits. They felt guilty about not having the older person at home. Decreased frequency of contact related to increased worry about the relative's welfare. Thus, from the perspective of mental health, parental incapacity poses challenges not only for the parent, but also for concerned family members (Smith & Bengtson, 1979).

Although the thrust of many services for the aged is to maintain the independence of the elderly in the community, it is not clear that community living is always to be preferred over institutional living. For example, a large study of older persons in Manitoba reported a surprising discovery (Myles, 1978). Given comparable levels of illness and disability, the institutionalized aged were less likely to report themselves to be in poor health than were other older persons. The author suggested that the institutionalized aged maintain this perception of their good health because nursing homes are organized so as to minimize the disruptive potential of physical incapacity.

Coping with Change: Common Issues

Our discussion thus far has identified events or transitions the older family is likely to face. In each event, and in many more we have not detailed, a common series of issues is raised. They seem to repeat themselves all along the lifeline of the family, no less so in late life. We will briefly discuss three issues of family life that never seem to achieve closure: autonomy versus dependency, connectedness versus separateness, and survival of the family as a functional unit.

Autonomy versus Dependency

The issue of autonomy and dependency can be seen at each stage of personal development, and the family is often the most central arena for seemingly unending conflict in this area. Adolescents and parents struggle with expectations to loosen family ties and authority yet still supply support. At this stage, parents may fear the dissolution of the family itself, while children may yearn for greater freedom to determine their own fate. In the parents' eyes, the teenagers may seem to demand autonomy yet deny responsibility, while to the teenagers, the drama is more one of control.

In the transitions of old age, one also sees the confrontation between autonomy and dependency. A previously independent adult encounters dependency brought on by retirement, widowhood, and sickness. The older parent may long for unprompted signs of care from their children yet fear being dependent on children. Children struggle with the ambivalence between duty to parents and duty to self. In a national survey that described common fears in late life, the fear of being a burden to one's children was consistently mentioned first (Harris et al., 1975). We suspect that all family members place a high value on autonomy and are threatened by changes in health or living that serve to abridge that value.

Connectedness versus Separateness

The struggle for autonomy involves both generations and is frequently a source of conflict. Often it reflects a second characteristic issue, the tension between connectedness and separateness. Some subsume this issue under the term *individuation,* the capacity to establish and maintain an identity and lifestyle that are not overly determined by family. Hess and Handel (1959) suggest that this is the major issue in family socialization during adolescence. But the issue of family connectedness versus individual separateness persists through later life. Children of the elderly struggle to sort out a reasonable and "balanced" degree of family involvement and caretaking responsibility. Parents may strongly condemn their adult children for reasons of attitude, sexual practice, or whatever. Guilt may be high as all parties negotiate around the issue of how strongly the family will continue to hold power over each other's behavior. Fundamental to these issues of autonomy/dependency and connectedness/separateness are those of power, authority, and control.

Will the Family Survive?

Finally and perhaps most basically, we propose that a recurrent issue facing the family as it ages concerns the fundamental question of whether the family will survive at all (Kuypers & Trute, 1978). Change involves confrontation with the unknown. It prompts concern over what will be lost and what will remain. For reasons that may become clear later, often the unknown in the older family is imagined to be the total loss of family life itself. Hence, parents may harbor a deep-seated apprehension that family life, as they know it, will be lost as children launch their more autonomous existence. Later the children may fear the loss of their hard-fought autonomy if they become more involved with their elderly parents in times of need. Face to face with a family transition (expectable or otherwise), the question of the family's very survival is partly at issue.

Family Involvement and Emotional Well-Being

A comment on the relationship between family life and mental health is in order here. We have thus far argued that the normal course of family life involves negotiation between generations and that the negotiation often embodies conflict. Such conflict is centered often on the normal and inevitable tension that surrounds recurrent issues of autonomy, connectedness, and survival. In making our argument, we have left unattended that question of how family involvement in late life relates to the health of its members.

It is often assumed that family relations influence the well-being of older family members. After all, families are or should be a source of assistance. Families provide a context in which self-concept is shaped. In the public mind, the relationship between family life and the mental health of the aged is unequivocal, one example being the notion that close intergenerational ties promote happiness or that a close-knit family will care for its elder members. All will feel satisfied in the expression of their "filial maturity."

Despite a cultural bias toward cordial and intimate family life, there is surprisingly little evidence that older people without such a supportive kin network are at the psychological disdvantage. Research has shown that intense interaction need not lead to greater happiness for older family members. For example, Kerckhoff's (1966a) study of retired couples found that husbands and wives who lived close to their offspring had lower morale than those who lived farther away. In a large national survey of Americans aged 58 to 63, married men living with kin were less likely to report themselves "happy" than were those who shared housing only with a wife (Murray, 1976). In a South Carolina survey of older widows, Arling (1976b) reported no association between morale and contact with kin, especially contact with children. Contact with friends and neighbors, on the other hand, did serve to reduce loneliness while increasing feelings of usefulness.

Given these data as well as our own personal observation of the intense ambivalences encountered by all family members as they adapt to their aging family, we must caution against a simple notion that *more equals better* or that *closer equals happier*. In fact, the least we hope to have accomplished thus far is to advise that the dynamics of older family life are complex, the issues of change are fundamental, and any image of what is a "good" or "happy" older family must be tempered.

We now turn our focus to the dynamics of the older family as it ages in hopes that this investigation will help direct the clinician to possible differences between older and younger families. Thus far we have implied that the older and younger family face similar concerns and issues. We will now begin to argue that the older family is, as well, quite different from the younger family and that these differences are crucial to explore (Kuypers & Trute, 1978).

The Older Family as an
Evolving System:

The argument of this section is that members of an older family have profoundly conflictual loyalties. While this conflict holds for all parties, it is particularly severe for the middle generation. Following closely from this assumption is that the younger generation is often driven to resist entering into an increased level of involvement with their family of orientation. The younger generation strives to hold on to levels of involvement negotiated in the past. However, the younger family member must often face the prospect of increased involvement by virtue of the losses and limitations experienced by older parents. The younger generation is squeezed. They need guidelines and support to order their choices. Culture provides inadequate or inaccurate normative guidance. Social supports are underdeveloped or hard to access, and the whole family is left vulnerable to moralisms concerning "duty" or "loyalty." The result is often that a family finds its ability to cope pushed to the limit. Social support services, if they exist at all, often do not follow a family system model. They may isolate the elderly from possible family supports and thereby further fractionate the family. Let us take our argument step by step.

Assumption 1: As Families Age, Intensity of Family Involvement will Decrease. Young couples make the choice to raise children with certain assumptions regarding the normal, expectable progression of the family as a unit. One of these assumptions is that the intensity of family life itself will decrease as children mature and eventually launch their own lives. Perhaps the herculean demands of an infant or toddler can be tolerated only because the caretaker knows that the intensity of the demand will decrease. The family is a base from which children must, by social and personal law, take leave. Intensity of day-to-day involvement, of doing for and being done for, of being "on call" and available to help, as well as the desirability of shared family living itself, all follow a natural cycle of waning intensity.

The crucial point for purposes of our discussion is that both the parenting and the parented generations order their thoughts and make plans about the future on the premise, absolute and strongly sanctioned by social mythology, that intensity of family life (family of orientation) will and should decrease. Neither generation expects or hopes for a reverse movement.

Assumption 2: As Families Age, Primary Loyalties Will Transfer. A second assumption is that as intensity decreases, so will the degree to which loyalty is primarily attached to the family of origin. We are socialized to believe that the expected life course entails (1) *separation* from parent and (2) the *formation* of primary alliance with nonfamily members. These become our spouses, children, and affinal families.

As loyalties are transferred, there is the assumption that prior loyalties will decrease in their claim on the person. Often parents have more to lose in this process. Children replace old loyalties with new ones, through marriage and sometimes friendship. The parent may find replacement difficult. Hence, when a crisis emerges in the older family, and if old loyalties are called upon, the children and parents face a different task. Children must balance multiple loyalties, often with considerable conflict and at great emotional cost. Parents must balance their hoped-for gain in recapturing some of the old loyalty with their desire to protect their children from undue responsibility. Neither generation can easily reclaim an old loyalty without considerable ambivalence.

Assumption 3: Parents Care for Children and Not the Reverse. Participation in young families also establishes a pattern around issues of authority, caregiving, and responsiblity. For the most part, the vectors of caregiving are one-way: parents caring until the care is not needed, and parents taking responsibility for the myriad decisions and choices around that function. Young children seldom experience their family role as providing care for their parents. In fact, many family theoreticians describe the family as dysfunctional if and when a child is given the caretaker role. The general point is that children and their parents participate in their young family with one set of assumptions about interdependency and do not expect or plan for a reversal.

How Older Families Interpret Change

Thus far these dynamics present no problem, for they require only a gradual and smooth loosening of family bonds and a lessening in the intensity of interaction. But this may not be the case— especially as the changes we have previously described emerged and the specter of aging presents itself.

Children become acutely and increasingly aware that the earlier expectations of separation, waning intensity, and unquestioned competence of their parents were impermanent. They are faced with the prospect, real or imagined, that a reversal in these assumptions about family life may occur.

Crisis theory helps explain this phenomenon. Crisis has been defined as an upset in a "steady state" (Caplan, 1964; Rappaport, 1962) prompted by the combination of (a) a hazardous event, (b) a subjective response to the hazardous event as threatening, and (c) an inability to respond with the adequate coping mechanisms (Parad, 1966).

We have thus far talked about some of the "events" in late life that confront the family. Crisis theory argues that we must also look at how the events are subjectively experienced. This analysis, then, helps us to understand how one will evaluate coping ability. We have already argued that the transition events involve basic and recurring issues. We have further implied that the natural progression of the family as it ages is toward less intense confrontation. Reversal is resisted. We will now show how these factors may combine to reduce the older family's capacity to cope with the events.

We propose that if an event involves an elderly family member, the *meaning attached to it* by the children will have greater crisis proportions than in younger families. There is a tendency to magnify the crisis subjectively. This tendency has its roots buried deep in cultural mythologies (stereotypes, prejudices, and fears) about aging. Culture defines aging by loss and decay (Kuypers, 1977). Signs of difficulty, therefore, may trigger a view of the future that involves *inevitable decline*. This exaggeration may produce fear that loss and decline have a natural progression into unrelenting and *increasing dependency*. The potential threat for the middle-aged children may be great if they imagine the future in this way. Not only does the path lead to senility and death, but the process of getting there increasingly involves the children. This violates their sense of the "natural" order of family growth.

Family members may find it relatively easy to become a resource in situations in which success and improvement are the expected and presumed outcome. This *hopeful expectation,* however, is often difficult to hold when the change involves an elderly person. The cultural view that aging is an inevitable and constant deterioration is deeply rooted. It is not surprising, therefore, that observers of an elderly person's developng situation may fear the personal implications if they acknowledge that a crisis exists in the first place. In other words, there is also pressure on the middle-aged child to *minimize the importance* of observed changes in a parent. A level of split and conflicting perception may develop. The observing child may be painfully aware of the developing crisis, but the feared anticipation of increasing dependency prompts denial of its implication.

This conflicting perception and consequent use of denial may have many consequences. First, the observer may maintain denial too long and thereby delay action until the crisis becomes full-blown and the denial cannot hold up. The observer may exclude the use of other coping mechanisms as long as the denial is maintained, limiting exploration of other solutions to the developing crisis. On another front, the conflict encourages the use of a third-party "rescue fantasy." If salvation is perceived in the hands of a culturally sanctioned helper (such as a doctor or social worker), the personal threat of a developing crisis is, as if by magic, erased. Perhaps the most devastating effect, however, lies in the fact that the use of denial establishes a family style around resolution of family problems—a style of avoidance and delayed action. Situations may escalate to crisis levels because early solutions are based on avoidance reactions.

Thus far we are suggesting that the middle generation cannot easily commit itself to action in times of older family crises. The middle generation in particular may have a limited capacity for visualizing a positive outcome. Stereotyped fears of what aging is all about distort perceptions of what the realistic limits of the problem may be, and denial is reinforced as an initial coping mechanism.

Not only do older family loss and change threaten to increase the intensity of family involvement; they may disruptively challenge lingering images of one's parents' competence, severely altering the historically reinforced pattern of responsibility, authority, and autonomy. As these issues emerge, the older family may experience a rather basic discontinuity. We propose that this discontinuity of family life, revolving around the many facets of interdependency, is often sufficient reason to explain the middle generation's profound conflict as the family ages.

Two additional factors come into play and in their own way influence the quality and intensity of older family life, especially around times of loss and change.

A first factor concerns the developmental tasks of the middle generation. Much has recently been written about the mid-life "crisis" (Sheehy, 1974; Levinson, 1978). One issue in this period involves the sense that the middle generation is forced into "harness" to care for the rest of the world. The mid-generation may feel overtaxed—economically, socially and personally—as it attempts to meet responsibilities to children and parents. The prospect of their young children leaving home may represent a longed-for release and may signal a new beginning for long-delayed personal plans. The possibility of taking on new caretaking responsibilities, this time for the older parents, may heighten the middle generation's sense of panic.

A second factor concerns the unique history of a given family as to the degree of resolution of basic conflicts. Older families leave behind them, unresolved, some of their most fundamental relationship problems. We suggested earlier that issues of dependency, individuation, and survival are never resolved. By virtue of this residue of abated yet lingering tensions, older families exist in a state of potential disruption, with yesterday's issues likely to reemerge as family intensity is increased in efforts to work together on a developing crisis.

The residues of "unfinished personal business" may involve quite basic issues. Graver, Betts, and Burnbom (1973) highlight the destructive part lingering authority conflict may play. Boszormenyl-Nagy and Spark (1973) argue that work with older families may resurrect unresolved conflicts around issues of loyalty, justice, and indebtness. Brody and Spark (1966) argue that unsettled sibling jealousies are a deterrent to effective family work. Albrecht (1954) argued that the efficacy of older family work is dependent on how the family resolved issues of individualization and autonomy.

We want to unite what these authors are saying independently: *that the historical baggage of younger families is particularly difficult to resolve because of the fundamental quality of the issues involved.* Small matters of family tensions are likely to lose their importance with time. The basic issues, if unresolved, act as time-hardened barriers to free expressions of caring and support.

This analysis leads to the conclusion that while members of the older family are struggling with recurrent and fundamental issues, they do so in a context that resists reversing the historically reinforced expectations of decreased intensity and decreased dependency. Children are squeezed by profoundly conflicting loyalties and share with their parents a real confusion about what is reasonable, fair, and workable. In other words, the natural forces that impinge on members of the older family lead to an increased level of vulnerability in times of transition and change. This is the very condition that increases the possibility that the older family may experience breakdown as it struggles to confront changes in its members.

Intervention

We have presented, for heuristic reasons, a bleak picture of the aging family's vulnerability to breakdown. We do not mean to suggest, of course, that all older families break down, but that, for many, the *conditions* for breakdown exist and must be understood. In this final section, we will begin a discussion of ways a clinician might help reduce vulnerability and prevent breakdown. In Figure 13.1 we suggest some means by which one can reduce the vulnerability of families and older individuals and reverse the malignant cycle of family breakdown dealing with the expectable transitions of aging. We call this the Family Support Cycle (Bengtson & Kuypers, 1981). This cycle shows a reversal of the Social Breakdown Syndrome (SBS) as described by Zusman (1966) and adapted by Kuypers and Bengtson (1973). The inner circle of Figure 13.1 shows the SBS reversed. The outer boxes in Figure 13.1 suggest activities that may help such a reversal to occur. In this section we are concerned only with the outer boxes and refer the interested reader to our previous work for a fuller description of the SBS.

The first step is to reduce vulnerability. This can be done by attending to various input factors indicated in boxes in Figure 13.1. Input A is time-consuming, but crucial: for the professional to spend time clarifying the event with the family—discussing realistically the level of probable impairment after a stroke, for example, or the progression of Alzheimer's disease. Most family members operate in a total information vacuum as they confront a disabling event. Input B involves discussion of the acceptable and limited involvement on the part of family members. The family and the professional should avoid overextension of family resources. The professional should recognize the personal anxieties concerning overtaxed resouces of time and effort.

Related to this, the counselor should alert the family participants to the existence of competing intergenerational demands (input C) and their expectability; at the same time, he or she should avoid being lured into "correcting" historically stabilized dynamics in the family, with their own unique history of roles and coalitions.

An important feature in the Family Support Cycle involves reduction of dependence on external and inappropriate labels—specifically, moralisms and cliche obligations that lead to guilt (input D). Open dialogue on this issue may yield multiple dividends. In combination with a clear articulation of expectations and resources within the family, fear and conflict can be reduced. Family members may be fearful of confronting such expectations openly, but frequently the dialogue itself releases guilt and lowers fears of unreasonable expectation. This can be followed (input F) by delimiting reasonable interdependencies and expectations for the family.

The Family Support Cycle argues for a collective redefinition of the event that has been labeled "hopeless." The professional can assist the older family at risk by identifying feasible and appropriate goals (input G). This may mean (1) resisting efforts of those involved to exaggerate

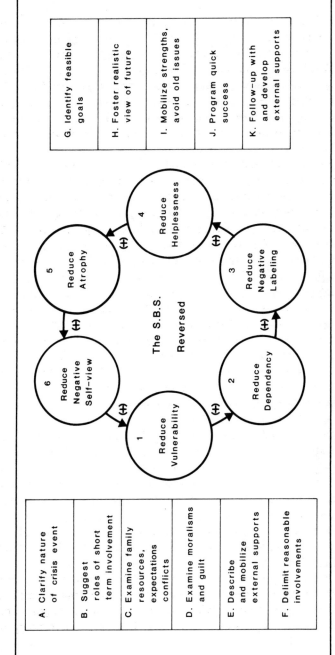

| A. Clarify nature of crisis event |
| B. Suggest roles of short term involvement |
| C. Examine family resources, expectations conflicts |
| D. Examine moralisms and guilt |
| E. Describe and mobilize external supports |
| F. Delimit reasonable involvements |

The S.B.S. Reversed

1 Reduce Vulnerability

2 Reduce Dependency

3 Reduce Negative Labeling

4 Reduce Helplessness

5 Reduce Atrophy

6 Reduce Negative Self-view

| G. Identify feasible goals |
| H. Foster realistic view of future |
| I. Mobilize strengths, avoid old issues |
| J. Program quick success |
| K. Follow-up with and develop external supports |

Figure 13.1 The Family Support Cycle: Reversal of the Social Breakdown Syndrome as Applied to the Older Family

(out of fear or helplessness) the extent of the crisis and (2) grieving the real losses they will confront as they begin to accept the limits to recovery. It is necessary (input H) to foster an honest, realistic appraisal of future developments—improvement and decrement.

Inputs in the Family Support Cycle also call for mobilization of realistic coping skills. This will reduce the atrophy of skills apparent prior to the crisis, and will reduce dependence on external definitions. The professional should focus on strengths (input I), emphasizing what the family *can* do as contrasted with what *might* or *should* be done. It may be useful (input J) to program some quick demonstration of success, to affirm a positive (and delimited) experience of mastery. It is certainly necessary to follow this up by demonstrations of interface with external support networks, realistically identified (input K). This final input is crucial. In indentifying and mobilizing support, by contacting concerned friends and neighbors, by coordinating professional networks, the isolation and fear in older families may be countered. More important, perhaps, by helping develop the network basis of intervention in older families, an important piece of prevention may be accomplished. The efforts, struggles, and successes of one family can be shared and advertised, so to speak, beyond the family. In going beyond the family, all involved will apply these new experiences to future crisis.

Conclusion

We conclude with a caution. As economics and policy shifts combine to encourage the family to assume more responsibility for its elder members, the limits of the family's capacity will be revealed. In our efforts to assist, we must become informed as to the unique strengths and weaknesses that unfold in older families. Our caution is that we cannot uncritically borrow from a theoretical and practice literature that is young-family focused. We must borrow selectively and construct our own perspective based on a clear belief that while the older family is similar to all other families, *it is also unique*. In knowing its uniqueness, we will be able to inform the limits of social science theory as well as to expand the limits of family intervention theory to better serve. To this end, we hope to have contributed.

NOTE

1. For purposes of discussion, the term "older family" refers to the nuclear family when parents and children are all adults.

14

Providing Services to Older Persons
and Their Families

ELLIE BRUBAKER

The practitioner providing services to older clients is frequently involved, either directly or indirectly, in work with the families of those clients. This is not only the case for practitioners who work with elderly clients within the community, but also applies across service settings, (community work, partial institutional, and total institutional situations). In addition to a variety of settings, practitioners involved with older families represent numerous disciplines. For example, the practitioner could be a social worker assigned to a geriatric unit of a state psychiatric hospital, a homemaker/home health aide providing services to an elderly individual in his or her home, a physician seeing an elderly resident of a long-term facility, or a physical therapist working with an elderly client on an outpatient basis in a hospital.

Whatever the practitioner's profession or setting, a service provider goes through a process in providing services to clients and their familes. Although that process may have variations, generally the service provider initiates a contact with the client, gathers information about that client, establishes service priorities, provides services to meet needs, evaluates successive services, and either continues a relationship with the client or terminates the relationship based on the evaluation made. Within this chapter, information will be provided about the practitioner's role at each stage in the process outlined above.

Initiating Relationships with
Clients and Their Families

The initial contact with any client is important to the relationship the professional and client will have. This contact is not only important in itself, but often sets the tone for and characterizes the continuing professional relationship. As a result, it is necessary that the practitioner establish a relationship of trust with the client beginning with the first contact, whether by telephone or face to face. If the client feels in the initial contact that the service provider is not someone to be trusted or relied upon, these feelings will probably occur throughout the relationship and will likely damage the client's reception of the services that the service provider has to offer.

In addition, it is important from the beginning contact that the practitioner clearly identify his or her role so that the client understands the services offered and does not have expectations that will be violated at a future date. As part of clarifying the service provider's role, the provider needs to explain what can and cannot be done for the client and what kinds of specific services will or will not be offered. The worker also must clarify, early in the relationship, the potential length of the relationship and come to some understanding with the client concerning that time period. If the client is expecting to meet with the worker once and the worker is expecting to meet with the client ten times, confusion may result.

For the elderly client it is particularly important to begin a relationship by establishing trust and clarifying expectations of the provider's role. Many elderly clients come into contact with service providers for the first time in old age. For those clients, the service provider is not someone whom they automatically trust and want to share information with, but someone about whom they may be uncertain. When possible, trust is facilitated by involving significant family members at the beginning of the process. This, of course, is not possible where such involvement would result in a breech of confidentiality. The following example reveals the advantages of establishing trust, clarifying expectations, and involving a family member with whom the older client feels comfortable in the initial contact.

Mrs. Johnson, an 80-year-old widow, was referred by her niece to an adult service worker at the county welfare department. The niece stated her concern that Mrs Johnson would soon have to discontinue independent living due to her inability to complete household tasks. After a brief telephone conversation, the worker requested a meeting with Mrs. Johnson and her niece to further determine Mrs. Johnson's needs. The niece stated that she did not want Mrs. Johnson to know that she had called and requested that the worker approach Mrs. Johnson alone. The worker indicated that this was possible but said that it would be much easier for

Mrs. Johnson to accept help if she fully understood why it was being offered. Also, because the niece had indicated that she and Mrs. Johnson had a close relationship, the worker requested the niece's presence at the first meeting to increase Mrs. Johnson's trust. Although hesitant, the niece agreed to do this as well as to talk with Mrs. Johnson first and share with her the reasons for the meeting. After their talk, the niece reported that Mrs. Johnson had revealed her fears about being able to remain in her own home. Mrs. Johnson had seemed relieved at the end of the conversation and expressed a desire for the worker to become involved, in the hope that she could provide some help.

As a result of having obtained Mrs. Johnson's trust, the worker was able to meet with her and describe how their relationship could proceed. At the end of the meeting, the worker explained that she would refer Mrs. Johnson to appropriate agencies (e.g., homemaker/home health aide services, Meals on Wheels) for needed services, following up to ensure that these services were meeting Mrs. Johnson's needs. Mrs. Johnson was initially confused about the worker's role, having thought that she would provide all the services herself, and this was discussed. Mrs. Johnson expressed concern about the possiblity of various people coming to her home; however, her niece agreed that if the agencies became involved, she would be with Mrs. Johnson at the time of their first contact as she was present at this meeting.

As a result of the niece's involvement and assurances, Mrs. Johnson began a trusting relationship with the adult service worker which enhanced future service provision.

Consequently, a trusting relationship, with boundaries clearly outlined, can facilitate utilization of services. If the elderly client lacks confidence in the worker, the relationship may be terminated without the client receiving needed help.

Gathering Information

Generally, data gathering begins prior to or at the time of the first contact with the client and continues throughout the relationship withthe client. Consequently, gaining client information is a process, although major efforts in this area must take place prior to determining client need and services to meet needs. It is vital for the service provider to identify needs and their causes. In order to examine the causes of problems, the professional must investigate the client's environment, including relationships to significant others. To assume that a complete assessment can take place without utilizing an ecological approach is to assume that the client exists without being influenced by his or her environment.

Since the elderly client is influenced by informal relationships and the majority of older persons have informal support systems (usually extended family), assessment of family relationships and of helping patterns is important. The knowledge of the clients within the context of their situation enables the practitioner to deal with problems as they arise. Consequently the practitioner requires knowledge concerning those to whom the client relates. For example, the practitioner may question the client about help received from children but not discover that the older client's siblings are involved in meeting the client's needs. (Research indicates that siblings of the elderly do meet needs; see Shanas, Townsend, Wedderburn, Friis, Milhoj, & Stehouwer, 1968; Lopata, 1973.) Without this knowledge, an existing resource system may be interfered with or a potential resource system may not be activated.

In addition to an awareness that older clients often interact with family members, the practitioner must gain information about what those relationships involve (Miller, Bernstein, & Sharkey, 1975). Social network theory provides a frame of reference for the practitioner seeking to assess older clients' needs and resources. Snow and Gordon (1980) emphasize that the transactions between clients and significant others are important and, if examined, can reveal a good deal of information about the clients involved in those transactions. That older individuals have family relationships is not enough information. The client must be viewed as an individual with unique relationships and idiosyncratic ways of handling those relationships. Several aspects of relationships with extended families may be helpful. These include types of family support available, frequency of family interactions, background information about the family, and family strengths and weaknesses.

Families, as well as others in the client's social network, can provide various types of support. This can include "instrumental" support "emotional or social" support, and "referral and information" support (Unger & Powell, 1980, P.569). However, the family may be unable to provide complete support in each area or unable to provide support in one specific area. For example, the family may be able to give affective but not instrumental support to their elderly relative. Awareness of the various types of support a social network can provide may help to prevent naive intrusions into a client's social network.

The service provider can also gain helpful information by examining how frequently members within a social network interact with one another. Unger and Powell (1980, p. 570) report that "Wellman (1979) and Unger (1979) both found a high positive correlation between the frequency of contact with network members and the extent of help given." Consequently a practitioner's assessment of the client's relationships to family members and their social network may provide information about the type and extent of existing or potential help.

It is valuable for the service provider to ask questions about how the family has interacted in the past. If family members and the client have had a conflictual relationship, it may be unlikely that the family will be eager to participate in service provision to their older relative. In addition, the client may be angered if unwanted family members are included in the service delivery process. Also, the practitioner is better prepared to deal with family conflict if aware of its potential (Brubaker & Brubaker, in press).

To gain perspective on older family interactions, Blazer (1978) calls for the physician to be aware and capable of evaluating family strengths and weaknesses. With the aging family some difficulties are similar to those experienced by any family, while some differ. Problems older families experience that are different from those of younger families could include historical problems with which the family has never successfully dealt. For example, a problem may have occurred years earlier in the family with resentments increasing over the years. The worker who is unaware of the potential for this situation may exacerbate a problem without realizing it.

Other problems different from those young families might face may include dealing with situations elderly alone face—for example, fixed income, adult children still struggling to achieve separation and independence from their parents (Lowy, 1979; Schmidt, 1980), decreased ability to care for oneself physically (McGreehan & Warburton, 1978), poor health (Johnson & Bursk, 1977), or an older person involved in "unhappy second marriage" (Simos, 1975, p. 3). Also, the adult children may feel guilt if they were not the ones to seek help when the aged parent experienced problems. On the other hand, if the family does refer the elderly member for services, the aged person may feel that their relatives have been disloyal (O'Brien & Wagner, 1980).

Johnson (1978, p. 30) suggests that "identification of factors which influence the affective quality of the older parent-adult child relationship" helps open up more areas for the practitioner to deal with. In order to gain the information necessary to guide service provision, older clients and their family members can be contracted. Rosen (1975) describes how information gained from elderly clients concerning their relationship with their families facilitated services provided to those clients.

In addition to questioning the older clients themselves about their support systems, it is possible for the practitioner to request the client for permission to contact the family. It may be that the older person has overstated or understated the amount of help received from informal support systems. For example, the older client could report that the family is providing help when in fact no help is forthcoming (Brody, Poulshock, & Masciocchi, 1978). This may occur out of loyalty, to prevent the practitioner from realizing that the family has not provided the desired help. The elderly client may state that the family is not helping when in fact they are providing support. This could happen if support is less than expected by the older person, or if the elderly person misunderstands the service provider's questions. The older client may have family who are willing to provide help to the elderly relative but who are unaware that help is needed. The aged relative may dislike the thought of becoming more dependent or have difficulty asking family members to provide help. However, if help is needed, the older individual may prefer that family members provide it as opposed to professionals.

The example below serves to illustrate the importance of gaining information about the older client-family relationship.

An intake worker at a community mental health center received a telephone call from Mrs. Jones, who asked for help with her mother, Mrs. Crowley. Mrs. Jones stated that her mother, aged 70, was "either senile or crazy." She requested that Mrs. Crowley be sent to a nearby state psychiatric hospital.

The intake worker questioned Mrs. Jones about her mother's behavior and discovered that Mrs. Crowley was living with Mrs. Jones and her husband. Recently, Mrs. Crowley had exhibited hostile behavior, throwing things at Mrs. Jones and verbally abusing her. This behavior was described as being unusual for Mrs. Crowley.

The worker said that she would like to meet with Mrs. Jones, her husband, and Mrs. Crowley to gain more information. During the data-gathering interview, the worker chose to investigate the possibility that family transactions were contributing to Mrs. Crowley's behavior. Questioning revealed that Mrs. Jones and her mother had always argued with each other and that their current living situation was a recent arrangement. Previously, Mrs. Crowley had lived with her daughter, Carol, but had moved to the Jones's because of Carol's impending divorce. Mrs. Crowley had expressed a strong desire to return to Carol's home. During the interview, Mrs. Jones's husband revealed that the entire family had felt under stress since Mrs. Crowley moved in and that all family members were becoming verbally abusive to one another.

The intake worker requested the family's permission to call Carol and gain information about her perspective. A telephone interview with Carol revealed that she would like for her mother to return to her home and that she could benefit from Mrs. Crowley's help with her children. The Jones family had been hesitant to contact Carol for fear of intruding on her during a difficult time.

Mrs. Crowley moved back to Carol's home; however, she and Mrs. Jones decided to continue to receive services from the mental health center to work on their relationship. Assessment which involved Mrs. Crowley's significant family members, examined past and current relationships, and focused on interpersonal transactions not only facilitated resolution of immediate problems but also allowed the family to work on future relationships.

Gathering information from the clients and their families allows expression of concerns and provides the practitioner with a broader perspective from which to view family relationships. The importance of facilitating family members' participation in the data-gathering process cannot be denied. Family members can benefit from the chance to express their feelings within a professional-client relationship.

Setting Service Priorities

The assessment process will have presented different aspects of the client's situation to the service provider. With this information the practitioner and client conjointly decide which needs should be met in what order. Prioritizing involves several aspects. First the client's needs are rated according to their significance. Second, the availability of resources to meet those needs is determined. Third, an attempt is made to make the best match of needs to resources. Family members will need to be included throughout this process. They are of vital importance to the client's sense of security, as well as to the success of the service plan.

Rating of Client's Need

How does the practitioner determine the significance of each of the older client's needs? This begins by focusing on each client as an individual, engaged in unique interactions with the formal and informal social systems to which he or she relates. This step has taken place during the data-gathering process. However, as client, family, and significant others become involved in setting service priorities, more information may become available to the practitioner.

Basic to establishing the importance of client needs is the older client's own view of what he or she requires. It is important that the aged client be involved in the decision-making process just as any other client would be involved. The older client does not relinquish his or her right to self-determination just because he or she is elderly. For the clients who are unable to make decisions on their own, a "representative proxy" can be selected (Salzberger, 1979). Salzberger suggests that clients unable to make their own decisions do not give up their *right* to decision making, but rather their opportunity. To ensure "right," it is appropriate for those clients that someone be chosen to make decisions for them which successfully represent their wishes. As Salzberger notes, the most representative proxies are often family members.

Finally, involvement of the family in need prioritizing is vital. Without the family's participation in this, the practitioner may lack the ability to engage the family in the remainder of the service provision process. Unless family members are clear as to what services are being provided and why, they may be uncertain about their role in the provision process. Friedman and Kaye (1980, p. 119) report a study of elderly homecare recipients whose families were not briefed about their relatives' homecare service provision. "In 19% of the cases . . . this resulted in disruptive influences upon the homecare plan."

Determination of Available Resources

It is inappropriate to go through the process of establishing needs and suggesting various services to meet needs if those services are in fact unavailable. If required services for clients are nonexistent, the responsible service provider will attempt to make known the need for those services to those who plan for programs within the community, transferring private troubles into public issues, as Schwartz (1969) suggests.

Along with this, the provider may encounter reluctance on the part of other professionals to become involved in the service plan. Kosberg and Haris (1978) report that practitioners from various professions are reluctant to serve the elderly. Should this be encountered, the provider whose services have been engaged by the client becomes an advocate, attempting to convince professionals of the worth of meeting the older client's need. Finally, the provider must seek out whatever services of exist to meet client need. This requires a knowledge of both formal and informal supports available to the client.

Matching Resources to Need

Planning service provision for the older client mandates that services be appropriately paired with need. To accomplish this, available resources are examined to determine their ability to meet long- and short-term client goals. It is valuable to couple societal and familial resources to best meet the needs of older clients. Getzell (1982) suggests that the extended family of the elderly should be supported by human service workers in providing care to their relatives. Streib (1972) refers to this process as "sharing functions." Markson, Levitz, and Gognalons-Gaillard (1973) cite research findings indicating that many elderly persons are institutionalized because of a lack of community resources to meet their needs. These authors suggest coordinated community services in the medical, social, economic, and home-help areas to satisfy those needs. Often community resources alone are not sufficient to prevent institutionalization of the elderly. By the same token, adult families often lack the varied resources required to maintain elderly relatives in the community. The combination of resources available to both family members and professional service providers may allow for thorough tailoring of services that conform to client needs. In addition, the more the older client and family are involved as active participants in service prioritizing, the greater the likelihood of services matching need.

Service Provision

Service provision flows from the establishment of service priorities. Because of the various professions that are involved in work with older clients, this chapter does not attempt to provide specific information about intervention with older clients and their families. Nevertheless, there are general areas of work that can lead to successful intervention in dealing with older clients and their families. Within this section, four areas of service provision will be described. Three types of clients' situations will be examined: (1) clients receiving family support, (2) clients involved with family but not helped by them; and (3) clients who lack family ties. In addition, prevention will be discussed as an aspect of service provision that cuts across types of client situations.

The gerontological literature provides substantial evidence that for the majority of elderly persons, family members provide needed help (Shanas, 1979a). To those persons, the service provider can offer support, education, and supplementary services. For the smaller number of elderly clients whose families are involved but not in a helpful way, the practitioner may wish to provide incentives to encourage family help, model a helping relationship to the older client, or recommend services that will free family members to become involved in supporting their older relative. An even smaller number of elderly lack any family help. These older clients can receive substantial support from the service provider. In addition, the provider can act as a liaison between that client and unrelated individuals who are willing to become "family" to an older person. Finally, primary prevention should be considered as part of the service delivery process.

Clients Receiving Family Support

Families who are providing help to their older relatives, and who expect to continue to do so, may have contacted the service provider for several reasons. The family may simply need answers to questions about the aging process or about resources that could facilitate their caregiving. The practitioner provides services in this situation by acting as an information and referral resource. It would be important that the practitioner not confuse a request for information with a request for services by taking over family functions that are being provided satisfactorily. However, it is helpful for the practitioner to share information with the family about the availability of additional services. This type of support can be beneficial to families' and older clients' helping processes. Beaulieu and Karpinski (1981) suggest that if families are supported by service providers, they in turn can increase their ability to support older relatives. Support can involve informational help, emotional support, educational help, and/or formal resources that complement those provided by the family.

Families involved in providing care can often benefit from education given by the practitioner. As one homemaker/home health supervisor stated, "The families with whom our agency works are often providing help before we become involved. In these situations our service provision primarily entails teaching the family to help their relatives through role modeling." Shared service delivery often allows the practitioner to provide services while teaching family members to take over those services.

Sharing services on a continued basis, without planned family "takeover," is also part of the service delivery process. Families often require aid that supplements their caregiving. For middle-aged children who have children of their own as well as social and career responsibilities, total responsiblity for an elderly parent is impossible, while partial responsibility is feasible and possibly desirable. In addition, family members may be unable to complete some tasks that practitioners are trained to do, as is evident in the following example:

> Mrs. Smith, an 80 year-old widow, lived alone in the community and received a good deal of support from her daughter, Mrs. Saxton. Mrs. Smith also had weekly visits from the county health nurse, who checked her physical condition and administered her medication. Mrs. Saxton had the time and ability to meet many of her mother's needs as they arose, but was unable to make medical determinations. The continuing involvement of the nurse allowed Mrs. Smith to remain in her own home. At the same time, Mrs. Saxton enjoyed being available to aid her mother in non-health-related areas.

Sharing service tasks does not require that the professional provider have an end goal of withdrawing from service provision, as this may be impossible. However, as Miller (1981, p. 421) suggests, practitioners should "supplement" families' services "only with the greatest possible involvement of the family."

Clients with Limited Family Involvement

Families often expect to aid their older relatives but are prevented from doing so by any number of barriers. For example, as noted above, family responsibilities may impede middle-aged children from helping their older parents. Finances are often a burden. Nelson (1982, p. 142) suggests the use of incentives and states that "government needs to foster family self-help in regard to care for the aged as the 'social service system' of first resort. Family policy must emphasize an incentive-based system of supports for existing family helping networks." Lebowitz (1978, p. 117) calls for the use of incentives such as "cash for work lost subsidies" and "tax deductions" to increase family involvement in the helping process. Also suggested are "respite services to provide rest and recovery time" for family caregivers (Lebowitz, 1978, p. 117).

Family conflicts may also hinder family support. In this situation, the practitioner may be able to act as a liaison or mediator between family and the older client. Counseling by the service provider may be helpful (Hayslip, Ritter, Ollman, & McDonnell, 1980), or the situation may require referral to another agency for work with serious family issues. Often the professional practitioner can engage in a relationship with the older client which models the type of interaction that is desired for the family to have with the client.

Clients Without Familial Resources

A small number of elderly (Cantor & Mayer, 1978, report 8 percent of their sample) lack an informal support system. For those persons, continuous, formal resources are a necessity (Cantor & Mayer, 1978). In these situations, however, formal resources systems can encourage volunteers to share services, perhaps by providing emotional support to the older client. For example, an elderly resident in a long-term care facility may require more emotional support than the staff is able to provide. A program that encourages community volunteers to visit that resident on a weekly basis, establishing a supportive relationship, may meet an important client need. The unavailability of informal support systems does not mandate that formal resources meet all needs. Rather, informal supports can be developed and encouraged by the practitioner.

Prevention

Primary prevention should be an aspect of all service provision endeavors. Service provision to the elderly is no exception. However, many services to older clients involve remedial or maintenance work rather than prevention. There is no reason families and the elderly cannot benefit from services that provide family life education. This type of service could alert older families to potential problems with aging relatives as well as prepare individuals to deal with issues before they become damaging.

Congregate meals, senior centers, and well-elderly clinics are excellent examples of primary prevention. Programs of this type contribute to the continuing emotional, social, and/or physical development of aging individuals. As with any age group, problems experienced by the elderly can often be prevented.

Evaluation

Evaluation of the service delivery process follows certain procedures regardless of the client's age. Evaluation involves determination of the success or failure of matching resources to need. If services were unsuccessful in meeting needs, either new goals are set or the service delivery process will be changed. If services have been successful, a decision will be reached about continuation of work with the client or termination of the client-practitioner relationship. It is necessary to include the client as a participant in the evaluation process, whether the client is 20 years old or 82. Similarly, when the client's family members have been involved, whether as clients or service deliverers, their inclusion in the evaluation of services in important.

The following example reveals the value of attention to the family during the evaluation phase:

Mr.Lindsey, age 78, was the resident of a long-term care facility. The nursing staff had developed a close relationship with both Mr. Lindsey and his wife, who visited for hours each day. Mrs. Lindsey often fed her husband, helped him to the bathroom and talked with him. The nurse's aides not only appreciated her help but also relied on her for information about Mr. Lindsey's comfort and needs. Several months after Mr. Lindsey had been admitted to the facility, the social service director requested a routine staff evaulation of Mr. Lindsey's condition and response to services. The nursing staff asked Mrs. Lindsey to be present at the evaluation meeting because of her involvement in meeting Mr. Lindsey's needs.

At the meeting it was quickly agreed that Mr. Lindsey's needs were being met at the facility and that he could benefit from continued treatment similar to that which he had been receiving. However, Mr. Lindsey had expressed anger about his roommate and the staff decided that a change of rooms might be beneficial. Mrs. Lindsey stated that it was her opinion that her husband was not angry at the roommate but rather, at the lack of privacy caused by having a roommate. She shared her own feelings of frustration at never being able to be alone with her husband and of her own need for intimacy with him. It was decided that Mr. Lindsey would remain in his present room but that it would be arranged for Mr. Lindsey and his wife to be alone for a period of time on a regular basis.

Mrs. Lindsey expressed her satisfaction with this. She also requested that her husband attend the next evaluation meeting, stating that he could enhance the meeting through his contributions.

As with each phase of the service delivery to the elderly, evaluation is facilitated when older clients and their families are involved as a vital part of the process.

Summary

Service providers, regardless of profession and setting, increase the effectiveness of service delivery by involving appropriate family members in the client-practitioner relationship. Family involvement can serve to facilitate a trusting relationship between the client and provider, clarify the client's situation, and help establish urgency of client needs. Significantly involved family, working with the practitioner, can enhance the actual delivery of services by making them more complete. Finally, family members can join with the client and practitioner in evaluation of the success of service provision.

Bibliography

ABRAHAMS, P., S. FELDMAN, & S. NASH (1978) "Sex role self-concept and sex role attitudes: enduring personality characteristics or adaptations to changing life situations?" Developmental Psychology 14: 393-400.

ADAMS, B. N. (1968a) Kinship in an Urban Setting. Chicago: Markham.

———— (1968b) "The middle-class adult and his widowed or still married mother." Social Problems 16: 50-59.

ADE-RIDDER, L. (1983) The Relationship of Marital Quality with Sexual Behavior and Interest, Morale, and Sex Role Orientation for Older Couples Living in Two Residential Environments. Unpublished doctoral dissertation, Florida State University.

ADLON, S. K. (1980) "Sex differences in adjustment to widowhood," pp. 239-246 in D. G. McGuigan (ed.) Women's Lives: New Theory, Research and Policy. Ann Arbor: Center for the Continuing Education of Women.

AHRONS, C. R. & M. E. BOWMAN (1982) "Changes in Family Relationships following divorce of adult child: grandmothers' perceptions." Journal of Divorce 5(1/2): 49-68.

AINSWORTH, M.D.S. (1972) "Attachment and dependency: a comparison," in J. L. Gewirtz (ed.) Attachment and Dependency. Washington, DC: B. H. Winston.

ALBRECHT, R. (1954) "Relationships of older parents and their children." Marriage and Family Living 16: 33-37.

ALBRECHT, S. L., H. M. BAHR, & B. A. CHADWICK (1979) "Changing family and sex roles: an assessment of age differences." Journal of Marriage and the Family 41: 41-50.

ALDOUS, J. (1969) "Occupational characteristics and males' role performance in the family." Journal of Marriage and the Family 31: 707-712.

———— (1978) Family Careers: Developmental Changes in Families. New York: Wiley.

ALLAN, G. (1977) "Sibling solidarity." Journal of Marriage and the Family 39: 177-184.

ALVIREZ, D. & F. BEAN (1981) "The Mexican-American family," pp. 271-292 in C. H. Mindel & R. W. Habenstein (eds.) Ethnic Families in America (2nd ed.). New York: Elsevier.

AMSDEN, D. J. (1982) Task Performance and Perceived Stress in Families Caring for an Elderly Relative. Unpublished master's thesis, University of Delaware, Newark.

ANDERSON, S. A., C. S. RUSSELL, & W. A. SCHUMM (1983) "Perceived marital quality and family life-cycle categories: a further analysis." Journal of Marriage and the Family 95(1): 127-139.

ANSPACH, D. F. (1976) "Kinship and divorce." Journal of Marriage and the Family 38: 323-330.

ARCHBOLD, P. (1980) "Impact of parent caring on middle-aged offspring." Journal of Gerontological Nursing 6: 79-85.

ARLING, G. (1976a) "Resistance to Isolation Among Elderly Widows." Aging and Human Development 7: 67-86.

——— (1976b) "The elderly widow and her family, neighbors, and friends." Journal of Marriage and the Family 38: 757-768.

ASCHENBRENNER, J. (1975) Lifelines: Black Families in Chicago. New York: Holt, Rinehart & Winston.

ATCHLEY, R. C. (1976a) Sociology of Retirement. Cambridge: Schenkman.

——— (1976b) "Selected social and psychological differences between men and women in later life." Journal of Gerontology 31(2): 204-211.

——— (1979) "Issues in retirement research." The Gerontologist 19: 44-54.

——— (1980) Social Forces in Later Life (3rd ed.). Belmont, CA: Wadsworth.

——— & S. S. CORBETT (1977) "Older women and jobs," in L. Troll, J. Israel, & K. Israel (eds.) Looking Ahead: A Woman's Guide to the Problems and Joys of Growing Older. Englewood Cliffs, NJ: Prentice-Hall.

ATCHLEY, R. C., L. PIGNATIELLO, & E. C. SHAW (1979) "Interactions with family and friends: marital status and occupational differences among older women." Research on Aging 1: 83-94.

AXELSON, L. J. (1960) "Personal adjustment in the postparental period." Marriage and Family Living 22: 66-68.

BADGER, E., D. BURNS, & P. VIETZE (1981) "Maternal risk factors as predictors of development outcome in early childhood." Infant Mental Health Journal 2(1): 33-43.

BAHR, H. M. (1976) "The kinship role," pp. 61-79 in F. I. Nye (ed.) Role Structure and Analysis of the Family. Beverly Hills, CA: Sage.

BAILEY, K. D. (1980) Methods of Social Research. Belmont, CA: Wadsworth.

BALES, F. (1958) "Task roles and social roles in problem solving groups," pp. 437-537 in E. Maccoby, T. Newcomb, & E. Hartley (eds.) Readings in Social Psychology. New York: Holt, Rinehart & Winston.

BALLWEG, J. A. (1967) "Resolution of conjugal role adjustment after retirement." Journal of Marriage and the Family 29: 277-281.

BARANOWSKI, M. D. (1982a) "Grandparent-adolescent relations: beyond the nuclear family." Adolescence 15(67): 575-584.

——— (1982b) "Relations with grandparents as a predictor of adolescents' attitudes toward the elderly." Presented at the annual meeting of the National Council on Family Relations, Washington, D.C.

BARKAS, J. L. (1980) Single in America. New York: Atheneum.

BART, P. (1968) "Social structure and vocabularies of discomfort: What happened to female hysteria?" Journal of Health and Social Behavior 9: 188-193.

BEAULIEU, E. M. & J. KARPINSKI (1981) "Group treatment of elderly with ill spouses." Social Casework 62(9): 551-557.

BELL, N. W. & E. F. VOGEL [eds.] (1960) A Modern Introduction to the Family. New York: Macmillan.

BENGTSON, V. L. (1973) The Social Psychology of Aging. Indianapolis: Bobbs-Merrill.

——— (1979a) "Ethnicity and aging: problems and issues in current social science inquiry," in D. Gelfand & A. Kutizk (eds.) Ethnicity and Aging: Theory, Research and Policy. New York: Springer.

——— (1979b) "Research perspectives on intergenerational interaction," in P. K. Ragan (ed.) Aging Parents. Los Angeles: University of California Press.

——— P. L. KASSCHAU, & P. K. RAGAN (1977) "The impact of social structure on aging individuals," pp. 327-353 in J. E. Birren & K. W. Schaie (eds.) Handbook of the Psychology of Aging. New York: Van Nostrand Reinhold.

BENGTSON, V. & J. A. KUYPERS (1971) "Generational differences and the developmental stake." Aging and Human Development 2: 246-260.

——— (1981) "Change, competence, crisis and intervention: a systems model of aging and family relations." Presented at the International Pre-Congress Workshop on Lifespan and Change in Gerontological Perspectives, Nijneger, Netherlands.

BENGTSON, V., G. OLANDER, & A. A. HADDAD (1976) "The generation gap and aging family members: toward a conceptual model," in J. J. Gubrium (ed.) Time, Roles, and Self in Old Age. New York: Human Sciences Press.

BENGTSON, V. & S. SCHRADER (1982) "Parent-child relations," in D. Mangen & W. Peterson (eds.) Research Instruments in Aging, Vol. II: Social Roles and Social Participation. Minneapolis: University of Minnesota Press.

BERARDO, F. M. (1967) "Social adaptation to widowhood among a rural-urban aged population." Washington Agricultural Experiment Station Bulletin 689. Pullman: Washington State University.

——— (1968) "Widowhood status in the United States: perspective on a neglected aspect of the family life-cycle." Family Coordinator 17: 191-203.

——— (1970) "Survivorship and social isolation: the case of the aged widower." Family Coordinator 1: 11-25.

BEREZIN, M. A. (1976) "Normal psychology of the aging process, revisited (I): Sex and old age: a further review of the literature." Journal of Geriatric Psychiatry 9: 189-209.

BILLINGSLEY, A. (1968) Black Families in White America. Englewood Cliffs, NJ: Prentice-Hall.

BLAU, Z. S. (1973) Old Age in a Changing Society. New York: Watts.

——— (1981) Aging in a Changing Society. New York: Watts.

BLAZER, D. (1978) "Working with the elderly patient's family." Geriatrics 33(2): 117-123.

BLENKNER, M. (1965) "Social work and family relationships in later life with some thoughts on filial maturity," in E. Shanas & G. F. Streib (eds.) Social Structure and the Family. Englewood Cliffs, NJ: Prentice-Hall.

——— (1969) "The normal dependencies of aging," in R. Kalish (ed.) The Dependencies of Old People. Ann Arbor: University of Michigan Institute of Gerontology.

BLOCK, J. H. (1973) "Conceptions of sex role." American Psychologist 28: 515-526.

BLOCK, M. R. & J. D. SINNOTT [eds.] (1979) The Battered Elder Syndrome: An Exploratory Study. College Park, MD: Center on Aging, University of Maryland.

BLOCK, M. & J. P. SINNOTT (1980) "Prepared statement," pp. 10-12 in U.S. House of Representatives, Elder Abuse: The Hidden Problem. Briefing by the Select Committee on Aging held in Boston, Mass. on June 23, 1979 (96). Washington, DC: U.S. Government Printing Office.

BLOOD, R. O., Jr., & D. M. WOLFE (1960) Husbands and Wives. New York: Macmillan.

BOOTH, A. & S. WELCH (1978) "Spousal consensus and its correlates: a reassessment." Journal of Marriage and the Family 40: 23-32.

BORNSTEIN, P. E., P. J. CLAYTON, J. A. HALIKAS, W. L. MAURICE, & E. ROBINS (1973) "The depression of widowhood after thirteen months." British Journal of Psychiatry 122: 561-566.

BOSSARD, J. H. & E. S. BOLL (1955) "Marital unhappiness in the life cycle." Marriage and Family Living 17: 10-14.

BOSZORMENYI-NAGY, I. A. & G. SPARK (1973) Invisible Loyalities: Reciprocity in Intergenerational Therapy. New York: Harper & Row.

BOWLBY, J. (1979) The Making and Breaking of Affectional Bonds. New York: Tavistock.

——— (1980) Attachment and Loss. Vol. III: Loss, Sadness and Depression. New York: Basic Books.

BREMER, T. & P. K. RAGAN (1977) "Effect of the empty nest on morale of Mexican-American and white women." Presented at the annual meetings of the Gerontological Society, San Francisco.

BRIM, O. G., Jr. (1976) "Theories of the male midlife crisis." Counseling Psychologist 6(1): 2-9.

BRODERICK, C. B. (1971) "Beyond the five conceptual frameworks: a decade of development in family theory." Journal of Marriage and the Family 33: 139-159.

BRODY, E. M. (1966) "The aging family." The Gerontologist 6: 201-206.

——— (1978) "The aging of the family." Annals of the American Academy of Political and Social Science 438 (July): 13-26.

——— & C. SPARK (1966) "Institutionalization of the aged: a family crisis." Family Process 5: 76-90.

BRODY, S. J. (1973) "Comprehensive health care for the elderly: an analysis. The continuum of medical, health, and social services for the aged." The Gerontologist 13: 412-418.

———, S. W. POULSHOCK, & C. F. MASCIOCCHI (1978) "The family caring unit: a major consideration in the long-term support system." The Gerontologist 18(6): 556-561.

BROTMAN, H. B. (1981) "Supplement to the chartbook on aging in America." 1981 White House Conference on Aging, Washington, D. C.

——— (1982) "Middle series projections, all ages and 65+, by race and sex, 1982-2050." November. (Mimeograph)

BROWN, E. M. (1982) "Divorce and the extended family: a consideration of services." Journal of Divorce 5(1/2): 159-171.

BRUBAKER, T. H. & E. BRUBAKER (1981) "Adult child and elderly parent household: issues in stress for theory and practice." Alternative Lifestyles 4: 242-256.

——— (in press) "Family involvement in long term care of older persons," in W. H. Quinn & G. A. Hughston (eds.) Independent Aging: Perspectives in Social Gerontology. Rockville, MD: Aspen Systems Corporation.

BRUBAKER, T. H., C. L. COLE, C. B. HENNON, & A. L. COLE (1978) "Forum on aging and the family: discussions with F. Ivan Nye, Bernice L. Neugarten, and David and Vera Mace." Family Coordinator 27: 436-444.

BRUBAKER, T. H. & C. B. HENNON (1982) "Responsibility for household tasks: comparing dual-earner and dual-retired marriages," pp. 205-219 in M. Szinovacz (ed.) Women's Retirement: Policy Implications of Recent Research. Beverly Hills, CA: Sage.

BRUBAKER, T. H. & E. A. POWERS (1976) "The stereotype of old: a review and alternative approach." Journal of Gerontology 31: 441-447.

BUEHLER, C. & J. HOGAN (1980) "Managerial behavior and stress in families headed by divorced women: a proposed framework." Family Relations 29: 525-532.

BULTENA, G. L. & V. WOOD (1969) "The American retirement community: bane or blessing?" Journal of Gerontology 24: 209-217.

BURGESS, E. W. [ed.] (1960) Aging in Western Societies. Chicago: University of Chicago Press.

———— & P. WALLIN (1953) Engagement and Marriage. Philadelphia: Lippincott.

BURR, W. R. (1970) "Satisfaction with various aspects of marriage over the life cycle." Journal of Marriage and the Family 32(1): 29-37.

———— (1973) Theory Construction and the Sociology of the Family. New York: Wiley.

————, R. HILL, F. I. NYE, & I. L. REISS [eds.] (1979) Contemporary Theories About the Family, Vol. 1: Research-Based Theories. New York: Macmillan.

BURSTON, G. R. (1978) "Do your elderly parents live in fear of being battered?" Modern Geriatrics (November 16).

BURTON, J. & D. B. HENNON (1980) "Consumer concerns of senior citizen center participants." Journal of Consumer Affairs (Winter): 366-382.

———— (1981) "Consumer education for the elderly." Journal of Home Economics (Summer): 24-28.

BUTLER, R. (1975) Why Survive? New York: Harper & Row.

———— & M. I. LEWIS (1973) Aging and Mental Health: Positive Psychological Approaches. St. Louis: Mosby.

———— (1976) Sex After Sixty: A Guide for Men and Women in Their Later Years. New York: Harper & Row.

———— (1977) Aging and Mental Health. St. Louis: Mosby.

CAINE, L. (1974) Widow. New York: Morrow.

CAMERON, P. (1968) "Masculinity-feminity of the aged." Journal of Gerontology 23: 63-65.

———— (1976) "Masculinity/feminity of the generations: as self-reported as stereotypically appraised." International Journal of Aging and Human Development 7(2): 143-151.

———— & H. BIBER (1973) "Sex thought throughout the lifespan." The Gerontologist 13: 144-147.

CANTOR, M. H. (1975) "Life space and the social support system of inner city elderly of New York." The Gerontologist 15(1): 23-27.

———— (1979) "Neighbors and friends: an overlooked resource in the informal support system." Research on Aging 1: 434-463.

———— (1980) "The informal support system: its relevance in the lives of the elderly," pp. 131-144 in E. F. Borgatta & N. G. McCluskey (eds.) Aging and Society. Beverly Hills, CA: Sage.

———— & M. J. MAYER (1978) "Factors in differential utilization of services by urban elderly." Journal of Gerontological Social Work 1(1): 47-61.

CANTOR, M. H., K. ROSENTHAL, & L. WILKER (1979) "Social and family relationships of black aged women in New York City." Journal of Minority Aging 4: 50-61.

CAPLAN, G. (1964) Principles of Preventive Psychiatry. New York: Basic Books.

CARLSON, J. (1979) "The recreational role," pp. 131-147 in F. I. Nye (ed.) Role Structure and Analysis of the Family. Beverly Hills, CA: Sage.

CARLSON, E. (1979) "Divorce rate fluctuation as a cohort phenomenon." Population Studies 33: 523-536.

CAVAN, R. (1962) "Self and role in adjustment during old age," pp. 526-536 in A. M. Rose (ed.) Human Behavior and Social Processes. Boston: Houghton Mifflin.

———— (1969) The American Family (4th ed.). New York: Crowell.

CHIRIBOGA, D. (1979) "Marital separation and stress: a life-course perspective." Alternative Lifestyles 2(4): 461-470.

————— & M. THURNHER (1975) "Concept of self," pp. 62-83 in M. Lowenthal, M. Thurnher, & D. Chiriboga, Four States of Life. San Francisco: Jossey-Bass.

CHRISTENSON, C. V. & J. H. GAGNON (1965) "Sexual behavior in a group of older women." Journal of Gerontology 20: 351-356.

CICIRELLI, V. G. (1977) "Relationships of siblings to the elderly persons' feelings and concerns." Journal of Gerontology 32 (May): 317-322.

————— (1979) "Social services for elderly in relation to the kin network." Report to the NRTA-AARP Andrus Foundation.

————— (1980) "Sibling relationships in adulthood: a life span perspective," in L. Poon (ed.) Aging in the 1980's. Washington, DC: American Psychological Association.

————— (1981a) Helping Edlerly Parents: Role of Adult Children. Boston: Auburn House.

————— (1981b) "Kin relationships of childless and one-child elderly in relation to social services." Journal of Gerontological Social Work 4(1): 19-34.

————— (1981c) "Effects of divorce, widowhood, and remarriage on adult children's relationship and services to elderly parents." Report to the NRTA-AARP Andrus Foundation.

————— (1982) "Sibling influence throughout the lifespan," pp. 267-284 in M. E. Lamb & B. Sutton-Smith (eds.) Sibling Relationships: Their Nature and Significance Across the Lifespan. Hillsdale, NJ: Erlbaum.

————— (in press a) "Adult children's attachment and helping behavior to elderly parents: a path model." Journal of Marriage and the Family.

————— (in press b) "Personal strains and negative feelings in adult children's relationships with elderly parents." Academic Psychology Bulletin.

CLARK, A. L. & P. WALLIN (1965) "Women's sexual responsiveness and the duration and quality of their marriage." American Journal of Sociology 71(2): 187-196.

CLARK, M. (1959) Health in the Mexican American Culture. Berkeley: University of California Press.

————— (1969) "Cultural values and dependency in later life," in R. Kalish (ed.) The Dependence of Old People. Ann Arbor: University of Michigan Institute of Gerontology.

————— & B. ANDERSON (1967) Culture and Aging: An Anthropological Study of Older Americans. Springfield, IL: Charles C. Thomas.

CLAYTON, P., J. HALIKAS, & W. MAURICE (1972) "The depression of widowhood." British Journal of Psychiatry 120: 71-78.

CLEVELAND, M. (1976) "Sex in marriage: at 40 and beyond." Family Coordinator 25: 233-240.

————— (1979) "Divorce in the middle years: the sexual dimension." Journal of Divorce 2: 255-262.

CLEVELAND, W. P. & D. T. GIANTURCO (1976) "Remarriage probability after widowhood: a retrospective method." Journal of Gerontology 31: 99-103.

COHEN, S. A. & B. M. GANS (1978) The Other Generation Gap: The Middle-Aged and Their Aging Parents. Chicago: Follett.

COHLER, B. J. & H. U. GRUNEBAUM (1981) Mothers, Grandmothers and Daughters: Personality and Childcare in Three-Generation Families. New York: Wiley.

COSTELLO, M. K. (1975) "Sex, intimacy, and aging." American Journal of Nursing 8: 1330-1332.

COTTRELL, W. F. & R. C. ATCHLEY (1969) Women in Retirement: A Preliminary Report. Oxford, OH: Scripps Foundation, Miami University.

CRAIG, J. & P. LEROY (1979) Methods of Psychological Research. Philadelphia: Saunders.

CRANO, W. D. & J. ARONOFF (1978) "A cross-cultural study of expressive and instrumental role complementarity in the family." American Sociological Review 43: 463-471.

CRAWFORD, J. K. (1979) "A case study of changing folk medical beliefs and practices in the urban barrio." Presented at the Pacific Sociological Association, Anaheim, California.

CRAWFORD, M. P. (1972) "Retirement and role-playing." Sociology 6: 217-236.

CROUCH, B. (1972) "Age and institutional support: perceptions of older Mexican Americans." Journal of Gerontology 27: 524-529.

CUBER, J. F. & P. B. HARROFF (1965) The Significant Americans. New York: Meredith.

CUMMING, E. (1963) "Further thoughts on the theory of disengagement." International Social Science Journal 15: 377-393.

——— & W. HENRY (1961) Growing Old: The Process of Disengagement. New York: Basic Books.

CUMMING, E. & D. M. SCHNEIDER (1961) "Sibling solidarity: a property of American kinship." American Anthropologist 63: 498-507.

CURRAN, B. W. (1978) Getting by with a Little Help from My Friends: Informal Networks Among Older Black and White Urban Women Below the Poverty Line. Unpublished doctoral dissertation.

DATAN, N. & L. GINSBERG (1975) Life-Span Development Psychology: Normative Life Crises. New York: Academic.

DECKERT, P. & R. LANGELIER (1978) "The late divorce phenomena: the causes and impact of ending 20-year-old or longer marriages." Journal of Divorce 1: 381-390.

DeNICOLA, P. & M. PERUZZA (1974) "Sex in the aged." Journal of the American Geriatrics Society 22: 380-382.

DENTLER, R. A. & P. PINEO (1960) "Sexual adjustment, marital adjustment, and personal growth of husbands: a panel analysis." Marriage and Family Living 22: 45-48.

DEUTSCHER, I. (1959) Married Life in the Middle Years. Kansas City: Community Studies.

——— (1962) "Socialization for post-parental life," in A. M. Rose (ed.) Human Behavior and Social Process. Boston: Houghton-Mifflin.

——— (1964) "The quality of post-parental life." Journal of Marriage and the Family 26: 52-60.

DIEKMAN, A. (1973) "Bimodal consciousness." Archives of General Psychiatry 45: 481-489.

DINKEL, R. (1944) "Attitudes of children toward supporting aged parents." American Sociological Review 9: 370-379.

DONAHUE, W., H. L. ORBACH, & O. POLLAK (1960) "Retirement: the emerging social pattern," pp. 330-406 in C. T. Tibbits (ed.) Handbook of Social Gerontology. Chicago: University of Chicago Press.

DOUGLAS, R., T. HICKLEY & C. NOEL (1980) "A study of maltreatment of the elderly and other vulnerable adults." Final report to U.S. Administration on Aging and the Michigan Department of Social Services, Ann Arbor, Michigan.

DUBERMAN, L. (1975) The Reconstituted Family. Chicago: Nelson-Hall.

DUFFY, M. (1982) "Divorce and the dynamics of the family kinship system." Journal of Divorce 5: 3-18.

DUVALL, E. M. (1977) Marriage and Family Development (5th ed.). Philadelphia: Lippincott.

EISENDORF, C. & M. P. LAWTON (1973) The Psychology of Adult Development and Aging. Washington, DC: American Psychological Association.

EKERDT, D. G. & R. BOSSE (1982) "Perceived good effects of retirement on health." The Gerontologist 22(5): 159-60.

ESTES, R. J. & H. L. WILENSKY (1978) "Life cycle squeeze and the morale curve." Social Problems 25: 277-293.

FARRAR, M. (1955) "Mother, daughter conflicts extended into later life." Social Casework 45: 202-207.

FELDMAN, S. S., Z. C. BIRIGEN, & S. C. NASH (1981) "Fluctuations of sex-related self-attribution as a function of stage of family life cycle." Developmental Psychology 17: 24-35.

FELDMAN, S. S. & S. C. NASH (1978) "Interest in babies during young adulthood." Child Development 49: 617-622.

——— (1979) "Sex differences in responsiveness to babies among mature adults." Developmental Psychology 15: 430-436.

——— & C. CUTRONA (1977) "The influence of age and sex on responsiveness to babies." Developmental Psychology 13: 675-676.

FENGLER, A. P. (1973) "The effects of age and education on marital ideology." Journal of Marriage and the Family 35: 264-271.

——— (1975) "Attitudinal orientation of wives toward their husbands' retirement." International Journal of Aging and Human Developmemt 6: 139-152.

FIELD, T. M., S. M. WIDMAYER, S. STRINGER, & E. IGNATOFF (1980) "Teenage, lowerclass, black mothers and their preterm infants: an intervention and developmental follow-up." Child Development 51: 426-436.

FINKLE, A. L. (1973) "Emotional quality and physical quantity of sexual activity in aging males." Journal of Geriatric Psychiatry 6: 70-79.

FOULKE, S. R. (1980) Caring for the Parental Generation: An Analysis of Family Resources and Support. Unpublished master's thesis, University of Delaware, Newark, Delaware.

FRANK, J. (1961) Persuasion and Healing. Baltimore: Johns Hopkins University Press.

FRANKLIN, P. A. (1977) "Impact of disability on the family structure." Social Security Bulletin 40: 3-18.

FRENCH, J.R.P., Jr., W. L. ROGERS, & S. COBB (1974) "Adjustment as person-environment fit," in G. Coelho, D. Haberg, & J. Adams (eds.) Coping and Adaptation. New York: Basic Books.

FRIEDEMAN, J. S. (1978) "Factors influencing sexual expression in aging persons: a review of the literature." Journal of Psychiatric Nursing and Mental Health Services 16: 34-47.

FRIEDMAN, S. R. & L. W. KAYE (1980) "Homecare for the frail elderly: implications for an interactional relationship." Journal of Gerontological Social Work 2(2): 109-123.

FRIEDMANN, E. & R. J. HAVIGHURST (1962) "Work and retirement," pp. 41-56 in S. Nosow & W. H. Form (eds.) Man, Work, and Society. New York: Basic Books.

FROMM, E. (1956) The Art of Loving. New York: Harper & Row.

FURSTENBERG, F. F., G. SPANIER, & N. ROTHSCHILD (1982) "Patterns of parenting in the transition from divorce to remarriage," in P. W. Berman & E. R. Ramer (eds.) Women: A Developmental Perspective. Washington, DC: U. S. Department of Health and Human Services, Public Health Service, National Institutes of Health. (NIH Publication No. 82-2298)

GAGNON, J. H. (1977) Human Sexualities. Glenview, IL: Scott, Foresman.

GALLEGO, D. (1980) "The Mexican American elderly: familial and friendship support system . . . fact or fiction?" Presented at the annual meeting of the Gerontological Society, San Diego.

GASS, G. Z. (1959) "Counseling implications of woman's changing role." Personnel and Guidance Journal 37: 482-487.

GEORGE, L. K. & S. J. WEILER (1981) "Sexuality in middle and late life." Archives of General Psychiatry 38: 919-923.

GETZELL, G. S. (1982) "Helping elderly couples in crisis." Social Casework 63(9): 515-521.

GIBSON, G. (1972) "Kin family network: overheralded structure in past conceptualization of family functioning." Journal of Marriage and the Family 34 (February): 13-23.

GILBERT, J. M. (1978) "Extended family integration among second generation Mexican Americans," in M. Casas & S. E. Keefe (eds.) Family and Mental Health in the Mexican American Community, Monograph 7. Los Angeles: Spanish Speaking Mental Health Research Center.

GILFORD, R. & D. BLACK (1972) "The grandchild-grandparent dyad: ritual or relationship?" Presented at the 25th Annual Meeting of the Gerontological Society, San Juan, Puerto Rico.

GLASS, S. P. & T. L. WRIGHT (1977) "The relationship of extramarital sex, length of marriage, and sex differences on marital satisfaction and romanticism: Athanasiou's data reanalyzed." Journal of Marriage and the Family 39(4): 691-703.

GLASSER, P. H. & L. N. GLASSER (1962) "Role reversal and conflict between aged parents and their children." Marriage and Family Living 24: 46-51.

GLENN, N. D. (1975) "Psychological well-being in the postparental stage: some evidence from national surveys." Journal of Marriage and the Family 37: 105-110.

GLICK, I. O., R. S. WEISS, & C. M. PARKES (1974) The First Year of Bereavement. New York: Wiley.

GLICK, P. (1979) "Future American families." Washington Cofo Memo 2 (Summer/-Fall): 2-5.

——— & A. J. NORTON (1977) Population Reports. Washington, DC: U.S. Bureau of the Census.

GORER, G. (1965) Death, Grief, and Mourning in Contemporary Britain. London: Cresset.

GOULD, R. (1972) "The phases of adult life: a study in developmental psychology." American Journal of Psychiatry 129(5): 521-532.

GOVE, W. (1972) "Sex, marital status, and suicide." Journal of Health and Social Behavior 13: 204-213.

——— (1973) "Sex, marital status, and mortality." American Journal of Sociology 79: 45-67.

——— (1979) "Sex, marital status, and psychiatric treatment: a research note." Social Forces 58: 89-93.

GRAVER, H., D. BETTS, & F. BURNBOM (1973) "Welfare emotions and family therapy in geriatrics." Journal of the American Gerontological Society 21: 21-24.

GREBLER, L., J. W. MOORE, & R. G. GUZMAN (1970) The Mexican American People: The Nation's Second Largest Minority. New York: Macmillan.

GREENBLATT, M. (1978) "The grieving spouse." American Journal of Psychiatry 135: 43-47.

GREENE, V. L. & D. J. MONAHAN (1982) "The impact of visitation on patient well-being in nursing homes." The Gerontologist 22: 418-423.

GRUNEBAUM, H. (1979) "Middle age and marriage-affiliative men and assertive women." American Journal of Family Therapy 7(3): 46-50.

GURIN, G., J. VEROFF, & S. FELD (1960) Americans View Their Mental Health: A Nationwide Interview Study. New York: Basic Books.

GUTMANN, D. L. (1975) "Parenthood: key to the comparative psychology of the life cycle," pp. 167-184 in N. Datan & L. Ginsberg (eds.) Developmental Psychology: Normative Life Crises. New York: Academic.

——— (1977) "The cross-cultural perspective: notes toward a comparative psychology of aging," pp. 302-326 in J. E. Birren & K. W. Schaie (eds.) Handbook of the Psychology of Aging. New York: Van Nostrand Reinhold.

HADER, M. (1965) "The importance of grandparents in family life." Family Process 4: 228-240.

HAGESTAD, G. O. (1978) "Patterns of communication and influence between grandparents and grandchildren in a changing society." Presented at the World Congress of Sociology, Uppsala, Sweden.

——— (1980) "Problems and promises in the social psychology of intergenerational relations," pp. 181-194 in R. Fogel, E. Hatfield, S. Kiesler, & J. March (eds.) Stability and Change in the Family. New York: Academic.

——— (1982) "Issues in the study of intergenerational continuity." Presented at the National Council on Family Relations Theory and Methods Workshop, Washington, D.C.

——— & M. SMYER (1982) "Dissolving long-term relationships: patterns of divorcing in middle age," pp. 155-188 in S. Duck (ed.) Personal Relationships 4: Dissolving Personal Relationships. New York: Academic.

——— & K. STIERMAN (1982) "Parent-child relations in adulthood: the impact of divorce in middle age," in R. Cohen, S. Weissman, & B. Cohler (eds.) Parenthood: Psychodynamic Perspectives. New York: Guilford.

HAGESTAD, G. O. & J. L. SPEICHER (1981) "Grandparents and family influence: views of three generations." Presented at the Society for Research in Child Development Biennial Meeting, Boston.

HALEY, W. E. (1983) "A family-behavioral approach to the treatment of the cognitively impaired elderly." The Gerontologist 23: 18-20.

HALL, C. S. & G. LINDZEY (1970) Theories of Personality (2nd ed.). New York: Wiley.

HANDEL, G. (1968) The Psychosocial Interior of the Family. Chicago: Aldine.

HARDY, J. B., T. M. KING, D. A. SHIPP, & D. W. WELCHER (1981) "A comprehensive approach to adolescent pregnancy," in K. F. Scott, T. F. Field, & E. Robertson (eds.) Teenage Parents and Their Offspring. New York: Grune & Stratton.

HARDY, S. B. (1981) The Woman That Never Evolved. Cambridge: Harvard University Press.

HARRIS, L. et al. (1975) The Myths and Realities of Aging in America. Washington, DC: National Council on Aging.

HARTSHORNE, T. S. & G. J. MANASTER (1982) "The relationship with grandparents: contact, importance, role conception." International Journal of Aging and Human Development 15(3): 233-245.

HARTUP, W. W. & J. LEMPERS (1973) "A problem in life span development: the interactional analysis of family attachments," in P. B. Baltes & K. W. Schaie (eds.) Life-span Developmental Psychology: Personality and Socialization. New York: Academic.

HAWKINS, J. L. (1966) "The Locke marital adjustment test and social desirability." Journal of Marriage and the Family 280(2): 193-195.

HAYS, W. C. & C. H. MINDEL (1973) "Extended kinship relations in black and white families." Journal of Marriage and the Family 35: 51-57.

HAYSLIP, B., Jr., M. L. RITTER, R. M. OLLMAN, & C. McDONNELL (1980) "Home care services and rural elderly." The Gerontologist 20: 192-199.

HEINEMANN, G. D. (1982) "Why study widowed women: a rationale." Women and Health 7 (Summer): 17-29.

HENNON, C. B. (1980) "Journey through divorce: personal reflections." Presented at the annual meetings of the National Council on Family Relations, Boston.

——— (1981) "A comparison of divorced and widowed elderly," pp. 142-159 in W. Dumon & C. Depaepe (eds.) Proceedings of the 29th International Child and Family Research Seminar on Divorce and Remarriage, Kotholieke Universiteit te Leuven, Leuven, Belgium.

——— (in press) When Your Adult Children Divorce. Madison: University of Wisconsin Extension Bulletin.

——— & T. BRUBAKER (in press) Social Support Networks for the Elderly. Madison: University of Wisconsin Extension Bulletin.

HENNON, C. B., R. N. MAYER, & J. R. BURTON (1981) "Empirical support for and the evaluation of an intervention model for elderly consumers." Journal of Consumer Studies and Home Economics 5: 13-21.

HENRETTA, J. C. & A. M. O'RAND (1980) "Labor force participation of older married women." Social Security Bulletin 43(8): 10-16.

HERNANDEZ, C. (1976) Chicanos: Social and Psychological Perspectives. St. Louis: Mosby.

HESS, B. (1979) "Family myths." New York Times, January 9: A-19.

——— & J. M. WARING (1978) "Changing patterns of aging and family bonds in later life." Family Coordinator 27(4): 303-314.

——— (1978) "Parent and child in later life: rethinking the relationship," in R. M. Lerner & G. B. Spanier (eds.) Child Influences on Marital and Family Interaction: A Life Span Perspective. New York: Academic.

HESS, R. D. & G. HANDEL (1959) Family Worlds. Chicago: University of Chicago Press.

HETHERINGTON, E. M., M. COX, & R. COX (1982) "Effects of divorce on parents and children," in M. E. Lamb (ed.) Nontraditional Families: Parenting and Child Development. Hillsdale, NJ: Earlbaum.

HEYMAN, D. K. & F. C. JEFFERS (1968) "Wives and retirement: a pilot study." Journal of Gerontology 23: 488-496.

HICKS, M. W. & M. PLATT (1970) "Marital happiness and stability: a review of research in the sixties." Journal of Marriage and the Family 32(4): 553-573.

HILL, R. (1965) "Decision-making and the family life cycle," pp. 113-139 in E. Shanas & G. Streib (eds.) Social Structure and the Family: Generational Relations. Englewood Cliffs, NJ: Prentice-Hall.

—— (1971) The Strengths of Black Families. New York: Emerson Hall.

—— N. FOOTE, J. ALDOUS, C. CARLSON, & R. MacDONALD (1970) Family Development in Three Generations. Cambridge: Schenkman.

HILTZ, S. R. (1981) "Widowhood: a roleless role," pp. 79-97 in P. J. Stein (ed.) Single Life: Unmarried Adults in Social Context. New York: St. Martin's.

HIRSCHFIELD, I. S. & H. DENNIS (1979) "Perspectives," pp. 1-10 in P. K. Ragan, Aging Parents. Los Angeles: University of Southern California Press.

HOOK, W. F., J. SOBAL, & J. C. OAK (1982) "Frequency of visitation in nursing homes: patterns of contact across the boundaries of total institutions." The Gerontologist 22: 424-428.

HOOKER, S. (1976) Caring for Elderly People: Understanding and Practical Help. London: Routledge & Kegan Paul.

HOROWITZ, A. (1982) "Predictors of caregiving involvement among adult children of the frail elderly." Presented at the 34th Annual Meeting of the Gerontological Society of America, Boston, Mass.

HUNT, M. (1969) The Affair. New York: World.

—— (1974) Sexual Behavior in the 1970's. New York: Dell.

—— & B. HUNT (1976) "The world of the formerly married," in S. Burden, P. Houston, E. Kripke, R. Simpson, & W. F. Stultz (eds.) The Single Parent Family: Proceedings of the Changing Family Conference V. Iowa City: University of Iowa.

IRISH, D. P. (1964) "Sibling interaction: a neglected aspect in family life research." Social Forces 42: 269-288.

JACKSON, J. J. (1972) "Marital life among aging blacks." Family Coordinator 21: 21-27.

—— (1980) Minorities and Aging. Belmont, CA: Wadsworth.

JASLOW, P. (1976) "Employment, retirement, and morale among older women." Journal of Gerontology 31(2): 212-218.

JOHNSON, C. L. & D. G. CATALANO (1981) "Childless elderly and their family supports." The Gerontologist 21 (December): 610-618.

JOHNSON, E. (1981) "Older mothers; perceptions of their child's divorce." The Gerontologist 21(4): 395-401.

JOHNSON, E. S. (1978) "Good relationships between older mothers and their daughters: a causal model." The Gerontologist 18(3): 301-306.

—— & B. J. BURSK (1977) "Relationship between the elderly and their adult children." The Gerontologist 17: 90-96.

JOHNSON, E. S. & B. H. VINICK (1982) "Support of the parent when an adult son or daughter divorces." Journal of Divorce 5 (1/2): 69-77.

KAHANA, B. & E. KAHANA (1970) "Grandparenthood from the perspective of the developing grandchild." Developmental Psychology 3: 98-105.

KAHN, M. (1970) "Nonverbal communication and marital satisfaction" Family Process 9: 449-456.

KALISH, R. A. (1979) "The new ageism and failure models: a polemic." The Gerontologist 19: 398-402.

—— & F. W. KNUDTSON (1976) "Attachment vs. disengagement: a life-span conceptualization." Human Development 19: 171-181.

KALISH, R. & E. VISHER (1981) "Grandparents of divorce and remarriage." Journal of Divorce 5(1/2): 127-140.

KEATING, N.C. & P. COLE (1980) "What do I do with him 24 hours a day? Changes in the housewife role after retirement." The Gerontologist 20: 84-89.

KEEFE, S. E., A. M. PADILLA, & M. L. CARLOS (1978) "The Mexican American extended family as an emotional support system," in J. M. Casas and S. E. Keefe (eds.) Family and Mental Health in the Mexican American Community, Monograph 7. Los Angeles: Spanish Speaking Mental Health Research Center, University of California.

——— (1979) "The Mexican American extended family as an emotional support system." Human Organization 38: 144-152.

KEITH, P. M. & T. H. BRUBAKER (1979) "Male household roles in life: a look at masculinity and marital relationships." Family Coordinator 28: 497-502.

——— (1980) "Adolescent perceptions of household work: expectations by sex, age, and employment situation." Adolescence 15(57): 171-182.

KELLAM, S. G., R. G. ADAMS, C. H. BROWN, & M. E. ENSMINGER (1982) "The longterm evolution of the family structure of teenage and older mothers." Journal of Marriage and the Family 44(3): 539-554.

KELLER, J. F., E. EAKES, D. HINKLE, & G. A. HUGHSTON (1978) "Sexual behavior and guilt among women: a cross-generational comparison." Journal of Sex and Marital Therapy 4: 259-265.

KERCKHOFF, A. C. (1964) "Husband-wife expectations and reactions to retirement." Journal of Gerontology 19: 510-516.

——— (1966a) "Family patterns and morale in retirement," pp. 173-192 in I. H. Simpson & J. C. McKinney (eds.) Social Aspects of Aging. Durham, NC: Duke University Press.

——— (1966b) "Norm-value clusters and the strain toward consistency among older married couples," pp. 138-159 in I. H. Simpson & J. C. McKinney (eds.) Social Aspects of Aging. Durham, NC: Duke University Press.

——— (1972) "Husband-wife expectations and reactions to retirement." In S. Chown (ed.) Aging. Baltimore: Penguin.

KERLINGER, F. (1972) Foundations of Behavioral Research (2nd ed.). New York: Holt, Rinehart & Winston.

KIMMEL, D. C. (1974) Adulthood and Aging. New York: Wiley.

KINSEY, A. C., W. B. POMEROY, & C. E. MARTIN (1948) Sexual Behavior in the Human Male. Philadelphia: Saunders.

KIRSCHNER, C. (1979) "The aging family in crisis: a problem in living." Social Casework 60: 209-216.

KITAGAWA, E. & P. HAUSER (1973) Differential Mortality in the United States: A Study in Socioeconomic Epidemiology. Cambridge: Harvard University Press.

KITSON, G., H. LOPATA, W. HOLMES, & S. MEYERLING (1980) "Divorcees and widows: similarities and differences." American Journal of Orthopsychiatry 50(2): 291-301.

KIVNICK, H. (1981) "Grandparenthood and the mental health of grandparents." Aging and Society 1 (November): 365-391.

——— (1982) "Grandparenthood: an overview of meaning and mental health." The Gerontologist 22: 59-66.

KNOPF, O. (1975) Successful Aging, the Facts and Fallacies of Growing Old. New York: Viking.

KNUDTSON, F. W. (1976) "Life-span attachment: complexities, questions, considerations." Human Development 19: 182-192.

KOHN, J. B. & W. K. KOHN (1978) The Widower. Boston: Beacon.

KORNHABER, A. & C. KORNHABER (1982) Presented at the Administration on Aging Forum on Intergenerational Relations, Washington, D. C.

KORNHABER, A. & K. WOODWARD (1981) Grandparents, Grandchild: A Vital Connection. Garden City, NY: Doubleday.

KOSBERG, J. I. & A. P. HARRIS (1978) "Attitudes toward elderly clients." Health and Social Work 3(3): 67-90.

KUNKEL, S. R. (1979) "Sex differences in adjustment to widowhood." M.A. thesis, Miami University, Oxford, Ohio.

KURLYCHEK, R. T. & T. S. TREPPER (1979) "Sex education for the middle and later years: rationale, suggested content, and consideration of approaches." Educational Gerontology 4: 333-340.

KUYPERS, J. A. (1977) "Aging: potentials for personal liberation." Humanities 13: 17-37.

——— & V. L. BENGTSON (1973) "Social breakdown and competence." Human Development 16: 181-201.

KUYPERS, J. A. & B. TRUTE (1978) "The older family as the locus of crisis intervention." Family Coordinator (October): 405-411.

LADNER, J. (1971) Tomorrow's Tomorrow: The Black Woman. Garden City, NY: Doubleday.

LANGDON, B. (1980) Statement presented to the House of Representatives Select Committee on Aging, 96th Congress, June 23, 1979, pp. 16-21. Washington, DC: Government Printing Office.

LAU, E. & J. KOSBERG (1978) "Abuse of the elderly by informal care providers." Modern Maturity (April/May): 10-15.

LAVERTY, R. (1962) "Reactivation of sibling rivalry in older people." Social Work 7: 23-30.

LEBOWITZ, B. D. (1978) "Old age and family functioning." Journal of Gerontological Social Work 1(2): 111-118.

LEE, G. R. & M. IHINGER-TALLMAN (1980) "Sibling interaction and morale: the effects of family relations on older people." Research on Aging 2: 367-391.

LESTER, D. (1968) "Punishment, experiences and suicidal preoccupation." Journal of Genetic Psychology 113: 89-94.

LEVINSON, D. (1978) The Seasons of a Man's Life. New York: Knopf.

LINDEMANN, E. (1944) "Symptomatology and management of acute grief." American Journal of Psychiatry 101 (September): 141-148.

LIPMAN, A. (1961) "Role conceptions and morale of couples in retirement." Journal of Gerontology 16: 267-271.

——— (1962) "Role conceptions of couples in retirement," pp. 475-485 in C. Tibbitts & W. Donahue (eds.) Social and Psychological Aspects of Aging. New York: Columbia University Press.

LITWAK, E. (1960a) "Occupational mobility and extended family cohesion." American Sociological Review 25 (February): 9-21.

——— (1960b) "Geographic mobility and extended family cohesion." American Sociological Review 25 (June): 385-394.

——— (1968) "The use of extended family groups in achievement of social goals," pp. 82-89 in M. B. Sussman (ed.) Sourcebook in Marriage and the Family (3rd ed.). Boston: Houghton Mifflin.

LONG, I. (1976) "Human sexuality and aging." Social Casework 57: 237-244.

LONGINO, C. F. (1980) "Retirement communities," pp. 391-418 in f. J. Berghorn & D. E. Schafer (eds.) The Dynamics of Aging. Boulder, CO: Westview.

——— & A. LIPMAN (1981) "Married and spouseless men and women in planned retirement communities." Journal of Marriage and the Family 43 (February): 169-177.

LOPATA, H. Z. (1973) Widowhood in an American City. Cambridge: Schenkman.

——— (1974) "Perceived adequacy of their support systems by American, urban widows." Presented at the International Sociological Association Eighth World Congress of Sociology, Toronto.

——— (1975) "Suppot systems of elderly urbanites: Chicago of the 1970's." The Gerontologist 15 (February): 35-41.

——— (1978) "Contributions of extended families to the support system of metropolitan area widows: limitations of the modified kin network." Journal of Marriage and the Family 40 (May): 355-364.

——— (1979) Women as Widows: Support Systems. New York: Elsevier.

——— (1981) "Widowhood and husband sanctification." Journal of Marriage and the Family 43 (May): 439-450.

LOWENTHAL, M. F. & D. CHIRIBOGA (1972) "Transition to the empty nest: crisis, challenge, or relief?" Archives of General Psychiatry 26: 8-14.

LOWENTHAL, M. F. & B. ROBINSON (1976) "Social networks and isolation," pp. 432-456 in R. H. Binstock & E. Shanas (eds.) Handbook of Aging and the Social Sciences. New York: Van Nostrand Reinhold.

LOWENTHAL, M. F., M. THURNHER, D. CHIRIBOGA, & Associates (1975) Four Life. San Francisco: Jossey-Bass.

LOWY, L. (1979) Social Work with the Aging. New York: Harper & Row.

LUCKEY, E. B. (1966) "Number of years married as related to personality perception and marital satisfaction." Journal of Marriage and the Family 28(1): 44-48.

LUDEMAN, K. (1981) "The sexuality of the older person: review of the literature." The Gerontologist 21: 203-208.

MAAS, H. & J. A. KUYPERS (1974) From Thirty to Seventy. San Francisco: Jossey-Bass.

MADDOX, G. (1975) "Families as context and resources in chronic illness," pp. 317-347 in S. Sherwood (ed.) Long-Term Care: Handbook for Researchers, Planners, and Providers. Flushing, NY: Spectrum.

MALDONADO, D. (1974) "The Chicano aged." Social Work 20: 213-216.

MANNEY, J. D. (1975) Aging. Washington, DC: Office of Human Development, U.S. Department of Health, Education and Welfare.

MARKSON, E. W., G. S. LEVITZ, & M. GOGNALONS-GAILLARD (1973) "The elderly and the community: reidentifying unmet needs." Journal of Gerontology 29: 503-509.

MARRIS, P. (1958) Widows and Their Families. London: Routledge & Kegan Paul.

——— (1975) Loss and Change. Garden City, NY: Doubleday.

MARTIN, E. F. & J. MARTIN (1978) The Black Extended Family. Chicago: University of Chicago Press.

MASTERS, W. H. & V. E. JOHNSON (1966) Human Sexual Response. Boston: Little, Brown.

MATTHEWS, S. H. (1979) The Social World of Old Women. Beverly Hills, CA: Sage.

McGREEHAN, D. H. & S. W. WARBURTON (1978) "How to help families cope with caring for elderly members." Geriatrics 33(6): 99-106.

McKAIN, W. C. (1969) Retirement Marriage. Monograph 3. Storrs, CT: Agriculture Experiment Station, University of Connecticut.

McTAVISH, D. G. (1971) "Perceptions of old people: a review of research methodologies and findings" The Gerontologist 11: 90-101.

MEDLEY, M. L. (1977) "Marital adjustment in the post retirement years." Family Coordinator 26(1): 5-11.

MELVILLE, M. (1980) Twice a Minority: Mexican American Women. St. Louis: Mosby.

MILLER, B. C. (1976) "A multivariate development model of marital satisfaction." Journal of Marriage and the Family 8(4): 643-657.

MILLER, D. A. (1981) "The 'sandwich' generation: adult children of the aged." Social Work 26(5): 419-423.

MILLER, M. B., H. BERNSTEIN, & H. SHARKEY (1975) "Family extrusion of the aged patient: family homeostasis and sexual conflict." The Gerontologist 15: 291-296.

MILLER, S. J. (1981) "Characteristics of one's spouse as predictors of one's own sense of well-being." Presented at the annual meetings of the Gerontological Society, Toronto.

MILLS, L. A. & R. B. CAIRNS (1981) "Life satisfaction and grandparenting in low income elderly black women." Presented at the biannual meeting of the Society for Research in Child Development, Boston.

MINDEL, C. H. (1979) "Multigenerational family households: recent trends and implications for the future." The Gerontologist 19: 456-463.

——— (1980) "Extended familism among urban Mexican Americans, Anglos, and Blacks." Hispanic Journal of Behavioral Sciences 2: 21-34.

——— (1982) "Kinship Relations," in D. Mangen & W. Peterson (eds.) Research Instruments in Aging, Vol. II: Social Roles and Social Participation. Minneapolis: University of Minnesota Press.

——— (1982b) "Assessing the role of support systems among black and white elderly." Presented at the annual meeting of the Gerontological Society of America, San Diego.

MINDEL, C. H. & R. WRIGHT (1982b) "Assessing the role of support systems among black and white elderly." Presented at the annual meeting of the Gerontological Society of America, San Diego.

MINNIGERODE, F. A. & J. A. LEE (1978) "Young adults' perceptions of social sex roles across the life span." Sex Roles 4(4): 563-569.

MIRANDA, M. (1975) "Latin American culture and American society: contrasts," in A. Hernandez & J. Mendoza (eds.) The National Conference on the Spanish Speaking Elderly. Kansas City: National Chicano Social Planning Council.

MOGEY, J. (1976-77) "Residence, family kinship, some recent research." Journal of Family History (1/2): 95-105.

MOORE, J. W. (1971) "Mexican Americans." The Gerontologist 2: 30-35.

MORGAN, M. (1969) "Middle life and the aging family." Family Coordinator 29: 37-46.

MORSE, N. C. & R. WEISS (1955) "The function and meaning of work and the job." American Sociological Review 20: 191-198.

MOYNIHAN, D. P. (1965) The Negro Family: The Case for National Action. Washington, DC: Office of Planning and Research, U.S. Department of Labor.

MUELLER, C. W. & H. POPE (1977) "Marital instability: a study of its transmission between generations." Journal of Marriage and the Family 39: 83-93.

MURILLO, N. (1971) "The Mexican American family," in N. N. Wagner & M. V. Haug (eds.) Chicanos. St. Louis: Mosby.

MURPHY, G. J., W. W. HUDSON & P.P.L. CHEUNG (1980) "Marital and sexual discord among older couples." Social Work Research and Abstracts 16: 11-16.

MURRAY, J. (1976) "Family structure in preretirement years," pp. 82-101 in M. Irelan et al., Almost 65: Baseline Data from the Retirement History Study. Washington, DC: U.S. Government Printing Office.

MYLES, J. F. (1978) "Institutionalization and sick role identification among the elderly." American Sociological Review 43: 508-521.

NADELSON, C. C., D. C. POLONSKY, & M. A. MATHEWS (1979) "Marriage and midlife: the impact of social change." Journal of Clinical Psychiatry 40(7): 292-298.

NADELSON, T. (1975) "A survey of the literature on the adjustment of the aged to retirement." Journal of Geriatric Psychiatry 3: 3-20.

NAVRAN, L. (1967) "Communication and adjustments in marriage." Family Process 6: 173-184.

NELSON, G. M. (1982) "Support for the aged: public and private responsibility." Social Work 27(2): 137-146.

NEUGARTEN, B. L. (1979) "The Middle Generation," pp. 258-266 in P. K. Ragan, Aging Parents. Los Angeles: University of Southern California Press.

——— & D. L. GUTMANN (1958) "Age-sex roles and personality in middle age: a thematic apperception study." Psychological Monographs 72(17): 1-33.

NEUGARTEN, B. L., J. W. MOORE, & J. C. LOWE (1965) "Age norms, age constraints, and adult socialization." American Journal of Sociology 70: 710-717.

——— & K. K. WEINSTEIN (1964) "The changing American grandparent." Journal of Marriage and the Family 26: 199-204.

NEUGARTEN, B. L., V. WOOD, R. KRAINES, & B. LOOMIS (1963) "Women's attitudes toward the menopause." Vita Humana 6: 110-151.

NEWMAN, G. & C. R. NICHOLS (1970) "Sexual activities and attitudes in older persons," pp. 227-281 in E. Palmore (ed.) Normal Aging. Durham: Duke University Press.

NEWMAN, S. (1976) Housing Adjustments of Older People: A Report from the Second Phase. Ann Arbor: Institute for Social Research, University of Michigan.

NIEMI, R. G. (1974) How Family Members Perceive Each Other. New Haven: Yale University Press.

NIMKOFF, M. F. (1962) "Changing family relationships of older people in the United States during the last fifty years," pp. 405-414 in C. Tibbitts & W. Donahue (eds.) Social and Psychological Aspects of Aging. New York: Columbia University Press.

NORTON, A. J. (1980) "The influence of divorce on tradtional life-cycle measures." Journal of Marriage and the Family 42: 63-69.

NYDEGGER, C. N. (1983) "Family ties of the aged in cross-cultural perspective" The Gerontologist 23: 26-32.

NYE, F. I. (1976) "Family roles in comparative perspective," pp. 149-174 in F.I. Nye (ed.) Role Structure and Analysis of the Family. Beverly Hills, CA: Sage.

————— & V. GEKAS (1976a) "Family role analysis: the Washington family role inventory." Technical Bulletin 82. Pullman: college of Agriculture Research Center, Washington State University.

————— (1976b) "The role concept: review and delineation," pp. 3-14 in F. I. Nye (ed.) Role Structure and Analysis of the Family. Beverly Hills, CA: Sage.

O'BRIEN, J. E. & D. L. WAGNER (1980) "Help seeking by the frail elderly: problems in network analysis." The Gerontologist 20(1): 78-83.

O'MALLEY, H. et al. (1979) Elder Abuse in Massachusetts: A Survey of Professionals and Paraprofessionals. Boston: Legal Research and SErvices for the Elderly.

ORTHNER, D. K. (1975) "Leisure activity patterns and marital satisfaction over the marital career." Journal of Marriage and the Family 37(1): 91-102.

PALMORE, E. (1981) Social Patterns in Normal Aging: Findings from the Duke Longitudinal Study. Durham, NC: Duke University Press.

—————, W. CLEVELAND, J. NOWLIN, D. RAMM, & I. SIEGLER (1979) "Stress and adaptation in later life." Journal of Gerontology 34: 841-851.

PARAD, H. (1966) "The use of time-limited crisis intervention in community mental health programming." Social Service Review 40: 275-282.

PARIS, B. L. & E. B. LUCKEY (1966) "A longitudinal study in marital satisfaction." Sociology and Social Research 50(2): 212-222.

PARKES, C. M. (1970) "The first year of bereavement: a longitudinal study of the reaction of London widows to the death of their husbands." Psychiatry 33 (November): 444-467.

PARKES, C. (1972) Bereavement. London: Tavistock.

PARNES, H. J., & G. NESTEL (1981) "The retirement experience," pp. 155-197 in H. J. Parnes (ed.) Work and Retirement. Boston: MIT Press.

PARRON, E. A. & L. E. TROLL (1978) "Golden wedding couples: effects of retirement on intimacy in long-standing marriages." Alternate Lifestyles 1(4): 447-464.

PARSONS, T. (1955) "The American family: its relations to personality and to the social structure," pp. 3-33 in T. Parsons & R. F. Bales (eds.) Family, Socialization and Interaction Process. New York: Macmillan.

PEASE, R. A. (1974) "Female professional students and sexuality in an aging male." The Gerontologist 14: 153-157.

PENALOSA, F. (1968) "Mexican family roles." Journal of Marriage and the Family 30: 13-27.

PETERS, G. A. (1971) "Self-conceptions of the aged, age identification and aging" The Gerontologist 11: 69-73.

PETERSON, J. A. (1979) "The relationship of middle aged children and their parents," pp. 27-37 in P. K. Ragan, Aging Parents. Los Angeles: University of Southern California Press.

————— & M. L. BRILEY (1977) Widows and Widowhood: A Creative Approach to Being Alone. New York: Associated Press.

PETERSON, J. A. & B. PAYNE (1975) Love in the Later Years. New York: Association Press.

PETROWSKY, M. (1976) "Marital status, sex, and the social network of the elderly." Journal of Marriage and the Family 38 (November): 749-756.

PFEIFFER, E. (1974) "Sexuality in the aging individual." Journal of the American Geriatrics Society 22: 481-484.

—— & G. C. DAVIS (1974) "Determinants of sexual behavior in middle and old age," pp. 251-262 in E. Palmore (ed.) Normal Aging II. Durham: Duke University Press.

PFEIFFER, E., A. VERWOERDT, & G. C. DAVIS (1974) "Sexual behavior in middle life," pp. 243-251 in E. Palmore (ed.) Normal Aging II. Durham: Duke University Press.

PFEIFFER, E., A. VERWOERDT, & H. S. WANG (1970) "Sexual behavior in aged men and women," pp. 299-303 in E. Palmore (ed.) Normal Aging. Durham: Duke University Press.

PIAGET, J. (1952) The Origins of Intelligence in Children. New York: International Universities Press.

PIHLBLAD, C. T. & D. L. ADAMS (1972) "Widowhood, social participation, and life satisfaction." Aging and Human Development 3(2): 323-330.

PINEO, P. E. (1961) "Disenchantment in the later years of marriage." Marriage and Family Living 23: 3-11.

—— (1969) "Development patterns in marriage." Family Coordinator 18(2): 135-140.

PLATERIS, A. (1978) Divorce and Divorce Rates: United States. Series 21, No. 29, Vital and Health Statistics. Rockville, MD: National Center for Health Statistics.

POWELL, M. C. (1981) The Widow. Washington, DC: Anaconda.

POWERS, E. A., P. M. KEITH, & W. GOUDY (1975) "Family relationships and friendships," pp. 67-90 in R. C. Atchley (ed.) Rural Environments and Aging. Washington, DC: Gerontological Society.

PRESTON, S. & J. McDONALD (1979) "The incidence of divorce within cohorts of American marriages contracted since the civil war." Demography 16: 1-25.

QUINN, W. H. (1983) "Personal and family adjustment in later life." Journal of Marriage and the Family 45: 57-73.

RAGAN, P. (1979) Aging Parents. Los Angeles: University of Southern California Press.

RAINWATER, L. (1966) "The crucible of identity: the lower class Negro family." Daedalus 95: 258-264.

RALEY, M. (1982) "Families in an aging society." Presented at the annual meetings of the National Council on Family Relations, Washington, D.C.

RAMIREZ, O. & C. ARCE (1981) "The contemporary Chicano family: an empirically based review," in A. Baron, Jr. (ed.) Explorations in Chicano Psychology. New York: Praeger.

RAPPAPORT, L. (1962) "The state of crisis: some theoretical considerations." Social Service Review 36: 211-217.

RASCHKE, H. (1977) "The role of social participation in post-separation and post-divorce adjustment." Journal of Divorce 1: 129-140.

RATHBONE-McCUAN, E. (1978) "Intergenerational family violence and neglect: the aged as victims of reactivated and reverse neglect." Presented at the 11th International Congress of Gerontology, Tokyo.

RENVOIZE, J. (1978) Web of Violence: A Study of Family Violence. London: Routledge & Kegan Paul.

RILEY, M. W. & A. FONER (1968) Aging and Society, Vol. I: An Inventory of Research Findings. New York: Russell Sage.

RIX, S. E. & T. ROMASHKO (1980) With a Little Help from My Friends. Washington, DC: American Institute for Research.

ROBERTS, W. L. (1980) "Significant elements in the relationship of long-married couples." International Journal of Aging and Human Development 10: 265-271.

ROBERTSON, J. (1977) "Grandmotherhood: a study of role conceptions." Journal of Marriage and the Family 39(1): 165-174.

ROBINSON, B. & M. THURNHER (1979) "Taking care of aged parents: a family cycle transition." The Gerontologist 19: 586-593.

ROLLINS, B. C. & K. L. CANNON (1974) "Marital satisfaction over the family life cycle: a reevaluation." Journal of Marriage and the Family 36(2): 271-282.

ROLLINS, B. C. & H. FELDMAN (1970) "Marital satisfaction over the family life cycle." Journal of Marriage and the Family 32(1): 20-28.

ROSEN, A. J. (1975) "Group discussions: a therapeutic tool in a chronic diseases hospital." Geriatrics 30 (August): 45-48.

ROSENBERG, G. S. & D. F. ANSPACH (1973) "Sibling solidarity in the working class." Journal of Marriage and the Family 35: 108-113.

ROSENMAYR, L. (1977) "The family: a source of hope for the elderly?" in E. Shanas & M. B. Sussman (eds.) Family, Bureaucracy, and the Elderly. Durham, NC: Duke University Press.

ROSOW, I. (1967) Social Integration of the Aged. New York: Macmillan.

——— (1973) "Social contacts of the aging self." The Gerontologist 13: 82-87.

ROSS, H. & J. MILGRAM (1982) "Important variables in adult sibling relationships: a qualitative analysis," in M. E. Lame & B. Sutton-Smith (eds.) Sibling Relationships: Their Nature and Significance Across the Lifespan. Hillsdale, NJ: Erlbaum.

ROWLAND, K. F. & S. N. HAYNES (1978) "A sexual enhancement program for elderly couples." Journal of Sex and Marital Therapy 4: 91-113.

RUBENSTEIN, D. (1971) "An examination of social participation of black and white elderly." Aging and Human Development 2: 172-188.

——— (1978) "On being socialized out of the human sexual response in the later years." Journal of Sociology and Social Welfare 5: 843-855.

RUBIN, I. (1965) Sexual Life After Sixty. New York: Basic Books.

——— (1970) Sexual Life in the Later Years. Sex Information and Educational Council of the U.S., Siecus Study Guide No. 12.

SAFILIOS-ROTHSCHILD, C. (1969) "Family sociology or wives' family sociology? A cross-cultural examination of decision making." Journal of Marriage and the Family 32(2): 290-301.

SALZBERGER, R. (1979) "Casework and the client's right to self-determination." Social Work 24(5): 398-400.

SANDERS, R. & G. SPANIER (1979) "Divorce, child custody, and child support." Current Population Reports, Series p-23, No. 84. Washington, DC: U.S. Bureau of the Census.

SANDLER, J., M. MYERSON, & B. N. KINDER (1980) Human Sexuality: Current Perspectives. Tampa, FL: Mariner.

SAUNDERS, L. (1954) Cultural Differences and Medical Care: The Case of the Spanish Speaking People of the Southwest. New York: Russell Sage.

SCANNELL, E. (1982) Displaced Homemakers' Financial Management, Locus of Control and Demographics: Implications for Curriculum. Unpublished doctoral dissertation, University of Wisconsin.

SCANZONI, J. H. (1975) Sex Roles, Life Styles, and Childbearing. New York: Macmillan.

SCHMIDT, M. G. (1980) "Failing parents and aging children." Journal of Gerontological Social Work 2: 259-268.

SCHRAM, R. W. (1979) "Marital satisfaction over the family life cycle: a critique and proposal." Journal of Marriage and the Family 411: 7-12.

SCHWARTZ, A. (1977) Survival Handbook for Children of Aging Parents. Chicago: Follett.

SCHWARTZ, W. (1969) Private Troubles and Public Issues: One Social Work Job or Two? New York: Social Welfare Forum, Columbia University.

SCOTT, F. (1962) "Family group structure and patterns of social interaction." American Journal of Sociology 68(2): 214-228.

SCOTT, J. P. & V. R. KIVETT (1980) "The widowed black older adult in the rural South: implications for policy." Family Relations 29 (January): 83-90.

SEELBACH, W. C. & W. J. SAUER (1977) "Filial responsibility expectations and morale among aged parents." The Gerontologist 17(6): 492-499.

SENA-RIVERA, J. (1979) "Extended kinship in the United States: competing models and the case of la familia Chicana." Journal of Marriage and the Family 41: 121-129.

SHANAS, E. (1973) "Family-kin networks and aging in cross-cultural perspective." Journal of Marriage and the Family 35: 505-511.

——— (1979a) "Social myth as hypothesis: the case of the family relations of old people." The Gerontologist 19(1): 3-9.

——— (1979b) "The family as a social support system in old age." The Gerontologist 19(2): 169-174.

——— & G. D. HEINEMANN (1978) National Survey of the Aged, 1975. Washington, DC: Administration on Aging. (Project HEW OHD 90-A-369)

SHANAS, E. & G. L. MADDOX (1976) "Aging, health and the organization of older people." Journal of Social Issues 30: 79-92.

SHANAS, E. & M. B. SUSSMAN [eds.] (1977) Family, Bureaucracy, and the Elderly. Durham, NC: Duke University Press.

SHANAS, E., P. TOWNSEND, D. WEDDERBURN, H. FRIIS, P. MILHOJ, & J. STEHOUWER (1968) Old People in Three Industrial Societies. New York: Atherton.

SHEEHY, G. (1974) Passages: Predictable Crises in Adult Life. New York: Bantam.

SHERMAN, R. H., A. HOROWITZ, & S. C. DURMASKIN (1982) "Role overload or role management? The relationship betwen work and caregiving among daughters of aged parents." Presented at the 34th Annual Meeting of the Gerontological Society of America, Boston.

SHIMKIN, D. B., E. M. SHIMKIN, & D. A. FRATE (1978) The Extended Family in Black Societies. The Hague: Mouton.

SIEGEL, J. (1976) Demographic Aspects of Aging and the Older Population of the United States. Series p-23, No. 59, U.S. Department of Commerce, Bureau of the Census, Special Studies.

SILVERMAN, W. & R. HILL (1967) "Task allocation in marriage in the United States and Belgium." Journal of Marriage and the Family 29: 353-359.

SILVERSTONE, B. (1982) "Adults and aging parents: an applied approach." Presented at the National Workshop on Aging, Boston.

——— & H. HYMAN (1976) You and Your Aging Parent. New York: Pantheon.

SIMOS, B. G. (1975) "Adult children and their aging parents." Social Work 18: 78-85.

SINNOTT, J. D. (1977) "Sex-role inconsistency, biology, and successful aging." The Gerontologist 17: 459-463.

—— (1982) "Correlates of sex roles of older adults." Journal of Gerontology 37(5): 587-594.

SLOCUM, W. L. & F. I. NYE (1976) "Provider and housekeeper roles," pp. 81-99 in F. I. Nye (ed.) Role Structure and Analysis of the Family. Beverly Hills, CA: Sage.

SMART, M. S. & R. C. SMART (1975) "Recalled, present, and predicted satisfaction in stages of the family life cycle in New Zealand." Journal of Marriage and the Family 37(2): 408-415.

SMITH, E. W. (1975) "The role of the grandmother in adolescent pregnancy and parenting." Journal of School Health 45: 278-283.

SMITH, K. F. & V. L. BENGTSON (1979) "Positive consequences of institutionalization: solidarity between elderly parents and their middle age children." The Gerontologist 19: 438-447.

SMITH, L. (1977) "Crisis intervention theory and practice." Community Mental Health Review 2: 1-13.

SMYER, M. & B. HOFLAND (1982) "Divorce and family support in later life: emerging concerns." Journal of Family Issues 3(1): 61-77.

SNOW, D. L. & J. B. GORDON (1980) "Social network analysis and intervention with the elderly." The Gerontologist 20(4): 463-467.

SNYDER, D. K. (1979) "Multidimensional assessment of marital satisfaction." Journal of Marriage and the Family 41(4): 813-823.

SNYDER, E. E. & E. SPREITZER (1976) "Attitudes of the aged toward nontraditional sexual behavior." Archives of Sexual Behavior 5: 249-254.

SOTOMAYER, M. (1973) A Study of Chicano Grandparents in an Urban Barrio. Unpublished doctoral dissertation, University of Denver.

SPANIER, G. B. & S. HANSON (1982) "The role of extended kin in the adjustment to marital separation." Journal of Divorce 5(1/2): 33-48.

SPANIER, G. B. & R. A. LEWIS (1980) "Marital quality: a review of the seventies." Journal of Marriage and the Family 42(4): 825-839.

SPANIER, G. B. & C. L. COLE (1975) "Marital adjustment over the family life cycle: the issue of curvilinearity." Journal of Marriage and the Family 37(2): 264-275.

SPICER, J. W. & G. D. HAMPE (1975) "Kinship interaction after divorce." Journal of Marriage and the Family 37: 113-119.

STACK, C. (1974) All Our Kin: Strategies for Survival in the Black Community. New York: Harper & Row.

STAPLES, R. (1981) "The Black American family," in C. H. Mindel & R. W. Habenstein (eds.) Ethnic Families in America (2nd ed.). New York: Elsevier.

STEINMETZ, S. K. (1977) The Cycle of Violence. New York: Praeger.

—— (1978) "The politics of aging, battered parents." Society (July/August): 54-55.

—— (1980a) "Prepared statement," pp. 7-10 in U.S. House of Representatives, Elder Abuse: The Hidden Problem. Briefing by the Select Committee on Aging held in Boston, Mass. on June 23, 1979 (96). Washington, DC: U.S. Government Printing Office.

—— (1980b) "Elder abuse: society's double dilemma." Hearing before the Senate Select Committee on Aging (97) May 28. Washington, DC: U.S. Government Printing Office.

—— (1980c) "Investigating family violence." Journal of Home Economics (Summer): 32-36.

—— (1981) "Elder abuse." Aging 315/316: 23-26.

—— (1983) "Dependency, stress and violence between middle-aged caregivers and their elderly parents," in J. I. Kosberg (ed.) Abuse and Maltreatment of the Elderly. Littleton, MA: John Wright-PSG, Inc.

—— (in press) "Violence in the family: an historical, statistical, and theoretical overview," in M. susman & S. Steinmetz (eds.) Handbook on Marriage and the Family. New York: Plenum.

STEVENS-LONG, J. (1979) Adult Life: Developmental Process. Palo Alto, CA: Mayfield.

STINNETT, N., L. M. CARTER, & J. E. MONTGOMERY (1972) "Older persons perceptions of their marriages." Journal of Marriage and the Family 34(4): 665-670.

STINNETT, N., J. COLLINS, & J. E. MONTGOMERY (1970) "Marital need satisfaction of older husbands and wives." Journal of Marriage and the Family 32(3): 428-434.

STREIB, G. (1968) "Family patterns in retirement," in M. S. Sussman (ed.) Sourcebook in Marriage and the Family. Boston: Houghton Mifflin.

—— (1972) "Older families and their troubles: familial and social responses." Family Coordinator 21: 5-19.

—— & R. W. BECK (1980) "Older families: a decade review." Journal of Marriage and the Family 42: 937-956.

STREIB, G. F. & C. J. SCHNEIDER (1971) Retirement in American Society. Ithaca, NY: Cornell University Press.

SUSSMAN, M. B. (1953) "The help pattern in the middle class family." American Sociological Review 18: 22-28.

—— (1965) "Relations of adult children with their parents in the United States," in E. Shanas & G. Streib (eds.) Social Structure and the Family: Generational Relations. Englewood Cliffs, NJ: Prentice-Hall.

—— (1977) "The family life of old people," in R. H. Binstock & E. E. Shanas (eds.) Handbook of Aging and the Social Sciences. New York: Van Nostrand Reinhold.

—— & L. BURCHINAL (1962) "Kin family network: unheralded structures in current conceptualizations of family functioning." Marriage and Family Living 24: 231-240.

SUTTON-SMITH, B. & B. G. ROSENBERG (1968) "Sibling consensus on power tactics." Journal of Genetic Psychology 112: 63-72.

—— (1970) The Sibling. New York: Holt, Rinehart & Winston.

SVILAND, M. A. (1975) "Helping elderly couples become sexually liberated: psychosocial issues." Counseling Psychologist 5: 67-72.

SWENSON, C. H., R. W. ESKEW, & K. A. KOHLHEPP (1981) "Stage of family life cycle, ego development, and the marriage relationship." Journal of Marriage and the Family 43: 841-853.

SZINOVACZ, M. (1980) "Female retirement: effects on spousal roles and marital adjustment." Journal of Family Issues 1: 423-440.

TERMAN, L. (1938) Psychological Factors in Marital Happiness. New York: McGraw-Hill.

THOMAS, L. E. (1982) "Sexuality and aging: essential vitamin or popcorn?" The Gerontologist 22: 240-243.

THURNHER, M. (1976) "Midlife marriage: sex differences in evaluation and perspectives." International Journal of Aging and Human Development 7(2): 129-135.

TIGER, L. (1978) "Omigamy: the new kinship system." Psychology Today (July): 14-17.

TINSLEY, B. R. & R. D. PARKE (1983) "Grandparents as support and socialization agents," in M. Lewis (ed.) Beyond the Dyad. New York: Plenum.

TOWNSEND, P. (1957) The Family Life of Old People: An Inquiry in East London. New York: Macmillan.

TREAS, J. (1977) "Family support systems for the aged." The Gerontologist 6 (December): 486-491.

——— & A. VanHILST (1976) "Marriage and remariage rates among older Americans." The Gerontologist 16 (April): 132-136.

TROLL, L. E. (1971) "The family of later life: a decade review." Journal of Marriage and the Family 33: 263-290.

——— (1980a) "Grandparenting," in L. W. Poon (ed.) Aging in the 1980's: Psychological Issues. Washington, DC: American Psychological Association.

——— (1980b) "Intergenerational relations in later life: a family system approach," in N. Datan & N. Lohmann (eds.) Transitions of Aging. New York: Academic.

——— & V. L. BENGTSON (1979) "Generations in the family," in W. Burr et al. (eds.) Contemporary Theories About the Family, Vol. 1. New York: Macmillan.

——— (1982) "Intergenerational relations throughout the life span," in B. B. Wolman (ed.) Handbook of Developmental Psychology. Englewood Cliffs, NJ: Prentice-Hall.

TROLL, L., S. J. MILLER., & R. C. ATCHLEY (1979) Families in Later Life. Belmont, CA: Wadsworth.

TROLL, L. & J. SMITH (1976) "Attachment through the life span: some questions about dyadic bonds among adults." Human Development 19: 156-170.

TRUDGEON, J. H. (1978) "The effects of divorce upon qualified retirement benefits." Labor Law Journal 29: 12.

TUCKMAN, J. & I. LORGE (1954) "Old people's appraisal of adjustment over the life span." Journal of Personality 22: 417-422.

UHLENBERG, P. & M. A. MYERS (1981) "Divorce and the elderly." The Gerontologist 21: 276-282.

UNGER, D. G. (1979) An Ecological Approach to the Family: The Role of Social Stress, and Mother-Child Interacton. Unpublished master's thesis, Merrill-Palmer Institute, Detroit.

——— & D. R. POWELL (1980) "Supporting families under stress: the role of social networks." Family Relations 29: 556-574.

U.S. Bureau of the Census (1972) Census of Population: 1970. Washington, DC: U.S. Government Printing Office.

——— (1974) Current Population Reports. Series p-25, No. 519, Table 1. Washington, DC: U.S. Government Printing Office.

——— (1977) Current Population Reports. Series p-25, No. 704, Table 8. Washington, DC: U.S. Government Printing Office.

——— (1978) Current Population Reports. Series p-25, No. 721, Table I. Washington, DC: U.S. Government Printing Office.

——— (1979) Current Population Reports, Series p-20, No. 349. Marital status and living arrangements, Table I. Washington, DC: U.S. Government Printing Office.

——— (1980) Current Population Reports. Series p-25, No. 870, Table 1. Washington, DC: U.S. Government Printing Office.

——— (1981) "Marital status and living arrangements: March 1981." Current Population Reports, Series p-20, No. 372. Washington, DC: U.S. Government Printing Office.

——— (1982) Material from the Aging Population: A 1980 Census Workshop. Training Activity No. 200-1, Data User Services Division, Washington, D.C., September 29-30.

U.S. Department of Health and Human Services (1980) Monthly Vital Statistics Report, Provisional Statistics, Annual Summary for the United States, 1979. Office of Health Research, Statistics, and Technology, National Center for Health Statistics. DHHS Publication (PHS) 81-1120, Vol. 28, No. 13, November.

URBERG, K. A. & G. LABOUVIE-VIEF (1976) "Conceptualizations of sex roles: a life span developmental study." Developmental Psychology 12(1): 15-23.

VERWOERDT, A. (1976) "Normal psychology of the aging process revisited (I)." Journal of Geriatric Psychiatry 9: 211-219.

WADDELL, F. [ed.] (1975) The Elderly Consumer. Columbia, MD: Human Ecology Center, Antioch College.

WAGNER, R. M. & D. M. SCHAFFER (1980) "Social networks and survival strategies: an exploratory study of Mexican American, Black and Anglo female family heads in San Jose, California," in M. B. Melville (ed.) Twice a Minority: Mexican American Women. St. Louis: Mosby.

WAKE, S. B. & M. J. SPORAKOWSKI (1972) "An intergenerational comparison of attitudes supporting aged parents." Journal of Marriage and the Family 34: 42-48.

WALES, J. (1974) "Sexuality in middle and old age: a critical review of the literature." Case Western Reserve Journal of Sociology 6: 82-105.

WALLIN, P. & A. L. CLARK (1963) "A study of orgasm as a condition of women's enjoyment of coitus in the middle years of marriage." Human Biology 35: 131-139.

——— (1964) "Religiosity, sexual gratification, and marital satisfaction in the middle years of marriage." Social Forces 42: 303-309.

WALSTER, E., E. BERSCHEID, & G. WALSTER (1973) "New directions in equity research." Journal of Personality and Social Psychology 2: 151-176.

WALSTER, E., G. WALSTER, & E. BERSCHEID (1978) Equity Theory and Research. Boston: Allyn & Bacon.

WARD, R. A. (1978) "Limitations of the family as a supporting institution in the lives of the aged." Family Coordinator 27: 365-373.

——— (1979) "The never-married in later life." Journal of Gerontology 34: 861-869.

WAXLER, N. E. & E. G. MISHLER (1970) "Experimental studies of families," pp. 249-304 in L. Berkowitz (ed.) Advances in Experimental Social Psychology, Vol. 5. New York: Academic.

WEED, J. (1980) National Estimates of Marriage Dissolution and Survivorship: United States. U.S. Department of Health and Human Services Publication (PHS) 81-1403, Office of Health Research, Statistics, and Technology, National Center for Health Statistics, Hyattsville, Maryland, November.

WEEKS, J. R. J& J. B. CUELLAR (1981) "The role of family members in the helping networks of older people." The Gerontologist 21 (August): 388-394.

WEINBERG, J. (1969) "Sexual expression in later life." American Journal of Psychiatry 126: 159-162.

WEISHAUS, S. (1979) "Aging is a family affair," in P. K. Ragan (ed.) Aging Parents. Los Angeles: University of Southern California Press.

WEISS, P. (1975) Marital Separation. New York: Basic Books.

WELLMAN, B. (1979) "The community question: the intimate networks of East New Yorkers." American Journal of Sociology 84: 1201-1231.

WEST, N. (1975) "Sex in geriatrics: myth or miracle?" Journal of American Geriatrics Society 23: 551-552.

WILLIAMSON, D. (1982) "Personal authority via termination of the intergenerational hierarchical boundary: Part II—the consultation process and the therapeutic method." Journal of Marital and Family Therapy 8: 23-39.

WOOD, V. (1982) "Grandparenthood: an ambiguous role." Generations (Winter): 22-23.

——— & J. F. ROBERTSON (1978) "Friendship and kinship interaction: differential effects on the morale of the elderly." Journal of Marriage and the Family 40 (May): 367-375.

——— (1976) "The significance of grandparenthood," in J. Gubrium (ed.) Time, Roles and Self in Old Age. New York: Human Sciences Press.

WYLIE, F. M. (1971) "Attitudes toward aging and the aged among Black Americans: some historical perspectives." Aging and Human Development 2: 66-70.

YARROW, M. R., P. BLANK, O. W. QUINN, E. G. YOUMANS, & J. STEIN (1971) Human Aging. Washington, DC: U.S. Government Printing Office. (Publication [HSM] 71-9051)

YORK, J. L. & R. J. CASLYN (1977) "Family involvement in nursing homes." The Gerontologist 17: 500-505.

YOUMANS, G. (1963) Aging Patterns in a Rural and Urban Area of Kentucky. Lexington: University of Kentucky Agricultural Experiment Station.

YOUNG, M. & P. WILLMOTT (1957) Family and Kinship in East London. London: Routledge & Kegan Paul.

ZUSMAN, J. (1966) "Some explanation of the changing appearance of psychotic patients: antecedents of the social breakdown concept." Milbank Memorial Fund Quarterly 44: 363-394.

About the Contributors

LINDA ADE-RIDDER is an Assistant Professor in the Department of Home Economics and Consumer Sciences, Miami University, Oxford, Ohio. She received her Ph.D. from Florida State University. Her professional interests include therapy and rsearch centering on marriage in later life, families, and women.

DEBORAH J. AMSDEN completed her master's thesis, "Task Performance and Perceived Stress in Families Caring for an Elderly Relative," at the Department of Individual and Family Studies, University of Delaware. She has given numerous workshops on aging, retirement, and family relationships. Currently, she is a home economist for the Cooperative Extension Service at the University of Delaware.

ROBERT C. ATCHLEY is Director of the Scripps Foundation Gerontology Center, Miami University, Oxford, Ohio. His books in the field of aging include *The Social Forces in Later Life* (third edition) and numerous journal articles and book chapters. He is editor of Gerontological Monographs for the Gerontological Society of America.

VERN L. BENGTSON is currently professor of Sociology at the University of Southern California as well as the Director of the Research Institute of the Andrus Gerontology Center in Los Angeles. He has published seventy papers presenting research on the social psychology of aging, family sociology, cross-cultural studies in behavior, and the methodology of social research. He is the author of *The Social Psychology of Aging, Youth, Generations, and Social Change,* and the six-volume Brooks/Cole Series in Social Gerontology.

ELLIE BRUBAKER is an Assistant Professor in the Department of Sociology and Anthropology, Miami University, Oxford, Ohio. She received her Ph.D. from Ohio State University. Her research interests are concentrated on practice and policy issues related to service delivery to older persons and their families.

TIMOTHY H. BRUBAKER is an Associate Professor in the Department of Home Economics and Consumer Sciences and a Fellow of the Scripps Foundation Gerontology Center, Miami University, Oxford, Ohio. His research interests focus on family relationships in later life, attitudes toward the elderly, and service delivery to the elderly and their families.

VICTOR G. CICIRELLI is Professor of Developmental/Aging Psychology in the Department of Psychological Sciences at Purdue University. A native of Miami, Florida, he earned his undergraduate degree at the University of Notre Dame and went on to earn PH.D.s at the University of Michigan and Michigan State University. He was a postdoctoral fellow at the University of Wisconsin's Institute for Cognitive Learning. He has published articles in a wide range of professional journals and is the author of the recent book, *Helping Elderly Parents: Role of Adult Children.*

CYNTHIA DOBSON is Assistant Professor and Social Sciences Bibliographer at Iowa State University. Her research has concentrated on the transition to old age, with an emphasis on role changes and maintenance of psychological well-being.

PAULA L. DRESSEL is Associate Professor of Sociology at Georgia State University and is the author of numerous articles in the areas of social gerontology and social planning. She is currently at work on a book detailing the political and cultural sources of job dissatisfaction among human service workers.

JOSEPH M. GARZA is Associate Professor of Sociology and former Director of Graduate Studies in Sociology at Georgia State University, where his present research interest is in middle- and later-life marriage. His most recent publications are on cohabitation and appear in the *American Journal of Psychoanalysis.*

GLORIA D. HEINEMANN is coordinator of the Interdisciplinary Team Training in Geriatrics (ITTG) program, Division of Geriatrics/Gerontology, Veterans Administration Medical Center, Buffalo, New York, and Assistant Professor in the Departments of Medicine and Social and Preventive Medicine, School of Medicine, State University of New York at Buffalo. Her research interests are in the areas of widowhood, aging and health, and long-term care for the elderly. She received her Ph.D. from the Department of Sociology, University of Illinois at Chicago. Prior to her present position, she was a senior research sociologist with the National Center for Health Services Research, Public Health Service, Department of Health and Human Services, Rockville, Maryland.

CHARLES B. HENNON is Family Life Education Specialist, Family Living Education, University of Wisconsin—Cooperative Extension, and Associate Professor of Child and Family Studies, School of Family Resources and Consumer Sciences, University of Wisconsin—Madison. He earned his Ph.D. in sociology from Case Western Reserve University. In addition to his ongoing interest in the elderly and divorce, he is doing research on family role transitions in later life and conducts extension programs on aging and the family.

JOSEPH A. KUYPERS is Associate Professor of Social Work at the University of Manitoba, Winnipeg, Manitoba, Canada. He is co-author (with Henry Maas) of *From Thirty to Seventy* (1974) and has published numerous articles in the areas of crisis, intervention, adult life cycle development, and competence. His current research and writing focus on crisis and the older family.

SHEILA J. MILLER is Associate Professor of Sociology and a Fellow of the Scripps Foundation Gerontology Center at Miami University, Oxford, Ohio. She is co-author of *Families in Later Life* and has published several articles dealing with family issues in gerontology. Most recently she has turned her attentions to long-term care.

CHARLES H. MINDEL is currently Professor of Social Work at the University of Texas, Arlington. He is the editor of *Ethnic*

Families in America. He has done research in the area of the elderly and their families with a focus on the ethnic and minority elderly.

JEAN PEARSON SCOTT is an Assistant Professor in the Department of Home and Family Life at Texas Tech University, Lubbock, Texas. She received her Ph.D. from the University of North Carolina at Greensboro. Her research interests are in rural aging, informal and formal support networks, and widowhood.

SUZANNE K. STEINMETZ, Ph.D., Professor in the Department of Individual and Family Studies at the University of Delaware, is author of *Cycle of Violence, Violence in the Family* (with M. Straus), *Behind Closed Doors: Violence in the American Family* (with M. Straus and R. Gelles), and numerous articles. Steinmetz has presented numerous keynote addresses, colloquia, and workshops nationally, on various aspects of domestic violence.

LILLIAN E. TROLL is a Professor II in the Psychology Department at Rutgers University in New Brunswick. She received a B.A., M.A., and Ph.D. from the University of Chicago Committee on Human Development and has published many articles on the subjects of families in later life, adult development and aging, and generations. She is the author of *Early and Middle Adulthood* and of *Continuations: Adult Development and Aging;* the co-author of *Looking Ahead: A Woman's Guide to the Problems and Joys of Growing Older* (with Joan Israel and Kenneth Israel), *Perspectives on Counseling Adults* (with Nancy Schlosberg and Zandy Leubowitz), *Families in Later Life* (with Sheila Miller and Robert Atchley), and *Review of Human Development* (with Tiffany Field, Aletha Huston, H. C. Qway, and Gordon Finley; and guest editor of the special issue of *Generations,* "Elders and Their Families."